Land of Tempest

Land of Tempest

Travels in Patagonia: 1958–1962

ERIC SHIPTON

Vertebrate Publishing, Sheffield
www.v-publishing.co.uk

Land of Tempest

Eric Shipton

 Vertebrate Publishing
Omega Court, 352 Cemetery Road, Sheffield S11 8FT, United Kingdom.
www.v-publishing.co.uk

First published by Hodder & Stoughton, London, 1963. This edition first
published in 2019 by Vertebrate Publishing.

A CIP catalogue record for this book is available from the British Library.

ISBN 978-1-912560-09-7 (Paperback)
ISBN 978-1-910240-31-1 (Ebook)

Produced by Vertebrate Publishing.

Contents

1 A Strange Land

Having a taste for strange country, I had long nursed a strong desire to visit Southern Patagonia; but the habit of travelling among the mountain ranges of Central Asia, like all agreeable habits, had been hard to break. Those ranges had provided an unlimited field, fresh opportunities kept occurring and each new venture suggested another batch of enticing projects; so Patagonia had receded ever further and more dimly into the future.

I once thought of applying for the job of British Consul in Punta Arenas, on the Straits of Magellan. I was Consul-General in Kunming at the time, and after a year of non-recognition by the Chinese Communist Government, it had become clear that I would have to move elsewhere. Having previously spent four years as a similar official in Kashgar, which had enabled me to travel in the Pamir, Kuen Lun and Tien Shan, it seemed an excellent way to achieve my purpose. However, I discovered that the post of Consul in Punta Arenas was an honorary one held by a local British resident. In any case, when I returned to England in the summer of 1951, I immediately became embroiled in the revival of the attempts to climb Everest, and soon found myself back in the Himalaya.

I celebrated my fiftieth birthday in the Karakoram. It was doubtless this melancholy event that impressed me with the urgency of making definite plans for an expedition to Patagonia before I became too senile for such an undertaking. Even so I might have done nothing about it, had it not been for Geoff Bratt.

Geoff was a young Australian student, working (in his spare time between more attractive activities) for his PhD at the Imperial College of Science. In 1957 the College had launched an expedition to the Karakoram and had invited me to lead it. Geoff was a member of the party and he had done much of the preliminary organisation. We often shared a tent, and a great deal of varied discussion. Occasionally, of course, we talked of travel and exploration; and I found that he, too, was less interested in mountaineering for its own sake than as a means of getting to strange and little known parts of the world. On the subject of Patagonia it was not difficult to arouse his enthusiasm; his warmth brought mine to the boil and we agreed to go there together the following year.

Patagonia is not a country. The name refers to the whole of the mainland of South America south of the Rio Negro in Latitude 40° S. The bulk of this vast territory, lying in Argentina to the east of the Andes, consists of prairie, some of it flat, much of it hilly, nearly all of it dry, treeless and covered with coarse grass and open scrub. It is a stark, inhospitable land which, until late in the nineteenth century, was inhabited only by a few scattered Indian tribes. It was only then, towards the end of the century, that white men came, mostly direct from Europe or from the Falkland Islands, to settle there as sheep farmers, first along the Atlantic coast, then gradually further inland. Indeed the settlement of Patagonia is so recent that even today many of the *estancieros* are the sons and daughters of those original pioneers.

The Chilean part of Patagonia, except for a small area in the extreme south, is utterly different. Most of it is wild, rugged and uninhabited, a region of tempest and torrential rain, of fantastic geographical form and strange natural phenomena. The Pacific coast immediately west of the Andes, is split by a complex network of fjords which bite deep into the mainland and form an archipelago, a giant jigsaw of islands, 1,000 miles long. The climate is subantarctic, and the glaciation so extensive that, although the mountains are not particularly high, they are as spectacular as any in the entire range. There are two great ice caps, which are the only examples of their kind outside polar regions. Many of the innumerable glaciers which radiate from these, flow down through dense 'tropical forest' (as Darwin described it) and thrust their massive fronts into the intricate system of waterways surrounding them. Parrots and humming-birds inhabit these forests.

There was no lack of interesting objectives. Apart from scores of unclimbed peaks, much of the region had never been visited. For example, the whole of the northern half of the main ice cap was untrodden ground, and with two exceptions none of the glaciers on the western side of the range had been explored. Although most of the channels had been charted since the voyage of the *Beagle* in 1831, for hundreds of miles along this tortuous, uninhabited coast, no one had penetrated inland, while the interior of many of the islands was unknown. The eastern side of the range was comparatively well explored, but even there, there was much interesting work to be done.

That so much of the region still remains unexplored is due almost entirely to the physical difficulties of travel there, for during the last fifty years many attempts have been made to penetrate it. The chief problem is presented by the weather, which is said to be some of the worst in the world. Heavy rain falls for prolonged periods; fine spells are rare and usually brief, and above all there is the notorious Patagonian wind, the savage storms which often continue for weeks at a stretch, with gusts up to 130 mph. The terrain too, is unusually difficult. Most parts of the main range, even many on the eastern side, can only be approached by water and, because of the weather, the use of small craft on the lakes and fjords is liable to be a hazardous business. The glaciers in their lower reaches are often so broken and crevassed that it is virtually impossible to travel on them, and lateral moraines rarely provide an easy line of approach, as they usually do in the Himalaya. In the foothills the forest often presents an impassable barrier, particularly on the western side of the range, where the wind has twisted the stunted trees into a low-lying mass of tangled trunks and branches. It is these obstacles which have prevented most expeditions to the area from achieving more than a limited objective or covering more than a very small proportion of the region.

The lakes of Southern Patagonia were explored towards the end of the last century by several expeditions, notably by that of Francisco Moreno, a distinguished Argentine geographer, who discovered Lago Argentino and Lago San Martin. The first expedition into the main range was made in 1914 by Dr Frederick Reichert, who succeeded in reaching the head of the Moreno Glacier from Lago Argentino. Later, in 1916 and in 1933, he made two attempts to cross the main ice cap, the first from the head of Lago Viedma and the second from Lago San Martin. Though on both occasions he was frustrated by appalling weather conditions, he was able to bring back the first detailed accounts of the remarkable Plateau. Several more explorers have since tried to cross it. Another dominant figure in the exploration of the region was the redoubtable Salesian priest, Father Alberto de Agostini, who made no fewer than twelve expeditions to various parts of it, including the mountains of Tierra del Fuego, which have contributed the major part of our knowledge of the main range. The only complete crossing of the range had been made south of the ice cap by H. W. Tilman in 1956. During the course of his long voyage in *Mischief* he landed with two companions at the head of the Calvo Fjord on the Pacific side, and crossed the range to the front of the Moreno Glacier and back, a journey as the crow flies of twenty-five miles each way, which took them six weeks of arduous travel.

Geoff and I had first to decide upon the kind of expedition we were to take, and to begin with we were confronted by something of a vicious circle. Until we had formulated some clear objective we could hardly expect to receive financial support, and until we could discover the kind of work most likely to evoke support it was hard to choose an objective; particularly in view of our ignorance of local conditions. Neither of us cared very much what we did, so long as it gave us the chance to make the acquaintance of this fascinating region, and acquaintance that I hoped might ripen into terms of intimacy. In fact, I regarded this first trip as a reconnaissance, to learn something of problems and possibilities of exploratory travel with the view, later, to tackling a more ambitious venture. Eventually, after a good deal of research, we found the Trustees of the British Museum willing to send a botanist with us and to furnish a grant to cover his share of the cost. The man chosen for the job was Peter James and his assignment was to make a comprehensive collection of plants, lichens and mosses. This was a most valuable advance, for it gave us a nucleus upon which to build our plans.

Before the war, Tilman and I used to boast that we could work out our plans for an expedition to the Himalaya in half an hour on the back of an envelope. Basic simplicity was the keynote of all our ventures together; we knew exactly the weight of the food and equipment we would need, what we would have to take from England and what we could obtain locally and, above all, its cost. We were never more than a few pounds out in estimating our expenses. Planning an expedition to a new continent where inflation was rife was quite another matter, and Geoff and I soon found ourselves floundering in such a morass of uncertainties and conflicting advice that I began to wonder if we would ever get it organised. Moreover, Geoff was faced with the stern necessity of passing, his final examinations in the summer of 1958, while I was engaged in forestry work in Shropshire; with the result that things moved slowly.

Fortunately, in July, John Mercer appeared on the scene. He had recently returned from his second visit to the Andes of Southern Patagonia and was anxious to go there again. Having heard of our plans he immediately offered to come with us; an offer we gladly accepted. With his first-hand knowledge to guide us, most of our troubles dissolved. A man of thirty-five, he had had a varied career as a geographer; his activities having ranged from a study of the glaciers of Baffin Land to an investigation of the population problems of Samoa. In 1949 he had made an attempt to cross the Ice cap from the vicinity of Lago Viedma. His main reason for wishing to return to Patagonia was to continue a line of study which he had begun, the object of which was to determine the dates of successive periods of glacial advance. As Geoff himself was keen to do some glaciological work, this fitted in very nicely.

Peter Miles, the last member of the party to be recruited, was an Anglo-Argentine from Venado Tuerto in the Province of Santa Fe. A farmer by profession, he was a keen amateur naturalist, and he undertook to make collections of birds and insects both for the British Museum and for the Darwin Institute in Buenos Aires.

With this battery of scientific objectives we were able largely to finance the expedition with grants from the British Museum, and Percy Sladen Trust and the Mount Everest Foundation.

For our field of operations we chose the section of the range embraced by the western arms of Lago Argentino, largely because it was the most easily accessible. To begin with, Lago Argentino had a small town, El Calafate, on its shore, while none of the other lakes of Southern Patagonia had a town within hundreds of miles. Secondly it could be reached by air and by reasonably good roads. But by far the most important consideration was the fact that there was a government launch operating on the lake, by means of which we would be able to reach our various bases. Our plan, which was indefinite and elastic, was to establish a series of these bases at the heads of the western fjords of the lake, spending three or four weeks at each, over a total period of three months.

Peter James, Geoff and I sailed for Buenos Aires from Tilbury on November 1. John travelled by way of the United States, where he had some private affairs to settle. In securing the cheapest available third class passages, we had been required by the shipping company to sign a document stating, in effect, that we realised what we were in for and that we would not complain. The reason became apparent when we reached Lisbon, where our meagre accommodation in the stern of the ship became congested with a multitude of Portuguese *emigres* bound for Rio and Santos. The small saloon, particularly in bad weather, was rather like an underground train in the rush hour, and the noise was shattering. It was an interesting experience but scarcely enjoyable, and we were not sorry when, on the 23rd, we reached Buenos Aires, where we were met by Peter Miles.

We found ourselves staying at the City Hotel, one of the best in the capital, which provided a remarkable change from the slum conditions of the voyage. Normally we would have chosen a more modest establishment, but we were guests of the British Council, for whom I had undertaken to give some lectures. Dr MacKay, the representative of the Council, and his assistant Mr Whistler, had made admirable arrangements for our stay, and we spent a busy week meeting a large number of people who could help and advise us. They also helped us to steer our baggage through the intricacies of the Argentine Customs which, without friends at court, can be a long and difficult business. Besides our camping, climbing and survey equipment we had brought an inflatable rubber dinghy and a small outboard motor; but the bulk of our luggage consisted of twenty-five large venesta cases to accommodate Peter James' botanical specimens. The Ministry of Foreign Affairs arranged for this equipment to be imported duty free.

The directors of Shell Argentine Ltd. generously placed a station-wagon at our disposal, which proved invaluable. On 1 December Peter Miles, Geoff and John left Buenos Aires in this vehicle which was loaded with as much of our baggage as it would hold. They completed the 2,000 mile drive to El Calafate by the evening of the 7th, having stopped a day in Comodoro Rivadavia to repair a broken main spring and a shattered windscreen. The rest of our baggage was sent on a ship sailing from Buenos Aires on 29 November and due to reach Santa Cruz a week later. In fact she took more than three weeks to make the voyage, with the result that our baggage did not reach El Calafate until Christmas Eve. I flew there on 4 December and Peter James, who had been invited to attend a botanical congress in Cordoba, followed on the 11th.

2   Some Pioneers

In shape the outline of Lago Argentino resembles a squid. The main body of water, which drains eastward into the Santa Cruz River, is forty miles long by fifteen miles wide. Two channels run westward from this and subdivide into eight sinuous tentacles. Some of the fjords so formed are more than thirty miles long, and penetrate deep into the foothills of the Andes. The country surrounding the main lake is, like most of the Patagonian pampas, dry, treeless and covered with coarse, yellow grass; it rises gently from the level of the lake at 600 feet to hills and undulating plateaux some 3,000 feet high. It reminded me very much of Tibet: the bleak, arid landscape, the level strata of the sandstone hills, the clear, exhilarating air, the pale blue sky and the keen wind blowing from the glaciers.

El Calafate, which lies halfway along the southern shore of the main lake, consists of a few houses, mostly built of wood, with corrugated iron roofs. It seemed to me such a perfect replica of a Wild West filmset, that I would hardly have been surprised to see a troop of cowboys galloping down the broad, dusty street, firing their six-shooters into the air. It has three small and, by modern standards, primitive hotels, and several stores which sell anything from onions to tweed suits, from gramophone records to farm implements. It is the only town within hundreds of miles, and it serves all the sheep *estancias* in the vicinity of the lake. It derives its curious name from a thorny bush, common on the Patagonian pampas, which has an edible berry like a blackcurrant. There is a local saying that any visitor who eats calafate berries is sure to return to Patagonia.

Though in that area there is little land left to be exploited for sheep raising, the country is sparsely populated. This is because the land is so poor, owing largely to the lack of rain, that on the average it requires four acres to keep one sheep; and as each *estancia* carries from 3,000 to 20,000 head, and some even more, the farmsteads themselves are few and far between. Some of the *estancias* are run by large companies, but for the most part they are owned by private individuals who comprise the cosmopolitan community. Among those we met were Britons, Spaniards, Germans, Danes, Norwegians, Hungarians, Turks and Yugoslavs.

The first *estanciero* I met was Carlos Santiago Dickie, generally known as 'Charlie'. He was wearing one of those old-fashioned caps with ear-flaps turned back over the crown. In his early sixties, his handsome, rather aristocratic face was framed by bushy grey side-whiskers which gave him something of the appearance of a Victorian country squire. His father had come to 'the Lago' from the Falkland Islands in the early years of the century. He had a prodigious zest for life, and a fund of thrilling stories that would have kept the editor of a popular magazine in copy for a year or more. He told them with great fluency and with such enjoyment that they were frequently interrupted by gusts of Rabelasian laughter, which were usually accompanied by an eruption of sparks from his pipe, with the result that his clothes and (as I saw later) the cover of his favourite armchair were pitted with burns. Though I saw a great deal of him then and later, he never exhausted his repertoire, nor did I ever hear one of his stories repeated. His wife came from Shropshire and they had met in England during the First World War, when she was a nurse and he a wounded soldier. They had a widespread reputation for generosity and kindness, and I often heard it said that Charlie would give the shirt off his back to anyone who needed it. This was indeed high praise among people to whom generous hospitality is second nature.

Another couple that we were most fortunate to meet was Mr and Mrs Atkinson, whose Estancia Lago Roca lay near one of the southern arms of the lake. They immediately invited us to make it our base whenever and for as long as we liked. They were both keen naturalists and their knowledge of the flora and the birds of the region was of great value to Peter James and Peter Miles who, later, accepted their offer so literally that the living room of the farm became littered with a wild confusion of drying plants and skins.

The most remote *estancia* in the district, and perhaps in Patagonia, is La Cristina, which lies at the head of one of the north-western arms of Lago Argentino. Almost surrounded by rugged mountains, the only practicable approach to it is by launch, and then only when the weather is calm enough to permit the voyage. When we reached El Calafate it had already been isolated by constant storms for three months, but the owners, Mr and Mrs Masters and their son Herbert, were in daily communication by radio with the Dickies. When they heard of our arrival they invited us to come and stay with them as soon as possible. As we had been hoping to make our first base somewhere in that vicinity, this suited us admirably. They had a small steam launch which they offered to lend us, but it was old and not very seaworthy, and they advised us to come by Government launch as soon as the weather moderated.

This vessel was operated by the National Parks Administration, the director of which, Senor Tortorelli, we had met in Buenos Aires. He had very kindly issued instructions to the local authorities to place the launch at our disposal when we required it. It was kept at Punta Bandera, a small settlement on the lake shore, forty miles by road west of El Calafate, and at the entrance of the southern fjord system. This was a splendid place for Peter Miles to begin his work, for there were enormous numbers of waterfowl in the shallow, reedy lagoons surrounding it; among them black-headed swans, widgeon, teal, steamer ducks, flamingos and several varieties of geese. None of the local inhabitants seemed in the least interested in shooting these birds, which would have been very easy prey.

The morning of 13 December was fine and calm. We set out in the launch from Punta Bandera at eight o'clock, and half an hour later passed through a narrow passage, known as Hell's Gate, into the northern channel. Here the scene changed abruptly. The low-lying yellow pampas gave place to tall rock precipices and steep, forested slopes on either side of the fjord while, ahead, a mighty rampart of ice-peaks burst into view. These were the mountains of the Cordon Darwin, as that part of the main range is called. Even remembering that I was viewing them from only 600 feet above sea level, I found it hard to believe that none of them was more than 10,000 feet high. We passed a score of icebergs, some smooth and rounded like giant mushrooms, some like craggy islands with cliffs of royal blue, one like a medieval castle with turrets and battlements standing more than 100 feet above the water. They were drifting eastward to the main lake; some of them would reach its farthest shore, to be stranded there, incongruous objects among the desert sand and scrub.

After a voyage of two and a half hours, the launch dropped anchor in a little landlocked bay at the southern end of the La Cristina valley. Herbert Masters was there to meet us when we came ashore and, having disembarked our baggage, we accompanied him to his house, a large bungalow with a corrugated iron roof, set in a garden gay with flowers and half surrounded by a grove of tall poplars. There we met his parents.

Mr and Mrs Masters were both eighty-two years old. They came from Southampton where he had been a seaman on a nobleman's yacht; but they had decided that this was no life for a married man, so in 1900, at the age of twenty-four, they had emigrated to Patagonia, where he had worked on various *estancias* to gain some knowledge of sheep farming. In those days it was a wild and desolate land; there were virtually no roads, the only means of transport were by horseback and bullock cart, and the journey from the coast to Lago Argentino took several weeks. It is difficult to imagine the impact of such conditions upon a young woman, brought up in an ordinary Victorian home, who had never left England before.

The valley was first visited in 1902 by H. Prichard, while on an expedition to discover the Giant Sloth, which was then believed to exist in Patagonia. The Masters came there not long afterwards, looking for a place to settle. They were captivated by its beauty, and immediately decided that it was to be their home. They acquired a lifeboat that had been salvaged from a wreck in the Straits of Magellan, and brought it to the lake by bullock cart, a journey of several hundred miles. Then, with none of the amenities which most of us take for granted as basic necessities, beyond the reach of medical help and with little resource save their courage, their staunch reliance upon themselves and each other, they calmly faced the years of toil and privation which they knew must intervene before they could win even a small measure of comfort and security. They named their *estancia* after their daughter, Cristina, who died there when still a young girl.

They started with a small flock of sheep. Living in tents before they had built themselves a house, they cleared and ploughed a small plot of land and planted the grove of poplars which now shields them from the wind-storms blowing down from the glaciers. Today they own 12,000 sheep which range over twenty square miles of country. They employ a *capitas* (headman) and a number of *peones*, mostly half-breed Chilean Indians, who do the shepherding and other work of the *estancia*. Their produce is taken to Punta Bandera in a barge towed by the steam launch (successor to the lifeboat). Their comfortable house, their well-appointed shearing sheds and farm buildings, are equipped with electricity generated by wind and water power. They have two cars which they keep in Punta Bandera and use once a year 'to go to town', by which they mean Rio Gallegos, on the coast.

Their story, of course, is not unique, for such was the pattern of the lives of most people who came to settle in Patagonia, little more than half a century ago. But what a lesson it should be to us in our pampered modern society.

Mr Masters was small and spare, and as active as most men in their prime. He held himself so erect that he always gave me the impression that he was leaning over backwards. He had lively, humorous eyes but a diffident, almost apologetic manner. But despite his apparent shyness, he made no attempt to hide his enormous pride in his wife, his 'Senora' as he called her. He once came to me with a photograph of an attractive girl in Victorian dress and, with a conspiratorial wink said, 'This is the one I left my home for.' I replied, 'Who wouldn't?' and meant it. Mrs Masters looked very frail, as though it would hardly require a Patagonian wind to blow her away; and her hands were knotted with arthritis. But she ran her house with quiet efficiency and very little outside help; she cooked delicious meals and worked in her garden, which obviously gave her tremendous pleasure. In her face there was a look of profound serenity.

Herbert, their only son, was fifty-seven. He was well over six feet tall and so towered over both his parents. He had been educated at a British school in Buenos Aires, but otherwise had spent his whole life on the *estancia*. He was very clever with his hands, a gift for which he had plenty of scope. Perhaps his most remarkable achievement was the building of a launch, about forty tons displacement, from timber cut and seasoned on the *estancia*. It was beautifully made from plans taken from a magazine, and it had taken him several years to complete. It was not yet in use, as he was waiting the arrival of a motor which had been ordered from abroad, but he hoped that it would soon replace the old steam launch.

Chief among his varied interests, however, was his radio, which amounted almost to a passion. He had built a powerful transmitter with which he spent a great deal of his time talking to other 'Hams' in every part of the globe. This was probably the origin of his extraordinary knowledge about distant lands, from Tibet to New Zealand, from the Congo to Alaska. Oddly enough he seemed to have no desire to travel. This hobby, of course, had practical value for he was in constant touch with El Calafate and Rio Gallegos and with various *estancieros* in the district, several of whom he had inspired with his enthusiasm. It was also a great joy to his mother to be able to have a cosy chat with Mrs Dickie every morning at ten o'clock.

It was easy to understand why the Masters had fallen in love with the valley as soon as they saw it, for it is an enchanting place. It lies in a climatic zone between the heavy precipitation of the main range and the dry conditions of the pampas to the east, so that while there is a great deal of forest, there is also plenty of open country. It is several miles wide and runs northward from the fjord to the foot of Cerro Norte, a beautiful peak standing at its head, twelve miles away. Its upper five miles contains Lago Pearson (named after the patron of Prichard's expedition), the source of a wide river that flows through flat grass-land to the fjord, and is joined by a tributary coming down over a series of fine waterfalls from another large lake, high up in the mountains. The valley is bounded on the east by forested slopes rising in a series of terraces to a range of barren mountains, which again reminded me of Tibet, particularly in the evening light when they glowed with soft and varied colour. To the west, the valley is contained throughout its whole length by a narrow ridge separating it from the Upsala Glacier. Its crest, which can be reached in an hour from the *estancia*, commands a superb view of that vast ice-stream: westward eight miles across it to the great peaks of the Cordon Darwin; southward to where it plunges on a three mile front into the waters of Lago Argentino; northward in an ever widening sweep to the ice cap itself. I little thought that, two years later, I would arrive at La Cristina after a journey from the Pacific coast across the whole length of that fascinating region.

The series of terraces on both sides of the valley, which cradle a score of small lakes among the forest, are formed by old lateral moraines, which mark the successive stages in the retreat of a glacier, which not so long ago filled the valley and was once united with the Upsala Glacier. The latter has itself retreated considerably in recent years, and when the Masters first came there it used to overflow the ridge at several points with long tongues of ice.

Though the bulk of our baggage had not yet arrived at El Calafate, we had the survey instruments and much of the camping equipment with us, so that a start could be made with the field work. On 16 December, Geoff and John went to the farther shore of the north-western fjord, where they were to spend a fortnight working on the Upsala Glacier and its lower tributaries. They were taken there in the steam launch which was operated by the *capitas* and one of the farm hands. It was a remarkable contraption, like a sort of marine version of Stevenson's Rocket; the engine made a prodigious noise and steam issued from a dozen unlikely parts of the vessel's anatomy. Geoff enlivened their departure by falling into the water with a box of provisions which he was carrying aboard. He spent most of the three-hour voyage huddled in the minute boiler room drying his clothes.

The rest of us spent ten delightful days in the La Cristina valley, which provided Peter James with an excellent opportunity to make a botanical survey of this intermediate zone. It contained a great variety of climatic conditions and he had to work extremely hard to cover the ground. He was out every day collecting from early morning until evening, while he spent most of each night sorting and pressing his specimens. Fortunately the Masters had an inexhaustible supply of old newspapers, for most of his drying equipment was contained in the baggage we had sent by sea. Peter Miles also had plenty to occupy him. Like Punta Bandera, the valley was teeming with waterfowl, and there were large numbers of plover and ibis, and a variety of birds of prey, such as condors, eagles, owls and hawks; but he was mainly interested in the smaller forest birds. Apart from foxes, wild animals seemed to be comparatively scarce, and we saw none of the small deer (huemul) which inhabit the forest, and are exceedingly shy. Herbert told us that there were still a great many pumas in the mountains, which killed a lot of sheep during the winter; but though he had shot plenty of them in his time, they were very hard to find.

On 23 December, the government launch came to fetch us and, bidding a most reluctant farewell to the Masters, we returned to Punta Bandera. From there we drove out to the Atkinsons' *estancia*, for Peter James had decided to spend the next fortnight collecting in the country surrounding Lago Roca and in the mountains to the south before tackling the flora of the rainforests in the main range.

The following day our baggage arrived in El Calafate, and Peter Miles and I spent Christmas Day unpacking it and transporting the collecting equipment to Lago Roca. Apart from some dehydrated meat and tea which we had brought from England, we obtained all the provisions that we required for our excursions into the mountains in El Calafate. We dealt mostly with a Yugoslav storekeeper named Tonko Simunovic, a huge man with courtly manners, who also acted as our banker and our post office. Letters we received were addressed to 'c/o Tonko, Lago Argentino'.

On 26 December, Peter and I were taken in the Government launch to Onelli Bay on the coast of the north-western fjord, ten miles south of Upsala Glacier front, where we had arranged to meet Geoff and John a couple of days later.

3   Lago Onelli

We disembarked on a spit of land half a mile wide, separating Lago Onelli from Onelli Bay. It was covered with dense forest, which also clothed the steep mountainsides surrounding the bay and extended 2,500 feet above it. Like all the forest in Patagonia it was composed of *Nothofagus*, which is said to be a first cousin to our beech, though personally I could see no resemblance. Though there are a great many varieties of this tree, only four extend to these southern latitudes; of these *Nothofagus Antarctica*, is the most common. Though we had seen plenty of woods at La Cristina, this was the first time we had been in the rain belt covering the main range, and the forest here was altogether different. There was a strange feel about it, eerie but not unfriendly, as though it belonged to another geological age, or perhaps to a Hans Andersen story.

As soon as the launch had departed, we went about making ourselves at home in a small clearing ten yards from the shore. Peter was a fastidious camper, and an excellent cook. Our stores were unpacked and neatly stored, while bunches of onions, garlic, and salami sausages, and backs of bacon were slung from poles. He was fond of his food, but for a man of his size (he weighed over seventeen stone) he did not eat a great deal, and could go for a long time with nothing at all. When I first met him in Buenos Aires dressed in his city suit, which looked as if it were about to burst, his sallow face under an Al Capone hat, he appeared corpulent, and I had grave doubts about his ability to survive an expedition of this sort. Now, in his rough expedition clothes, his appearance was completely transformed and he resembled the toughest of lumberjacks. I already knew that this was the real Peter Miles; physically immensely strong and very tough, well used to rough living and able to endure a great deal of hardship. He was a splendid companion, humorous and versatile in his talk (some, perhaps, might have thought he talked too much), an excellent raconteur and remarkably even-tempered.

It was a lovely evening and we cooked and ate our supper by a large fire, Peter was as thrilled as I was with our situation on the shore of this huge, uninhabited fjord, at the gateway to an unexplored part of the range. We slept on the beach, but in the night there was a sharp shower which sent us scrambling to our tent. But the rain did not last long, and by morning it was fine again. Indeed during the whole of our stay in the Onelli region we were blessed with a spell of weather very rare in Patagonia, and except for a few rain storms it was fine and almost windless the whole time.

We set off early to reconnoitre our surroundings, first making our way westward through the forest. Many years ago Mrs Masters' brother had made a bold attempt to establish an *estancia* here to breed cattle; but he had abandoned the project together with much of his stock. As a result, the surrounding forest was inhabited by wild cattle and horses, which were confined to comparatively narrow bounds by the precipices and glaciers. Within these bounds, however, they had trampled a network of tracks, which was a great help to us in moving about.

When we reached the eastern shore of Lago Onelli we found that end of the lake so filled with icebergs that there was little water to be seen. We then went round to the northern shore and climbed up through the forest above it, making for a prominent hill standing 1,000 feet over the lake. On the way we had an alarming encounter with a wild bull. He was only a few yards away when we saw him, and he looked as if he was about to charge; however, he thought better of it and trotted off, bellowing, into the undergrowth.

As we had expected, the hill commanded a splendid view of the surrounding country. We could see the whole of the lake, which measured three miles by two miles. The entire western and north-western shores were occupied by the fronts of two great glacier systems, which joined each other a mile beyond. The western ice-stream, which we called the Onelli Glacier, entered the lake as a low, comparatively smooth tongue, but the northern front presented a continuous cliff of ice-standing 200 feet above the water. Every now and then as we watched, huge blocks of ice calved from this cliff and fell into the water with an impressive roar. The waves started by these avalanches spread right across the lake; though, from where we stood, they looked like ripples on a pond, we discovered later that this was not quite the case. The blocks of ice breaking from the glacier fronts drifted down the lake and pressed themselves into a confused mass at its eastern end, which we had seen that morning. Our first objective was to establish a base at the western end of Lago Onelli, and for this our rubber dinghy would be needed; for there was obviously no way round the northern side of the lake, and on its southern side there was a river to cross and also one place where a precipice fell sheer into the water. Returning to camp, we spent the afternoon unpacking the dinghy and motor, assembling them and going for a cruise in the bay to try them out.

The following morning we carried the dinghy and motor and 80 lb of food through the forest and along the northern shore of Lago Onelli, until we found a narrow channel running through the mass of icebergs. Here we launched the boat, stowed the food and rowed cautiously through the channel until we reached the open water beyond. There we started the motor, set a course for the south-west corner of the lake and sat back to enjoy ourselves.

It was a perfect day, cloudless and still; the sun was so warm that we might have been on one of the Italian lakes. The blue water and the dark green forest, fringed with emerald at its upper limit, contrasted beautifully with the immense cirque of glaciers and ice mountains which opened to our view. We watched several avalanches falling into the lake from the glacier front, and we could now appreciate the size of the wave caused by the ice-blocks, some as large as houses, hitting the water; but by the time they reached us they had so broadened that we scarcely felt them. When we reached the south-west corner of the lake we found a little cove partly enclosed by the lateral moraine of the Onelli Glacier which projected far into the water. Bordering the cove there was a grassy glade covered with flowers, and sheltered on two sides by the forest and on the third by a high ridge of the moraine. We landed the stores at this delightful spot, which later became known as 'Pedro's Camp'.

It was only one o'clock when we started back, so we spent some time cruising along the northern and southern shores. When eventually we reached the packed icebergs towards the eastern end of the lake we found that the channel which we had come through that morning had widened, so instead of stopping the motor and getting out the oars, I merely throttled down to a slow speed. As we drew near to the point where we had embarked, we reached a narrow passage between two bergs. I was just about to stop the engine when the propeller guard struck a submerged ledge of ice; the motor was wrenched from its fastening and I turned in time to see it sinking beneath the surface. I made a grab at it, but it was just out of reach, and a moment later it disappeared.

At first I was not particularly worried, for by then we were only ten yards from the shore and I thought that we were in shallow water, though it was too heavily charged with glacier mud to see more than a foot below the surface. I scrambled on to the berg, of which the submerged ledge was part, and stayed there to mark the spot while Peter went ashore and returned with a twelve-foot pole. To our dismay we found that even with this we could not reach the bottom. We then discovered that the berg, which we had thought was grounded, was in fact afloat and had already drifted over the spot where the accident had happened, so that this was now impossible to locate. Neither of us was prepared to dive to the bottom of more than twelve feet of icy water and grope about beneath the ice, so there was nothing for it but to abandon our precious motor.

Very crestfallen we returned to camp, where we found that John and Geoff had arrived overland from their Upsala Camp, where they had spent a profitable time on their respective glaciological tasks. To save carrying it through the forest they had left most of their equipment behind; so the next day, while Geoff did a survey station on top of the hill we had climbed, and Peter began collecting, John and I took the dinghy round the coast to fetch it. The prospect of a twelve-mile row gave us cause to regret the loss of the motor; but again the day was fine and calm, and pulling gently over the smooth, sunlit water, which reflected the forest and the ice peaks around us, was a most pleasant occupation. After rounding the point of Onelli Bay we passed a number of very large icebergs drifting down from the Upsala Glacier front, with cliffs and caverns of vivid blue, some of them worn into fantastic shapes. We gave these monsters a wide berth, for sometimes weird noises would emanate from one or other of them; it would begin to pitch like a ship in a rough sea, and occasionally the whole mass would turn turtle causing a tremendous commotion in the surrounding water. As we approached it the glacier front itself was a spectacular sight, consisting of an ice cliff nearly three miles wide and 200 feet high, which was constantly calving fresh bergs into the fjord. We returned to camp by six o'clock.

Lago Onelli drained into the bay by a short but wide and rapidly flowing river. After supper that evening we struck camp and I ferried the party in three relays across the mouth of the river to the far side, and from there we carried the dinghy and our equipment through the forest to the south-east corner of Lago Onelli, which we reached at eleven o'clock as night was falling. It was mid-summer and we were in Lattitude 50° S, so that the night was very short, and it never became really dark, particularly when the sky was clear.

The next day I took the equipment in the dinghy, keeping close in to the southern shore of the lake, while the others walked along it as far as they could. I rowed to a point beyond the line of precipices which rose sheer from the water, unloaded my cargo on to some rocks a few feet above the water, and returned to ferry the others, one at a time, round the cliffs. While I was bringing John across we heard an avalanche fall from the glacier, two miles away across the lake. Five minutes later we reached the place where I had dumped the loads to find that a heavy swell was beating against the rocks where they lay and all but washing them away. We had to stand well off the shore, or the dinghy would have been ripped on submerged rocks now revealed by the backlash of the waves. At length the swell subsided and we were able to land and carry the equipment to a safe place in the forest above.

We were lucky to escape serious consequences resulting from my inexperience; for when the last man had been brought across and we were reloading the equipment into the boat, we heard a prolonged roar from across the lake and watched a series of ice towers collapse and crash into the water. It looked as though the glacier front were under an artillery bombardment. We hastily unloaded the boat and carried it and the equipment well clear of the lake. Five minutes later the waves came; this time they were many times larger than before and completely submerged the rocks where I had originally dumped the loads. The lesson was well and cheaply learnt.

We reached 'Pedro's Camp' in the middle of the afternoon and pitched our tents on the soft grass of the meadow. There was ample firewood and a stream of clear water nearby. After a brew of tea, Peter went off with his gun and butterfly net and Geoff set up his theodolite on the crest of the moraine.

The work on which John was engaged was unusual and fascinating. The history of most glaciers is marked by alternate periods of advance and retreat, and it is of great value to know when these periods occurred, not only to the glaciologist but also as evidence of past weather cycles. It is rarely possible to discover this information with any precision, but in wooded country when the advance of a glacier has penetrated the forest on either side, one often finds living trees that have been pushed over by the moraine marking the limit of the advance. By cutting an appropriate section from such a tree and studying the rings, one can determine the year when it was disturbed and thus date the climax of that particular advance. The technique has been employed with considerable success in North America, but it had never been tried in the Southern Hemisphere.

During the next two days, while Geoff was busy surveying the main glacier fronts, I went with John across the Onelli Glacier in search of suitable trees for his investigation. We camped in the forest beside a vast icefall forming part of the northern glacier system, where John obtained some excellent specimens from an old lateral moraine. The *Nothofagus* there were unusually large, many of them fully eighty feet high. It seemed odd to be sitting in the dark shade of these ancient trees, looking out across a huge expanse of ice, riven and twisted and dazzling white. Another thing that never quite lost its strangeness for me was the sight of flocks of green parrots flying over these glaciers, uttering the same raucous cries that hitherto I had associated only with Indian jungles and such tropical places. Wrens were by far the most common birds in the forest; they used to perch a few feet away to scold us wherever we went. A species also much in evidence was a woodpecker, the male of which was crested with a beautiful red cockade. Occasionally we saw hummingbirds hovering like large bees about the red flowers of the weigela bushes, but they were comparatively rare.

The amazing spell of fine weather continued into the New Year. On 1 January, Geoff, John, and I carrying three or four days' food, set out to explore the Onelli Glacier. We found the going so easy that in a few hours we had almost reached its upper basin, which consisted of a wide amphitheatre where a number of steep icefalls coming down from the surrounding mountains converged on to the centre. The largest of these originated in a broad saddle, which we assumed must lie on the main continental watershed. Geoff and I were anxious to reach a point from which we could look into the unexplored country on the Pacific side of the range. For this purpose we had chosen a peak standing above the north-west corner of the amphitheatre, which seemed to be high enough to command a view over the saddle. Leaving the northern side of the glacier we plunged immediately into dense forest. It was slow, strenuous work forcing our way through this, for the ground was steep and broken by lines of cliffs which had been invisible from below, hidden by the trees. But it was considerably worse when we reached the 'emerald band' at the upper limit of the forest. This was composed of a tangled mass of dwarf *Nothofagus*, their twisted trunks trained by the prevailing wind to grow almost horizontally, their branches intertwined like ivy to form a kind of lattice about six feet deep. It was appalling stuff to struggle through, even with comparatively light loads; most of the time we were stepping from branch to branch; often our footholds would break and we became firmly entrapped in the mass beneath.

It was eight o'clock by the time we had cleared this zone, and found a suitable ledge on which to pass the night. According to our aneroid the altitude was 2,800 feet, which seemed a paltry height to have reached after a long day's toil. All the same, our bivouac was a splendid viewpoint, and as we ate our supper we watched the sunset colours spreading over a wide expanse of forest, glacier and lake to the rose-red mountains beyond the fjord. I was asleep long before dark, but I awoke at one o'clock. There was no moon; the Southern Cross and 'Magellan's Cloud' were near the zenith, and the peaks around the amphitheatre were etched against a sky so brilliant with stars that here and there the ice shone with a phosphorescent glow.

We slept longer than we had intended and it was nearly seven o'clock before we started. An hour's easy climbing took us up 1,400 feet, to the first buttress on the northern ridge of our mountain. John had injured his arm in the forest the day before and it was giving him some trouble; so, as it looked as though we were in for some hard rock climbing, he decided to turn back. Geoff and I put on the rope, and after three or four difficult pitches, we reached the top of the buttress. From there the ridge swept upwards for 2,000 feet, steep, narrow and serrated. Though the rock was loose and we had to treat it with care, it was not particularly difficult, and we could move together most of the time. The sun was warm and the air was still. To our left we looked straight down into the great amphitheatre; to our right there was a vertical drop to a tributary of the Onelli Glacier, which was fed entirely by ice avalanches falling from the southern face of the mountain.

Climbing such a ridge in such conditions was sheer joy, and we were in high spirits when, at a height of 6,500 feet, we reached the point where it ran out into what appeared to be an easy snow slope leading to the summit. We found, however, that our troubles had not begun. The surface of the slope was unlike any I had ever seen; it was composed of balls of ice like large glass marbles, which slipped like quicksilver beneath our feet and threatened to carry us down on a rolling mass over the brink of the precipice below. At first we could find no way of dealing with this phenomenon; but after some experimenting, we discovered that, by flogging the surface with our ice-axes, we could cause it to avalanche in sections, and scoop steps in a comparatively compact layer beneath. It was a delicate operation and very hard work, and it took us nearly an hour to climb the first 100 feet; but beyond that the slope became less steep, and the ice marbles gradually gave place to soft snow.

At the top of the slope we were confronted by a more formidable obstacle, which had hitherto been hidden from us by the convexity of the slope. This was an ice-cliff running right across the face of the mountain, overhung by a cornice decorated with icicles, and separated from the snow below by a bergschrund, like a moat beneath a castle wall. At first it looked a hopeless proposition, and I felt a pang of disappointment that, after such an exhilarating climb, we were to be denied access to the summit, which a moment before had seemed within easy reach.

It was 12.30. A bank of cloud had begun to billow across the saddle from the west, but as this was a daily occurrence at this hour, it did not worry us. We still had ten hours daylight in hand. On close examination of the wall, we found that, towards the left, just at its lowest part, there was a break in the cornice and the bergschrund was spanned by a snow bridge. This happy combination of circumstances provided the one chance of climbing the wall, which at this point was only about twenty-feet high.

I anchored myself securely below the lip of the bergschrund while Geoff made his way slowly across the bridge. The surface of the wall was composed of a deep layer of rotten snow which had to be hacked away before he could cut hand and foot holds in the ice beneath. We had no ice pitons and it was very difficult work, as he was constantly thrown off balance by the overhanging snow above. When he was halfway up, the step on which he was standing broke away and he fell. He landed on a snow bridge, which, to my amazement and relief, held him. But in falling he had driven his right crampon deeply into the flesh of his left leg between the calf and the shin.

It was a nasty wound and must have been painful, but now Geoff s blood was up and he firmly vetoed my suggestion that we should abandon the climb. So, having bound up his leg with a silk scarf, he took over my position, and I crossed the bridge to tackle the wall. I was more fortunate, and after a long struggle I was able to reach the top of the cliff, where I found myself on a slope of hard ice, 100 feet below the main west ridge of the mountain. I brought Geoff up, and at 2.15 we reached the crest, where we paused for a snack.

There was a cold breeze blowing from the north and, as our clothes were thoroughly soaked by contact with the wet snow on the wall, we were not inclined to linger. Also our goal was still a long way off. The ridge, however, was broad and easy, and, two hours later, at 4.15, we reached the summit, 8,100-feet high. To our surprise and delight we found we were standing on the continental divide. The weather to the west was not as clear as we might have wished, but looking down across the saddle we could see the dark tracts of forest on the Pacific side, broken in the far distance by a narrow arm of water which must have been the upper reaches of the Penguin Sound. The country to the north-west fell away gently in a wide glacier valley, very bleak and inhospitable. By contrast, the sunlit valleys of the Onelli basin looked warm and green and lovely.

We allowed ourselves only half an hour on the summit before starting to descend, for our time was running rather short. Climbing down the ice-cliff was more difficult than I had expected and I spent far too long over it. Geoff, however, decided to save time by jumping down from a point where the wall overhung the bergschrund. He cut steps down to the brink and stood contemplating the drop of nearly thirty feet with evident distrust. I suggested that he should cut an ice bollard, hitch the rope round it, and slide down. He was turning round to carry out this manoeuvre when his foot slipped. He just managed to swing himself round and leap forward so that he fell with his feet under him, and landed, shaken and winded but otherwise unhurt, on the soft snow slope, well clear of the bergschrund. After this spectacular performance we had no further excitement and, climbing down the ridge as fast as the unstable rock would allow, we reached our bivouac just before ten o'clock, with plenty of daylight to spare. We were too tired to have much interest in food, but we consumed several pints of tea.

The sun was already high when we awoke the next morning, and for a long time we basked luxuriously in its warmth before rousing ourselves to prepare a leisurely breakfast. Starting at noon, we climbed down precipitous slopes to the 'Avalanche Glacier', and that evening we joined John at a rendezvous on the southern side of the Onelli Glacier. From there we went up into the great amphitheatre where, in its farthest recesses we found little isolated pockets of forest, like dark green gems set in a wilderness of ice.

Our time in this fascinating valley was all too short, but we had arranged for the launch to pick us up on 8 January, and we had to make our way back to Onelli Bay in time to meet it.

4 'Vulcan Viedma'

Returning to El Calafate on 8 January, we met Barny Dickinson and John Cotton, two Argentine mountaineers who, at my invitation, had come to join us for their summer holidays. We had intended to collect fresh supplies and go almost immediately to the head of Seno Mayo, the westernmost arm of Lago Argentino, for our second sortie into the main range. But one engine of the launch had broken down, and the captain was unwilling to venture out again until it had been repaired; as a result we had to defer this project for three weeks. We decided that Geoff, John and I would travel north to Lago Viedma in the station-wagon, which unfortunately was not large enough to take us all, while the other four went south-westward to the head of the Brazo Sur, and beyond to Lago Frio.

I was particularly anxious to visit the region around Lago Viedma to investigate the belief that there was an active volcano among the glaciers to the west. Since the discovery of the great lakes of Southern Patagonia there had been persistent reports of volcanic activity somewhere in the vicinity of the ice cap. For example, nearly fifty years ago some travellers had described showers of volcanic ash falling near the western end of Lago Viedma; deposits of volcanic ejecta had been found on several of the glaciers farther north; and, according to de Agostini and others, settlers near the shores of Lago San Martin had seen, on several occasions, columns of smoke rising from the ice cap to the west.

Dr Reichert's expedition of 1933 had reached the ice cap by ascending the O'Higgins Glacier from the southernmost branch of Lago San Martin. For sixteen days they were confined to their tents on the edge of the plateau by violent storms, and by the time these had abated their supplies were nearly exhausted. However, they pressed on westwards and reached a point close to the main divide. Visibility was still bad, but when they were at their farthest point, it cleared for a few minutes and they saw, looming out of the mist, 'a volcanic cone, 3,000 metres high', from which clouds of steam were issuing. For some reason Reichert's discovery did not receive the recognition it deserved, and in the subsequent speculation about the existence and whereabouts of the volcano it seems to have been largely ignored. His route to the ice cap was followed twice, in 1957 and 1958, by parties led by Hugo Corbela, but no fresh evidence had emerged.

In 1954–1955 the American Air Force made a series of survey flights over the range. Examining the photographs taken on these, Professor Keller of the University of Chile and Dr Lliboutry, a distinguished French glaciologist, found what they thought to be an active vent on a large rock outcrop in the upper basin of the Viedma Glacier. Lliboutry himself flew over the place in 1952, and the observations he made seemed to confirm this belief. Describing them he wrote, 'I distinctly saw a crater of ashes on a level with the glacier. At the firn line there is an irregular brown marking which could not be explained by any moraine deposit, and is perhaps the evidence of a relatively recent eruption of ashes.' No one had ever visited this peculiar outcrop, which had come to be known as 'Vulcan Viedma', and we were anxious to find out whether or not it really was a volcano erupting through an ice-sheet some thousands of feet thick.

We left El Calafate in the station wagon on 10 January. There was a fair earth road running northward along the valley of Rio Leon, the river by which Lago Viedma drains to Lago Argentino. But it involved the crossing of three ferries, one over Rio Santa Cruz and two over Rio Leon, and as the middle one was out of action we were forced to make a long detour to the east by a very rough pony track over the hills. There we saw large numbers of guanacos, long-necked animals resembling the llamas of Bolivia and Peru. Though in the more remote parts of Patagonia these creatures are still fairly plentiful, their numbers are now only a small fraction of what they were fifty years ago. They are large animals which can find little cover among the small scrub of pampas and are therefore easy to shoot; with the result that they have been mercilessly killed for their skins which, particularly those of the young beasts, make excellent rugs. They are supposed to be protected, but they are still being slaughtered, and there is grave danger that before long they will become extinct.

Another creature, extremely common both in the hills and the flat country bordering the lakes, was the rhea, the South American equivalent of the ostrich. When I first saw them, these huge birds looked singularly out of place against a background of glaciers. They have most peculiar breeding habits: a dozen or more females lay a single clutch of as many as sixty or seventy eggs; after which they take no further part in the matter, and leave the business of incubating the eggs and rearing the chicks entirely to the males. Unlike the guanaco, though they have been and are still hunted, their numbers do not seem to be diminishing.

Descending from the hills in the late afternoon we rejoined the road at a place called Punta del Lago, consisting of a store and an inn, at the eastern end of Lago Viedma. Continuing round the northern side of the lake, the road gradually deteriorated into a very rough track, which sometimes vanished for long stretches among the sand dunes, rocks and scrub which composed the desolate landscape. The station wagon suffered heavy punishment, and most of the time we were grinding along in bottom gear. Soon after leaving Punta del Lago we called at an *estancia* belonging to some friends of John, where we had dinner: then we drove on until dark and slept under the lee of a clump of calafate bushes.

At eight o'clock the next morning we reached the Rio de Vuelta, which flows from the eastern valleys of the Fitzroy range. This was the end of the 'motor road', for the swift river was spanned by a suspension bridge only wide enough to allow the passage of horses. At the bridge we found some twenty men, gathered round fires on which they were preparing their barbecue breakfasts. They were ranchers and *peones*, tough looking characters, from the scattered *estancias* across the river. They had come there that morning to meet the mail bus which was due to arrive from the Atlantic port of Santa Cruz, 250 miles away. We tried to enlist their help to transport our baggage to the foot of the range, now some fifteen miles away; but they were too absorbed in the enjoyment of their breakfast to take any interest in our problem, so we returned to a *puesta* that we had passed a couple of miles back.

Unlike most parts of Central Asia, where pack transport is usually available even in the most remote places, it is extraordinarily difficult to obtain in Patagonia. It took us the whole day to negotiate the hire of a horse and a man to come with it. By nightfall, however, we had overcome the stubborn opposition of the man in charge of the *puesta*, and the next day we reached Estancia Rio Tunnel, at the north-west corner of Lago Viedma.

The farm was owned by an old Norwegian lady and her three sons, all in their late thirties. Mrs Halversen greeted us in a gruff, unsmiling manner, like a matriarch who has a poor opinion of men in general; but we soon discovered that this air masked a most kindly disposition. 'The Boys', she told us, were away at one of the *puestas*; they were often absent for days at a time, and one never knew when they would be back; but meanwhile her *capitas* would have orders to do what he could for us. She was far from reticent, and as she bustled about her kitchen-cum-sitting-room, cooking and serving our meals, she spoke with much emphasis on such a bewildering variety of subjects and in such a strange mixture of Spanish, Norwegian and English, that it was very hard to follow the gist of the discourse.

We slept in one of the farm buildings, and after an early breakfast the *capitas* produced a pony to carry our baggage up the valley of the Rio Tunnel. As all the men on the farm were busy bringing in sheep for shearing, no one could be spared to accompany us, which meant that one of us would have to bring the pony back. As there was no pack-saddle available our baggage was put into an enormous canvas bag which was then slung across the pony's back. It made an extremely awkward load which was constantly slipping to one side or the other, or becoming snagged on rocks or tree stumps. Fortunately for us the pony was a philosophical creature, and placidly submitted to our clumsy handling of him and his load.

The first section of the valley was a difficult gorge, and to avoid this we had to climb 2,000 feet up very steep grass slopes and over a col. Beyond this the path led across a precipitous scarp formed by a landslide. Here there were several passages where it was difficult enough for a man to find adequate foothold, let alone a badly loaded pony, and where a slip would have sent the animal plunging down to the river, 1,000 feet below. However, he displayed an astonishing aptitude for mountaineering, and we reached the other side of the scarp with no more serious mishap than the loss of part of our supply of sugar which, during one critical passage, had poured out of a hole in the canvas bag.

We now entered a beautiful open valley of gentle pastureland interspersed with patches of forest, dominated by the graceful spires of Fitzroy and Cerro Torre. After five hours' marching we reached a glacier lake enclosed by vertical rock walls. It was obvious we could take the pony no farther, so after a late lunch, while John and Geoff pitched camp in a pleasant glade, I rode back down the valley, using the folded canvas bag as a saddle.

The pony was as willing as he was even-tempered and I had no difficulty in urging him to a steady canter over the smoother parts of the way. At one point, as we were descending a steep slope, the improvised girth slipped and I fell head over heels down the slope. The friendly animal stopped and eyed me pityingly as I scrambled back and recovered the 'saddle' from under his belly. After that I bore in mind the Tibetan dictum, 'If your horse can't carry you up hill he is no horse; if you don't lead him down hill you are no man', and we reached the *estancia* with no further mishap, just in time for supper.

As soon as the meal was over I set out once more, despite the protests of Mrs Halversen and the *capitas* who obviously thought I was mad. It was 8.45 and I still had two hours daylight before me. This time I made my way through the gorge, and climbing as fast as I could, reached the middle section of the valley as the last remnant of the light was fading from the surrounding snows. I slept on a soft bed of leaves in the forest, and was woken at dawn by gentle rain falling on my face. When I reached their camp two hours later, Geoff and John were still asleep.

After I had left them the previous afternoon, they had reconnoitred a complicated route through the glaciers blocking the head of the valley. This enabled us that day to reach a pass, 4,300 feet high, leading directly on to the Viedma Glacier. It was the pass that Reichert had discovered in 1916, on his first attempt to cross the Ice cap. From there the Viedma Glacier appears as a vast triangular sheet of ice descending gently from the Plateau of which it forms a kind of lobe. It penetrates the eastern rim of the Plateau as an ice-stream nearly ten miles wide but contracts rapidly, and after flowing for twelve miles it reaches Lago Viedma on a front of two miles.

The general altitude of the plateau itself is about 5,000 feet, but it is intersected by a number of separate ranges of much greater elevation. One of these, the Cordon Mariano Moreno, stretches for fifteen miles across the head of the Viedma Glacier, and contains peaks up to 11,600 feet. We had no difficulty in identifying the 'Vulcan Viedma' lying close under the eastern flanks of this range; it looked like a long, black island in a sea of ice, and it was the only feature of its kind in the whole basin.

Early on the morning of 15 January, carrying enough food for eight days, we climbed down 800 feet from the pass to the glacier, and set off towards the 'Vulcan'. Although the slope of the glacier was almost imperceptible, and its surface had appeared from the pass to be perfectly smooth, we found that much of it was so broken that it might have formed part of an icefall. A series of deep longitudinal valleys intersected by transverse crevasses, forced us to make long detours. Later we were confronted by a wide river flowing swiftly over the surface of the ice, and we had to explore far along its tortuous course to find a place where it was shallow enough to ford. We passed a number of spectacular 'Moulins', huge circular shafts plunging vertically into the glacier, their smooth walls echoing the sinister roar of subterranean rivers. Geoff had brought a 600-foot line with a lead weight attached for measuring the depth of these monsters; but each time we tried the line became entangled, presumably by unseen cascades below, and we achieved little.

About three or four miles from the side of the glacier we came to a place where pumice was scattered on the surface of the ice over a very wide area. It was rapidly decomposing; most of it had already disintegrated into a fine silt, and even the largest lumps were so sodden that it was difficult to pick them up without crushing them. This suggested that the pumice was of fairly recent origin, for it would not be long before the whole lot was washed away. It was an exciting find, and even Geoff, who had been very sceptical about Lliboutry's discovery, was forced to admit that the outcrop we were approaching might after all turn out to be a volcano.

In the middle of the afternoon we reached a medial moraine which, running as straight as a Roman road down the centre of the glacier from the southern end of the 'Vulcan', provided us with easy going. We were surprised to find that the heaps of debris, some of them thirty or forty feet high, contained no pumice, nor indeed any kind of volcanic rocks. As we went, we watched a dense bank of cloud pouring over the Mariano Moreno range from the west. So closely did it cling to the contour of the mountains, so sharply was its edge defined against the blue sky, that it might easily have been mistaken for part of the ice cap, but for its rapid movement as it cascaded across the main divide, plunged down the eastern side and vanished.

We reached the southern end of the 'Vulcan' at 7.30, and pitched our tent under a massive, overhanging boulder. That night a storm broke with considerable violence, and continued, with occasional lulls, for more than a week. Had it come twelve hours earlier we would have had a very rough time reaching our objective against the wind and driving rain. As it was, under the lee of the outcrop and with the protection of our boulder, we lay in comparative comfort while it spent its first fury.

On the morning of the third day there was a lull in the storm and we ventured out to investigate the 'Vulcan'. It was three and a half miles long and perhaps a mile wide, with its highest point at the northern end standing some 1,500 feet above the surface of the glacier. A few hours sufficed to explore every part of it. It was composed almost entirely of sedimentary and metamorphic rocks, and there was no sign whatever of any volcanic or thermal activity, either contemporary or ancient. Wherever the mysterious deposits of pumice we had found on the glacier had come from, it was certainly not from here. I was already prepared for this disappointment by the absence of volcanic material on the medial moraine and by the nature of the rocks around our camp; but I had still been hoping for some freak phenomenon to be revealed on the northern part of the outcrop. Geoff on the other hand was delighted that his scepticism had been vindicated. Nevertheless the pumice had furnished one more piece of evidence of the existence of the elusive volcano somewhere in this great wilderness of ice.

Near its centre, the outcrop was almost bisected by a deep, circular valley, or amphitheatre, and it was obviously this that Lliboutry had mistaken for a crater. It contained a large lake basin which was then almost empty; but a series of concentric shorelines and many stranded icebergs showed that from time to time the water was dammed back by the glacier on the eastern side of the outcrop to form a lake, 400 feet deep. On the southern part of the outcrop there were several smaller lakes with grassy shores, where we collected a dozen species of flowering plants and a variety of water insects. We were surprised to find, also, some animal droppings, probably those of deer or hares. We took some for identification, but unfortunately they had disintegrated by the time we got home.

In several places round the perimeter of the outcrop there were wide ravines, up to 100 feet deep, separating the rock from the glacier. At first we took them for 'melt pits' (troughs formed by the rock becoming heated by the sun and melting the adjacent ice), and we were puzzled by their extraordinary size; for they were much larger than any I had found even in the Himalaya where the sun is far stronger. Later, however, we realised that they were not 'melt pits' at all, but that these huge trenches had been scoured out of the solid glacier ice by the force of the wind.

That afternoon Geoff and I experienced an impressive sample of that wind. It had been comparatively calm for the previous hour or so, and we were just completing our investigation of the northern end of the 'Vulcan' when, without any warning, the tornado struck with incredible violence. I did not see what happened to Geoff, but I was blown off my feet by the first blast. The wind whipped the snow from the surface of the glacier and hurled it along as a dense cloud of spray. As the temperature was well above freezing, the snow had melted by the time it reached us and in a few moments we were completely drenched, as though we had been subjected to the concerted aim of a fireman's hose. We were roped together, and fortunately only a few hundred yards directly to windward of a gap leading to the amphitheatre; so, although we could see nothing, we had only to allow ourselves to be hurled up the slope towards it. There, funnelled by the gap, the wind was stronger than ever and we had to crawl through on hands and knees until we reached a steep gully beyond. As we made our way back to camp, keeping well under the lee of the main ridge of the 'Vulcan', over which the wind and spray still thundered, we speculated upon our chances of survival had we encountered such a storm on the peak above Lago Onelli.

Having investigated the 'Vulcan', we had intended to attempt to climb one of the peaks of the Mariano Moreno range; but as the weather showed no sign of improving, we decided to travel right down the Viedma Glacier to some forest bordering its southern flank, where John could pursue his quest for trees that had been disturbed by the ice. The wind had abated by the next morning and, though it was still fairly strong, it was at our backs, helping rather than impeding us. We followed the medial moraine for ten miles, and it was only when we left it to cross to the side of the glacier that we ran into difficult ice. That evening we camped by a stream in a sheltered hollow, deep in the forest. Soon after we had got there the storm revived some of its former violence, which it maintained for the next thirty-six hours.

We built an enormous fire, feeding it with the largest of the dead tree-trunks that we could shift. A peculiarity of *Nothofagus* wood is that it burns much more completely than most woods of the northern hemisphere, and it leaves so little ash, that however large a fire we made at night, it was always completely dead by the morning. During the day, from its warm environment, we watched with snug satisfaction the solid curtains of rain driving horizontally across the steep valleys above, and the tall trees bending with the wave-like rhythm of rippling corn.

On the second morning we awoke to a strange stillness. Though it was less than 2,000 feet above sea level, the summer forest lay under a deep blanket of snow. Our stock of food was almost finished so, as John was satisfied with his collection of tree-sections, we set out across the glacier at 6.30 after a very meagre breakfast. There was a dense mist, and though we had reconnoitred a route the previous day we had some difficulty in finding our way through the shattered ice. By mid-morning the weather had changed back to its former regime of wind and rain, which lashed our faces and soaked our clothes; but at least we could see where we were going. At three o'clock we celebrated our arrival at the foot of the pass by consuming the last of our food, a tin of condensed milk. From there it was a long, weary plod over the pass to our former camp site by the Rio Tunnel, where we had left a cache of supplies. We reached it late in the evening, wet and tired and hungry.

The drenching rain did not encourage us to make a second sortie towards the Ice cap, so we returned down the valley; and after two days at the north-west corner of the lake surveying the front of the Viedma Glacier, we started back to El Calafate.

5 Seno Mayo

When we returned to Lago Argentino on 27 January, the hills at the far end of the lake were covered with snow to within a few hundred feet of the water's edge. The others were back at Lago Roca from their expedition to the south-west. They had had a rough time with the weather, but the two Peters had added valuable material to their collections, and they were busy drying and sorting their specimens, ably assisted by their long-suffering hostess. The launch had both engines working again, so on 31 January, we all set out for the head of the Seno Mayo, taking with us provisions for a month. Cotton was nearly at the end of his holiday, and it was arranged that the launch should return to collect him after a few days.

The Seno Mayo is one of the most spectacular fjords of Lago Argentino. The narrow channel lies between precipitous forest, intersected by glaciers so steep that it looks as though the slightest disturbance would be enough to send them plunging bodily into the lake. At the head of the fjord, overshadowed by a magnificent rock spire known as Cerro Mayo standing 7,000-feet high above the water, the valley is blocked by a great ice-stream (the Mayo Glacier) which crosses it at right-angles and butts against the northern wall. Beyond this, the valley continues westward and penetrates so deeply into the main range that its actual head can only be half a dozen miles from the waters of one of the Pacific fjords. Apart from the botanical, zoological and glaciological work, our chief objective was to find a way into the basin of the upper valley, to explore it and, if time and weather allowed, to cross the range to the Pacific side.

We landed at noon on a wide, thickly wooded promontory jutting out from the southern shore of the fjord, a mile short of the glacier barrier. It was the first time that Peter James had been in the rainforest, and he was very excited by the abundance of flora, mosses and lichens. He could not wait to begin his collecting; and as soon as he set foot ashore he started running around like a terrier just released from its kennel, utterly oblivious of anything but his quarry. This intense absorption in his work was characteristic, and it never flagged throughout the whole expedition.

It was a fine afternoon and, after lunch, the rest of us set out to explore our lovely surroundings. Making our way through the forest to the far side of the promontory, we found that it was separated by a wide stretch of open water from the Mayo Glacier. Our passage along the southern shore was blocked by a vertical rock wall rising straight out of the lake for 3,000 feet and crowned with ice. This gigantic precipice was festooned with waterfalls which, in windy weather, never reached the base of the cliff, for they were caught at various levels by the stronger gusts and sent swirling upwards, so that the whole vast wall looked as though it were smouldering.

That evening Peter Miles and I went fishing in a creek beside the camp. In little more than an hour, using a spinner, we succeeded in landing eight rainbow trout, each weighing two or three pounds. We cooked them by wrapping them in newspaper and baking them in the hot ashes of the campfire.

The promontory provided the naturalists with an excellent base, from which they had easy access to the upper limits of the forest; so they decided to stay there. Its isolation from the Mayo Glacier, however, made it inconvenient for the rest of us; so, using the rubber dinghy, we ferried ourselves and our kit and fifteen days' food across to the northern shore of the fjord. There was a powerful westerly wind blowing, and it proved a difficult operation, which took us most of the day to complete. The wind was extraordinarily warm; this was a sure portent of storm, and during the next two days the weather was very rough. Indeed during the next three or four weeks there were only five days when it did not rain heavily, and calm spells were rare.

On 2 February we tried to find a way across the barrier formed by the Mayo Glacier. It was much more formidable than we had expected; everywhere the ice was broken and twisted into a chaotic mass of ridges and spires, intersected by a labyrinth of deep crevasses. It was impossible to choose a route for more than a few yards ahead; often we cut steps laboriously to the crest of a ridge only to find that we could not descend on the far side. Cotton was wearing a pair of clumsy, ill-fitting crampons, and three times he slipped and was only saved by the rope from falling into the chasms beneath. Matters were not improved by the wind and driving rain. By the middle of the afternoon we were barely halfway across, and our rate of progress was becoming slower and slower; so we abandoned the attempt and returned to camp, thoroughly soaked and cold.

For the next two days, when it rained incessantly, Cotton and I were both laid up with influenza and felt very sorry for ourselves. The launch was due to come on the 5th to fetch Cotton; and John, who had been suffering from toothache, decided to return to El Calafate with him. So, that morning, we ferried them across the fjord to the promontory.

Our camp on the northern shore had been badly chosen; it was exposed to the wind and was now very wet; so when we returned, Geoff, Barny and I cast around for a better home. Deep in the forest, not 200 yards from the shore, we found the ideal place. An overhanging cliff, 100 feet high, formed a roof over a wide area of dry, mossy ground, completely screened from the weather by thick undergrowth and tall trees. Several dead branches had fallen inside the cave, which provided us with enough dry firewood to last us for weeks; while twenty yards away there was a small lake of clear water. We lost no time in moving into this delightful abode where, free from the cramping confinement of tents, we could spread ourselves with complete abandon, and lie in luxurious comfort by a blazing fire.

In Barny we found an excellent companion. He was thoughtful and considerate, and had a most equitable temperament; he always seemed to be enjoying himself whatever the conditions and appeared quite impervious to discomfort, to minor personal misfortunes such as the loss of his pipe, and even to painful physical injury. He was slow in thought and in action, but his judgement was sound, and for us his more placid nature was most salutary. Geoff and I were prone to argue, often with considerable vehemence, over a wide range of subjects, from the behaviour of glaciers to abstract scientific or philosophical matters about which we knew nothing. Barny took no parts in these debates, but listened with an amused or, when we became particularly acrimonious, a puzzled expression on his face. But he was far from dull. Though it was not easy to draw him out, he had a wonderful fund of personal anecdotes; and, as a regular contributor to *Blackwood's Magazine*, he was a practised raconteur. As a bomber pilot during the war, he had been shot down over Germany, and some of his best yarns were of his attempt to evade capture by posing as a German officer, of his efforts to get out of various prison camps and of his eventual escape, some time after the war had ended, from his much harsher though less efficient confinement by the Russians. He told his tales with a kind of reluctant diffidence, and with a spontaneous humour, as if he had only just realised the comic side of his various predicaments.

On the 6th, Geoff and I tried to get round the barrier by climbing across the rock face against which the ice was pressing. To reach it we had to cross a small section of the glacier which demanded the use of crampons. Before tackling the rock, I left mine by a small tree in a place that I thought I could not mistake. A series of terraces enabled us to traverse nearly half a mile across the face and to reach a corner, from which we could see into the upper valley. But beyond this point the rock face was smooth and vertical, and we could go no farther; nor could we see any way through the tangled ice beneath us.

On the way back, I went to the place where I had thought I had left my crampons and found that they were not there. I was so certain that I had identified the right place, that I almost convinced myself that they had been removed by one of the condors that were circling overhead. This ludicrous theory delighted Geoff, and for a long time afterwards I had to suffer his taunts about my 'cramponivorous condors'. Two days later I found the wretched things neatly folded under another tree.

That evening I fished in a small lagoon which, though only a couple of hundred yards from the glacier, was fed by a stream from the forest. With my second cast, a particularly clumsy one, I caught a four-pound trout, which provided us with a substantial supper.

Our failure to cross the ice barrier now faced us with the unpleasant alternative of climbing more than 2,000 feet up through dense, precipitous forest to look for a high-level route into the upper valley. Fortunately the next day was comparatively fine and we succeeded in reaching a prominent spur running down from the Cerro Mayo, where we did a theodolite station. From the spur we looked down a vertical cliff of some 2,000 feet to a lake, which formed a continuation of the fjord beyond the ice barrier. We also had a clear view of the southern section of the basin and of a fairly low gap leading to the Pacific.

When we returned to the cave, we found that our camp had been visited by foxes. They had evidently had a wonderful time, for we found several bags of sugar and oats ripped open and the contents strewn all over the ground; while much of our cheese and nearly all our bacon had vanished.

The view from the spur had not been encouraging. The ground beyond looked so precipitous that Geoff and I had decided, before committing ourselves to the high-level route, to make one more attempt, the next day, to break through the ice-barrier. This time we kept close to the rock wall against which the glacier was pressing. By using some convenient rock ledges we made fair progress. Then, just as we seemed to have reached a complete impasse, with overhanging ice-cliffs hemming us in on all sides, we discovered a tunnel which ran for 200 yards under the ice and emerged beyond the cliffs. After some more strenuous climbing we struck better going and eventually reached a narrow inlet from the lake beyond. It lay between a mass of impassable ice-cliffs and a sheer rock wall, which was in fact the bottom of the precipice we had looked down the previous day. The only chance of making any further progress was by using the dinghy, but the inlet was so closely packed with small icebergs that we were very doubtful whether we could force a way through.

However, we decided to try, and the following day we returned with Barny, carrying our food and equipment together with the boat. We reached the inlet at 3.30. Inflating the dinghy, we found three punctures which had to be repaired. Then we started upon the most unusual combination of mountaineering and boating. The dinghy was not really big enough to take all three of us and the baggage as well. So first of all Geoff and I embarked with the baggage and by heaving at the icebergs and cutting away their edges with our ice axes, we succeeded, with a good deal of labour, in clearing a channel to a rock ledge, twenty yards away. It had been intended that Geoff should land there with some of the baggage, and that I should take the boat back for Barny. But meanwhile the ice had closed the channel behind us, and it was obvious that I would not be able to clear it and propel the boat by myself. Fortunately, there was a wide crack running obliquely up the wall from the ledge, and by climbing this I was able to reach a point thirty feet immediately above the place where Barny was standing. From there I lowered a double rope, and by pulling on one while Barny heaved himself up with the other, he managed to reach me, and we climbed down the crack to join Geoff in the ledge.

After that we continued the voyage all together in the grossly overloaded dinghy. Our main worry was that the boat would be punctured on some jagged edge as we shoved and hacked at the floating ice. One particularly large and stubborn monster forced us to disembark and carry the dinghy and the kit across it. We were reluctant to do so for the bergs were apt to capsize; indeed we had seen several of them do so on their own account. During the operation Barny's ice axe fell into the water and was lost. He was unusually upset by this mishap, which surprised me, for he had already borne the loss of his whole supply of tobacco with complete equanimity, until I discovered that the axe was one he had borrowed from Cotton.

The total distance that we had to cover to the opposite shore of the inlet was not more than 300 yards; but it took us four hours of very hard work to get there. It was late in the evening when we landed, and blowing a full gale. We had just time before dark to fill the boat with rocks to prevent it from being blown away, and to scramble up into the shelter of the steep forest, where we spent a wet and uncomfortable night.

Having passed the barrier we had hoped to complete the journey to the head of the main valley mostly by water so as to avoid crossing the numerous steep ridges and cliffs along the shore. But the force of the wind and the roughness of the lake made this quite impossible in our tiny boat; so we were forced to continue by land. It was slow and very laborious work, for there were hardly any beaches along the lakeside, and we spent most of the time scrambling up steep slopes of tangled undergrowth and down into the ravines beyond; often covering the same ground several times, to find a way and then to relay our loads.

For some reason, Barny suffered the most; before long his coat was badly torn and what was left of his trousers hung in shreds about his bleeding legs. Geoff, however, was in his element. He had spent much of his early youth 'bushwhacking' in the forests of his native Tasmania, and was justly proud of his ability, not only to get through any kind of scrub, but to find his way back with unerring precision. He had scored his greatest triumph some days before when, climbing through the forest to the spur, Barny had lost the rubber heel to his boot, and he had found it in the dense undergrowth on the way back.

While in the forest, of course, we did not feel the wind, but the noise that it made was most impressive; the individual gusts swept down the valley with a mighty roar like that of a major avalanche. On the night of the 10th, however, there was a lull, and the next morning dawned calm. It was already apparent that we could not attempt to cross the gap to the Pacific, and we now decided to seize the opportunity of the calm spell to make a long march to the head of the valley and back without our loads. The main reason for this decision was that there was one section of the route where the use of the boat was unavoidable. This was the neck of a big lagoon into which several glaciers flowed from the northern side of the basin. Even had it been possible to cross these glaciers, which we could see it was not, the detour involved would have taken many days.

We launched the dinghy and, rowing quickly along the shore, reached the mouth of the lagoon at nine o'clock. By that time, however, it had started to blow again, and I was having such difficulty rowing against the wind that I decided to drop Barny on the eastern shore and return for him when I had taken Geoff across the channel, which was nearly half a mile wide. But the force of the wind and the size of the waves continued to increase, and I had a hard struggle to reach the western shore. By the time we had landed, it was obvious that if I returned to fetch Barny I might well be unable to get back again; and that if I failed to do so, Geoff would be stranded on the wrong side of the channel. Clearly we must both return forthwith, or go on and leave Barny behind for the rest of the day. With a guilty feeling that we were taking advantage of his good nature, we decided on the latter course. Of course he well understood the situation, and we learned later that he was trying to signal to us to go on without him.

We carried the boat well beyond the reach of the waves, filled it with boulders, and then pressed on as fast as we could, through intermittent squalls of heavy rain, to the head of the valley. There, in the shelter of a cirque of huge rock walls, we found that the vegetation was much more luxuriant and the trees far larger than any we had seen hitherto. Having reconnoitred a route up the glacier to the pass, in case one day we might have a chance of returning there, we started back at two o'clock.

When we returned to the lagoon in the late afternoon, the wind was blowing with great force and we had some difficulty in launching the boat. As soon as we removed the boulders holding it down, it was swept up like a kite, dragging us along with it. Once on the water we were sent skimming over the waves like a leaf, with little control over our direction.

Violent gusts came alternately down from the lagoon and down the main valley. Swirling spirals of spindrift warned us of their approach and as a rule we managed to turn the boat so that they hit us astern. One blast, however, caught us broadside and we nearly capsized. But our main efforts were directed at preventing ourselves from being driven into a bay packed with floating ice, from which it would have been difficult to extricate ourselves. There was a heavy swell beating against the eastern shore of the channel, and when we reached it we were hurled unceremoniously on to the rocks where we were welcomed by Barny. He was remarkably cheerful considering that he must have spent a miserable day. However, he had not wasted his time, for he had found an alternative route back to camp which, though it involved some difficult rock climbing, saved us many hours of toil and further aquatic adventures.

For the return journey, reluctant to repeat the passage through the ice-filled bay, we decided to attempt a high-level route which, in any case looked much less formidable from this side. Luckily, during the critical phases, the weather was calm; but on the last day the wind was as violent as ever, and we had to move roped together even on easy slopes. At one point Barny was blown off his feet and, in falling, injured his back. Though, as a result of this, he was largely crippled for the next few weeks he continued to maintain that the trip had been one of the most enjoyable he had ever experienced.

After a day's rest at the base camp, where the naturalists were still hard at work with their collections, and Peter James was now approaching his total of 4,000 specimens of lichen and flowering plants, Geoff and I set out to reach the head of the Mayo Glacier. Once again we plunged into the maze of séracs and ice-ravines. It was exasperating work; hours of strenuous acrobatics resulted in little apparent progress, it was impossible to choose a route for more than a few yards ahead and we often had to return to try another line. Fortunately the day was fairly calm, though this gave us cause to wonder what the return journey might be like in really rough conditions. It was late in the evening when at last we broke through to relatively smooth ice, and at 9.30 we reached the side of the glacier below an isolated patch of forest.

Being tired and hungry we did not bother to look for a good camp site, but pitched our tent on the first piece of flat moraine we could find. Our carelessness was soon punished; for during the night there was a storm of wind and very heavy rain, and by morning the ground we were on had become the bed of a stream. The deluge continued for thirty-six hours without a pause; and when at last, on the second morning, it slackened to a drizzle, I climbed up into the forest to find a more congenial site. There I lit a fire, stripped off my anorak, sweater and shirt, and went back to fetch Geoff, whom I had left peacefully sleeping in his sodden sleeping bag.

When, carrying the tent and the rest of the gear, we returned to the fire, it was still burning brightly, and my shirt and sweater were nearly dry; but my anorak was nowhere to be seen. Presently, however, I discovered a piece of charred material, two inches square, which was all that remained of the precious garment. Later Geoff used it to patch his trousers. The prospect of returning down the glacier in the sort of conditions we had lately experienced had already caused us some concern; now, bereft of my anorak, I found it distinctly bleak. Although I had already become accustomed to the peculiarities of the region, it did seem a little odd to be sitting comfortably in the forest and worrying about our ability to get down a short stretch of glacier below.

But the fates were kind; that very evening the weather suddenly cleared, and for the next three days there was not a breath of wind and scarcely a cloud in the sky. First we went up to the head of the Mayo Glacier to examine a peculiar moraine that we had seen there, which we found to have been formed by a colossal landslide from one of the neighbouring peaks. Then we discovered an easy pass to the head of the Ameghino Glacier, and climbed to the summit of a rock peak above it, where for three hours we sat in the warm sun gazing at a magnificent panorama of nameless mountains.

Mingled with our contentment there was some feeling of sadness, for our time together in that enchanting land was drawing to its close. For my part I was determined to return. The potion of the calafate berry had already cast its spell.

6   The Elusive Volcano

The main purpose of my second visit to Patagonia in the southern summer of 1959–1960 was to locate and investigate the mysterious volcano. There was little doubt that it must exist, and there was something most intriguing in the idea of this lonely vent hidden somewhere in the great expanse of the ice cap. For an active volcano is not normally an unobtrusive phenomenon, easily concealed. The problem of finding it had a strong appeal.

We had already followed one clue and found it to be false. But the 'Vulcan Viedma' could not, in any case, have accounted for the volcanic deposits found on the O'Higgins Glacier some thirty miles farther north; nor for the eruptions reported to de Agostini by the settlers on the shores of Lago San Martin, for these were supposed to have been seen in the direction of the ice cap west of the lake.

Dr Lliboutry, who devoted a section of his book *Nieves y Glaciares de Chile* to a review of the question, was inclined to the opinion that the active vent or vents causing these phenomena were not located on any of the mountains rising above the ice cap, but rather that they were fissure volcanoes erupting periodically though the ice-sheet itself, and covered by snow during their intervening periods of quiescence. He had noticed on the American Air Force photographs, a number of peculiar markings similar to those he had seen on the Viedma Glacier, on the various glaciers radiating from the northern part of the ice cap, which he identified as bands of volcanic ash. From a study of these and other evidence he concluded that the main focus of the eruptions was situated about lat. 48° 50' S, Long. 73° 40' W; that is to say almost in the centre of the northern half of the ice cap, no part of which had ever been visited. Soon after my return I went to see Dr Lliboutry in Grenoble, and he kindly discussed his views in detail. He was not, however, sanguine about the possibility of making a detailed exploration of the area overland, owing to the difficulty of the approach and the appalling weather conditions prevailing on the ice cap. He considered that the only practicable method would be by using helicopters, based at a point within striking distance of the area, and making sorties there during spells of fine weather. The cost of such an undertaking, however, would be enormous.

It is most strange, particularly in view of what transpired later, that the report of Dr Reichert seems to have received so little consideration. Presumably this was because it was thought that his glimpse of the phenomenon was so brief that he and his companions might easily have mistaken snow blowing from a mountain-top for vapour issuing from a volcanic vent; and also because none of the other travellers, such as de Agostini and Corbela, who had been near the place he reached had seen a sign of anything that could be described as a 'volcanic cone', let alone an erupting volcano. Nevertheless, a man of Reichert's standing as an explorer and scientist should have been given more credence.

My original intention was to investigate the area indicated by Lliboutry, and I proposed to attempt to reach it from the head of the Brazo Oeste (western arm) of Lago San Martin. Several valleys drained into this fjord from the west, and although, so far as I could discover, none of them had been explored, I hoped that one at least would afford access to the ice cap. A good deal of time and effort would no doubt be needed to find a way but, as the main obstacle to the exploration of any part of the ice cap was the violent wind, this route would have the advantage of involving the shortest distance to be travelled on the plateau. Also the exploration of the valleys themselves would provide a most interesting secondary objective.

My plan was to establish an advanced base near the edge of the plateau, and from there, lightly laden with a tent and a few days' food, to make a series of swift excursions on skis during spells of fine or moderate weather, so as to cover as much of the area as possible. In the light of my subsequent experience, this plan seems somewhat naive; but my brief acquaintance with Patagonian winds, and still more the horrific stories that I had heard about conditions on the ice cap had so impressed me, that I did not contemplate a long sojourn on the plateau itself.

It was not possible to reach the Brazo Oeste overland, and from the scanty information that I could get, it appeared that the only boat available on Lago San Martin was extremely unreliable. However, I was fortunate enough to obtain the loan of an inflatable boat known as a 'Zodiac' manufactured by Messrs. R.F.D. Ltd., of Godalming. It was the ideal craft for the job. A replica of that used by Dr Bombard for his crossing of the Atlantic, it was capable of withstanding almost any weather conditions, and a surprising amount of battering against rocks and ice. When assembled it was fifteen feet long, and though it could carry well over a ton, it could be packed up into a handy load. Also, the British Seagull Company lent me two 4-h.p. outboard motors.

Partly to circumvent the problem of finance, I decided to recruit my party from South America. First I invited Peter Miles. Though not a mountaineer, I had found him a most useful man to have on an expedition of this kind; and I hoped that, besides helping with the exploration of the valleys and carrying loads to our advanced base, he would be able to continue the zoological work he had done during the previous season. He was very keen to come again, but he had recently got married, and he asked if he could bring his wife, Martha, with him. He told me that she was strong and thoroughly used to rough conditions, having done a lot of deep-sea sailing. As a further recommendation he said that she was a very bad cook, and therefore would not mind our spartan diet. As I thought that Peter Miles would probably have to spend most of his time at the lower camps in the forest, I readily agreed to his proposal.

For the work on the ice cap I invited Jack Ewer, an Englishman teaching at the University of Chile in Santiago, and Peter Bruchhausen of the Antarctic Institute in Buenos Aires. Jack, who was forty, had had a lot of mountaineering experience and an expedition to Antarctica to his credit. Finally, while I was preparing things in London, Bill Anderson asked if he could join the party and offered to pay his expenses. Though he had not done much mountaineering, his experience for two years as leader of a party at Hope Bay in the Antarctic was sufficient qualification, and he was a great help to me in the preliminary organisation.

At Rio, on my way out to Buenos Aires, I received a letter from Jack which contained some startling news. He told me that, with the co-operation of the Instituto Geographico Militar in Santiago, he had made an exhaustive study of the photographs taken by the American Air Force. He had found two pictures which had evidently escaped the notice of Professor Keller and Dr Lliboutry, for they showed definite evidence of volcanic activity near the summit of the highest peak of a range named by de Agostini 'Cordon Pio XI'. The peak, which was called 'Lautaro' by Lliboutry, stood high above the Plateau, well to the south of the area suggested by him, and in a position corresponding very closely to the 'volcanic cone' seen by Reichert.

I had with me a photograph of Lautaro taken by Corbela; it bore no resemblance to a cone, and certainly did not look like a volcano. Moreover, remembering the 'Vulcan Viedma' I was somewhat sceptical of Jack's discovery. However, when I met him in Buenos Aires and he showed me the pictures I had to admit that the evidence was too convincing to be ignored, and that we must divert our attention from the unexplored northern half of the ice cap to Lautaro, which could best be reached from the Brazo Sur (south arm) of the lake and up the O'Higgins Glacier. This change of plan altered the whole character of our task, for instead of finding a new route to the Plateau and there searching over a wide area of untrodden ground, we would be approaching by ways already traversed and aiming at a definite objective.

In the middle of December the party assembled in Buenos Aires where we bought most of our provisions. On the 22nd we embarked on a tanker bound for Comodoro Rivadavia, an oil town on the Atlantic coast of Patagonia, where we arrived on the 26th. Once again the Shell Company gave us generous and invaluable help, which solved our difficult problem of reaching Lago San Martin. Mr de Wit, the company's manager, entertained us and provided us with three vehicles for the outward journey of 600 miles.

Leaving Comodoro at seven o'clock on the 27th, we drove all day through undulating, semi-desert country along the coast, where the monotony of the landscape was relieved only by the sight of seals, guanacos, rheas and an occasional armadillo. San Julian, which we reached that evening, is a place of grim associations; for there Magellan's mutineers were left, presumably to die of slow starvation, and fifty years later Drake hanged Doughty, his second-in-command. To the modern traveller the country has a certain melancholy charm; but to those first voyagers, with the prospect only of appalling hardship and danger ahead of them, it must have seemed utterly dismal, and one cannot but feel some sympathy with the mutineers. Today San Julian is a port of some 3,200 inhabitants, and a centre of the local sheep industry. Like the other towns along the coast it is not a beautiful place.

From there we travelled westward for some 250 miles, through Tres Lagos, which consisted of a post office, a gendarmerie and a hotel-cum-store, and, late the next evening, we reached a place called Lago Tarr, near the south-east corner of Lago San Martin, where we found an inn.

Unlike Lago Argentino, Lago San Martin is almost completely surrounded by mountains, and its shores are very sparsely inhabited. Also it has no large, compact body of water, and consists rather of eight interconnecting fjords. Oddly enough, though it lies to the east of the Andes, it drains from its long north-western arm through the range to the Pacific.

Hitherto we had been travelling on a metalled road, but beyond Lago Tarr we followed a very rough track for another forty miles. Three times one of the vehicles got stuck in stream beds, and the last three miles of the track was a terrifying traverse across a steep unstable mountain slope. At three o'clock we reached a small *estancia*, El Condor, on the shores of the Maipu Fjord. The owner, Senor Fernandez, and his family received us with the usual open-handed hospitality that one finds everywhere in Patagonia.

Unlike the Brazo Oeste, the fjord from which I had originally intended to approach the ice cap, the Brazo Sur was accessible overland by a three-day journey across the mountains. However, as packhorses were scarce, it was decided that Bill, Peter Bruchhausen and I should take the bulk of the baggage in the Zodiac, while the other three followed by land with the three animals our host could provide. Señor Fernandez expressed grave concern about our venturing on the lake in such a tiny craft, and I doubt if we succeeded in convincing him that it was seaworthy.

Fortunately, the storms, which had apparently been raging for the past few weeks, had now died down, and at 9 a.m. on New Year's Eve we started on our fifty-mile voyage. The day was clear and still, and instead of the long cold struggle against powerful headwinds and drenching spray that we had anticipated, we found ourselves gliding over smooth water under a warm sun. By noon we had cleared the network of narrow channels at the exit of the Maipu Fjord and entered the main lake. I noticed that there was much less forest than I had seen among the inner fjords of Lago Argentino; at first the scenery reminded me of Lake Como, though on a very much larger scale. Gradually, however, the panorama of ice mountains opened to westward, clear except for some small white clouds that hung motionless over the higher peaks. At four o'clock we rounded a headland and were confronted to the south-west by a splendid view of the O'Higgins Glacier sweeping up from its broad front of ice-cliffs on a lake, to its source on the ice cap. Suddenly I noticed that one of the white clouds, far away in the background, seemed, unlike its neighbours, to be in a state of considerable agitation. We were able to observe it for an hour before it was lost to view; and three times we saw it shoot swiftly upwards to form a great mushroom-topped column. There appeared to be only one explanation for this peculiar phenomenon: that our volcano had chosen this very season to resume its activity!

At 6.15 we reached the mouth of a wide river connecting the Brazo Sur with the main lake, where there were two small farms, one on either side. Landing on the northern bank, we received a tempestuous welcome from a middle-aged woman who had run down from the farm at our approach. She embraced us as if we were dear relations whom she had not seen for years, and conducted us to her house, where we met her husband and daughter and two grandchildren.

Luis Mansilla was an elderly man with a sad, care-worn face; he rarely spoke and sat in meditative silence by the stove. It was clear that his household revolved about the dynamic personality of his wife, Doña Carmen, a woman of enormous vitality and, as we had already discovered, powerful emotions. She talked incessantly and displayed the volatile temperament of a *prima donna*; tears, laughter and passionate rage followed each other with such bewildering speed that Peter, our only linguistic contact, could find no explanation for her sudden changes of mood. She was for ever baking bread and a large tubful of dough was kept constantly in a corner of the kitchen: every now and then she would launch a vigorous attack, pummelling it like a boxer with a punch-ball, without the slightest interruption of her verbal flow. The finished article was always excellent.

The original settlers in this remote corner of Patagonia came there from Puerto Natales on the coast of southern Chile, nearly fifty years ago, making the long trek to their unknown destination by way of El Calafate and Tres Lagos. Doña Carmen had been there with her husband since 1925. One would imagine that, for a woman of her temperament, the loneliness must have been well-nigh intolerable; she told us that for the first seven years she had not seen another woman. Their present house, which had only been standing a few years, was built of rough timber and contained three very sparsely furnished rooms and a small kitchen. The walls of all these rooms were completely covered with newspapers, among which I was surprised to find several pages from English journals, twenty-five years old.

We hoped that we would be able to hire some packhorses to help us on the next stage of our journey, and that evening, Peter broached the matter. However, the mere suggestion evoked such a storm of abuse from Doña Carmen that it was clear that a great deal of patient diplomacy would be needed to secure her co-operation. Our unexpected arrival had provided her with a heaven-sent opportunity to talk, and she was not prepared to let us go without a struggle. She painted a horrific picture of the hardship and dangers of the glacial regions above, which no one but a fool would wish to visit. In any case it was New Year's Eve and she flatly refused to discuss our plans until after the fiesta the following day.

Early next day the neighbours arrived from across the river, dressed in their Sunday best, and the assembled company settled down to a prolonged orgy of eating and drinking. At eleven o'clock Peter and I set out for a long walk to reconnoitre our surroundings. This was certainly a tactical mistake and we would have been better advised to curb our impatience and sacrifice our stomachs in the interest of goodwill. However, we partly atoned for our lapse when we returned in the evening to find the party still in progress, and our hosts and their guests in a distinctly mellow condition.

The next day Doña Carmen, suffering the normal reaction to the gaiety of the previous day, was in a difficult temper; but, by dint of much wood-chopping and hard work in her vegetable plot, we succeeded in so far mollifying her that she ordered her daughter, Maria, to go and catch three ponies. On January 3, with two of the ponies heavily laden with our baggage and Maria mounted on the third, we set out, accompanied by two foals. Following a steep, ill-defined track through the forest for three hours, we reached the crest of the ridge separating the valley of the Brazo Sur from that of the O'Higgins Glacier. On the way we experienced a great deal of trouble with the packponies, whose awkward loads kept slipping under their bellies. Fortunately, Maria had inherited the philosophical temperament of her father; her mother would certainly not have tolerated our incompetence for a moment, and had she been our guide, we would soon have been left to our own devices.

From the crest of a ridge we descended to a shelf formed by an old lateral moraine of the O'Higgins Glacier, and made our way westward along it for several miles through pleasant, wooded country interspersed with grassy glades, until we reached the upper limit of the forest. There we chose a site for our first camp and dumped the loads. On the way back, Maria was shaken out of her habitual calm by the discovery that the two foals were missing. Mounted on one of the packponies I accompanied her on a fruitless search, conducted at a breakneck speed through a trackless forest and over steep mountainsides, which only the onset of darkness forced her to abandon. We got back to the farm at 11.30 that night, by which time I was too tired to feel upset by the scolding of our irate hostess. The foals turned up on their own the following day.

On 4 January, Jack and Peter and Martha Miles arrived from El Condor with five pack-ponies, accompanied by their owner, Aloyso Altamirando. A wizened brown nut of a man, with an expression of infinite resignation on his face, he had come to the lake with the original settlers nearly fifty years ago, and now farmed a small piece of land between El Condor and the Brazo Sur. With the help of his ponies we were able to carry up the rest of our baggage, and the next day, we set off after a touching farewell from Doña Carmen, who burst into tears at our departure.

So far things had gone remarkably well. In little more than a fortnight since leaving Buenos Aires, we were established at our first camp with provisions enough to last us for eight weeks. At this point, however, our satisfaction was marred by the departure of Bill Anderson. In an undertaking of this kind, when conditions must inevitably subject people's tempers to a good deal of strain, the mutual compatibility of the members of the party is a matter of vital importance. It was already clear that Bill and I did not see eye to eye and as it was better that we should part company while it was still possible to do so, he went back with Altamirando and the ponies.

7 The Nunatak

Opposite the site of our first camp, the O'Higgins Glacier, one of the largest flowing from the ice cap, was about two and a half miles wide. But it was in a state of rapid decline, and now flowed through a moraine trench (the top of which formed the shelf on which we had our first camp) between 800 and 1,000 feet deep. The sides of the trench were completely devoid of vegetation, which showed that they had not long been exposed. Altamirando told us that when he had first seen it in 1914, the surface of the glacier was almost level with the shelf. This would mean that the depth of the ice had decreased by some 800 feet in forty-seven years. Mrs von Rensell Atkinson, who accompanied Dr Reichert in 1933, has told me that the descent from the shelf to the glacier was then not more than 200 feet, which shows that the shrinkage had been far more rapid in the last twenty-seven years than during the previous twenty. Since 1933 the front of the glacier had retreated five miles. No other glacier that I have seen in Patagonia (or anywhere else for that matter) shows anything like this rate of decline. The extraordinary shrinkage of the O'Higgins Glacier is as difficult to explain as the fact that the Moreno Glacier, 120 miles farther south, has evidently not diminished appreciably during the last 200 years, while its neighbours have suffered a considerable net recession over the same period. Lliboutry suggests that the latter phenomenon might be explained by the shape of the Moreno's basin, which allows the unrestricted flow of the ice from the upper to the lower parts of the glacier. He admits that this explanation should also apply to the conditions of the Viedma Glacier, whose basin is quite as open, but which has retreated considerably; but he suggests that this apparent anomaly might be accounted for by thermal activity centred round the 'Vulcan Viedma'. As we have seen, the evidence for the existence of such activity has now been refuted, but the suggestion might be worth considering as an explanation of the phenomenal recession of the O'Higgins Glacier; though this would presumably imply that the present phase of volcanic activity on the ice cap began not much more than fifty years ago.

From our first camp onwards we had to carry everything ourselves, and the next two weeks was a period of hard work. We aimed at getting enough supplies to the ice cap to last us for a month; and this, together with our equipment (which included skis), necessitated three relays between each succeeding camp. In my original plan for the expedition I had not visualised Martha accompanying us far above the forest, though Peter, besides his zoological collecting, was to have helped with the exploration of the valleys leading to the Plateau from the Brazo Oeste. Now, however, with our change of plan, the situation was radically altered. They had both set their hearts on reaching the ice cap, and I could hardly expect them to be content to stay behind at the first camp for the six or seven weeks that we expected to be away. So I accepted their proposal to come with us and take their share in the work that lay ahead. Thereafter Martha, who had never done any backpacking before, carried a load of 30 or 40 lb. and bore the unpleasant conditions we met with as much stoicism as any of us.

First we had to descend 800 feet from the shelf into a curious bay of 'dead' ice (i.e. ice which has been left stranded by the recession of the parent glacier) formed by a gap in the mountains, through which, a few decades ago, a portion of the O'Higgins Glacier had flowed to join a tributary of another glacier running down to the Brazo Sur. This minor ice-stream was now making a vigorous thrust over the 'dead' ice, to form instead a tributary of the O'Higgins Glacier.

Our second camp, on the far side of the bay, was placed in a desolate waste of mud and boulders. We left there a cache of food together with one of our three tents. On our return in February we found that they had been buried by a mud avalanche. A mile or so beyond this place, following the edge of the glacier, we reached the entrance of a side valley. Formerly this had been occupied by a tributary glacier, but we found that its place had been taken by a large lake. With a good deal of difficulty we found our way round this obstacle, through a labyrinth of ice ridges, pinnacles and chasms not unlike the Mayo Glacier. This section of the route was a terrifying experience for poor Martha who was new to glacier travel and had not, of course, worn crampons until a few days before.

It was in this part that the rapid degeneration of the glacier was most apparent. There were day-to-day changes along our route, with new crevasses opening and ridges and pinnacles disintegrating; and when, a fortnight later, three of us had occasion to return there, it was obvious that a large part of the ice over which our route lay was about to collapse into the lake.

During all this time the weather was continuously bad, and strong wind and soaking rain were our daily portion. However, we were still sheltered from the full force of the westerly gales, which we could often see raging over the ice cap and, though conditions were most unpleasant, they were never bad enough to stop us.

On 14 January we reached the upper basin of the O'Higgins Glacier, where we established our fourth camp, and from there, on the 15th, Jack, Peter Bruchhausen and I reconnoitred forward to the edge of the Plateau. Returning to camp that evening, I fell into a hidden crevasse and dislocated my shoulder. Hanging on the rope with my right arm paralysed, I was quite unable to do anything to help matters. Fortunately, while Peter held the rope, Jack managed to reach down, grasp my arm and pull the joint back into place. The excitement of my situation must have acted as an anaesthetic, for I remember nothing but the relief of regaining the use of my arm and of being able to help my companions to extricate me. After that I rested for three days to give my shoulder a chance to recover, in which it was greatly helped by Martha's skilful massage, while Jack and the two Peters continued the work of relaying the loads.

On 19 January we carried the last relay to the edge of the Plateau, where we pitched our fifth camp on a comfortable ledge on a large rock outcrop. It commanded a superb view, and as by a lucky chance the weather had cleared we enjoyed that evening the first fruits of our toil. Northwards across the wide basin of the O'Higgins Glacier, the massive range of Cerro O'Higgins was delicately coloured in the golden twilight, looking with its remote summits, its armoury of hanging glaciers, as impressive as any Himalayan giant. To the north-west a vast sweep of almost level snow stretched away to some unexplored ranges on the northern part of the plateau, and to the gently curved saddle, rimmed by a line of dark blue which gave us the impression that we were looking over to the Pacific. But for us, by far the most exciting part of the view was to the west, where the Cordon Pio XI rose steeply above the plateau to a long line of peaks, silhouetted against the gaudy sunset sky. About 300 feet below the summit of the highest of these (Lautaro), the ice slope on the northern side was gashed by a black fissure, from which there flowed a steady stream of vapour, mounting virtually to a great height, then to be carried away by a southward air-current. It was a wonderful sight. Undoubtedly this was the volcano that Reichert had seen twenty-seven years before and about which there had been so much speculation.

It was still fine the next morning, and we set off on skis westward across the plateau to lay a dump of three weeks' supplies. Soon after we started we saw an eruption of ash from the volcano, which blackened the snow over a large area of mountainside. As there was no wind it was very hot; the snow soon became soft and sticky and our loads seemed inordinately heavy. Peter Bruchhausen was suffering from acute pain in his foot, and in the afternoon Jack and I carried his load forward in relays. Nevertheless, we succeeded in covering two-thirds of the distance to the foot of the volcano before laying our dump; but we were all very tired when we returned to camp at 9.30 that evening.

The following morning was again clear, though there were unmistakable signs that the fine spell was about to end. I was most anxious that we should carry our camp forward to the dump without delay because I was afraid that a heavy fall of snow or drift might bury it, and although we had done our best to fix its position by compass bearings, it would, in any case, be difficult to find in thick weather. Also we had left ourselves rather short of food at our present camp. However, though we prepared for an early start, it was obvious that the party was in need of a rest, particularly Peter Bruchhausen who had had a hard struggle to get back the previous evening. So I decided to take a chance on the weather and give the party an off day, the first that Jack and Peter Bruchhausen had had since leaving the farm more than a fortnight before.

That night the weather broke and for the next four days the violence of the wind and driving sleet made it impossible to venture out on to the Plateau. On the fifth day, however, the storm abated, and we struck camp and set off in the afternoon hoping to reach the dump by nightfall. But Peter Bruchhausen found that, despite the enforced rest, his foot was worse; skiing caused him such agony that it was useless for him to attempt to come any farther. Reluctantly it was decided to send him back. He pleaded to be allowed to go alone, but that was obviously out of the question so, that very evening, Jack and I started to escort him down the glacier. We accompanied him as far as our first camp in the forest, where there was plenty of food, and from there he made his way slowly back to the settlement on the Brazo Sur. Later it was found that the cause of the trouble was a kind of cyst which had formed in the upper part of his foot; it continued to lame him until he was able to have it removed by a doctor.

His departure was very sad both for us and for him, for he was extremely keen, and was bitterly disappointed not to be able to take part in the work on the ice cap, particularly after he had borne his full share of the toil of the last few weeks. It was also a bad blow to our prospects of achieving much on the ice cap, for the mountaineering strength of the party, already depleted, was now severely weakened. Peter and Martha Miles were not mountaineers, and though this fact made their performance all the more remarkable, it would have been foolish, for example, to take them on an attempt to climb Lautaro in the conditions we were likely to meet. Nor, because of the complexity of the crevassed areas we had seen, was it a job for Jack and me to tackle on our own.

After some forced marches, Jack and I rejoined the others at the fifth camp, which we reached just in time to take advantage of another brief spell of clear weather. In it we made our way across the plateau to a nunatak near the foot of the volcano, where, with supplies relayed forward from the dump, we established a well-stocked base, about halfway between Lago San Martin and the Eyre Fjord on the Pacific coast.

For the next fortnight the weather was very bad indeed, with heavy rain, some snowstorms and incessant wind, with occasional gusts of extreme violence. In one of these, two pairs of skis were blown away and never seen again. I do not believe that our small mountain tents would have survived for long in such conditions, had they not been protected from the full force of the wind by a rock cliff; though this had the minor disadvantage that when it snowed the tents were buried in drift.

One night, after a spell of particularly heavy rain, a pond two feet deep, formed on the concave platform occupied by the Miles' tent. Nothing could be done to drain it, so they brought their sodden sleeping bags and squeezed themselves into our tent (designed for two), where we remained tightly packed until, thirty-six hours later, a lull in the weather enabled us to extricate their flooded tent and construct another platform for it. But three nights later they were in trouble again. A violent gust from an unexpected quarter tore their tent from its moorings, snapped most of its guy ropes and broke one of its poles. Once again they were forced to accept our meagre hospitality for two nights until the damage could be repaired. Both Peter and Jack were very large men, and we were so closely constricted that movement was almost impossible. This had some slight advantage in keeping us warm, because by then everything was wet; but sleep was difficult to achieve, and we spent most of these nights singing and talking. Peter had a good voice and a fine repertoire of songs, and as the party was composed of a Roman Catholic, a Protestant, a materialist and an agnostic we had plenty of scope for religious discussion.

When we had been at the nunatak for about ten days, a final disaster befell us. Instead of the usual Primus stoves, I had supplied the party with petrol stoves of a cunning and compact design. We had two of these with us, and for some time they had been causing trouble. Each had a right-angled section in the feed pipe, which became blocked, either by volcanic dust or lead in the petrol, or both, and as the pipe was welded on to the tank, it was impossible to clear the blockage. Finally, at about the same time, both stoves ceased to function altogether, and there was nothing we could contrive to remedy the situation. So thereafter, we had to subsist on uncooked food and cold drinks. Fortunately we did not have to melt snow for water, of which there was an ample supply on the nunatak.

We had planned to make a journey from our nunatak base into the unexplored northern part of the plateau, where we expected that we might find more evidence of volcanic activity among the ranges there. Though Jack, a mighty optimist, would still have been more than willing to undertake it, I must confess that the battering that we had received from the weather had already robbed me of much of my zest for such an expedition. As for Peter and Martha, whose stoic endurances had been unfairly tested, and who in any case would have been left behind at the nunatak, there was little doubt as to where their inclinations lay. Now, however, with the failure of our stoves, even Jack was induced to admit that life on the open plateau, with our obviously inadequate tentage and no means of cooking or melting snow, might well prove intolerable. So we decided to limit our objective to making a collection of rocks from such outcrops on the mountain that we could reach. In this task we were helped by the advent of one fine day.

Apart from a few minor mishaps, such as Peter and Martha falling into crevasses and Jack cracking a rib, our journey back was uneventful and increasingly pleasant as the rigours relaxed and one by one we savoured the delights of getting back to normal conditions.

Our return to the farm swept Doña Carmen into an ecstasy of emotional outpouring. It happened that I arrived an hour ahead of the others, so that I bore the full brunt of her rapture. She kept moving me about from one place to another, as though she were trying to find just the right position for a new piece of furniture, plying me with food and talking all the time. I was slightly mortified by her constant repetition of the phrase 'Pobre viejo' ('Poor old man'), until I remembered how ancient my grey beard made me appear. It was quite a relief when the others arrived to divert her attention; though she continued to scold and cherish us like truant children whom she had despaired of ever seeing again.

A few days later we set sail in the Zodiac. One of the motors had been ruined by our clumsy handling and, despite a following wind, our speed was slower than on the outward journey. When we had been going an hour or so we were surprised to see a vessel approaching us. She turned out to be a boat, belonging to a strange character known as 'El Catalan', which we had seen lying at the other end of the lake at the end of December; she had then been out of commission. When we came alongside we found that she was carrying an expedition from the University of Chile, led by Eduardo Garcia. They were bound for Cerro O'Higgins. I was glad that Doña Carmen, whom we had left utterly dejected that morning, would so soon have company again.

That afternoon the wind, which had been moderate before, freshened considerably. Low clouds raced overhead, and the grey water became uncomfortably rough. Peter succumbed to sea-sickness, and lay miserably in the bows; and we all became very cold. I was glad when we reached the calm of the narrow channels at the entrance of the Maipu Fjord, where we were overtaken by nightfall and ran the Zodiac ashore in a sheltered cove on a small wooded island. It was raining gently, but we soon had a large fire blazing, and were content to lie most of the night before its grateful warmth.

The achievements of the expedition had been disappointing. True, we had established beyond all doubt the existence and position of the mysterious volcano, thanks to the timely circumstance of its renewed activity; and we had collected enough material to learn something of its structure. That, certainly, had been our main objective; but with less miscalculation and a little more luck, we should have made much better use of a month's supplies carried to the Plateau with so much toil. We had covered little fresh ground, and we knew no more than before about the northern part of the ice cap, which was by far the largest part of this strange region. But we had learnt some valuable lessons; and when failure acts as a spur to fresh enterprise, it cannot be counted a total loss.

8   Preparing for a Journey

My first two expeditions to Patagonia had provided me with the experience I needed to attempt a more ambitious venture. There was no doubt as to my choice of an objective. The idea of landing somewhere on the uninhabited Pacific coast and making a journey across the unexplored northern half of the ice cap, stood out with challenging simplicity. I was anxious, too, to discover whether the volcanic activity which we had located that year extended to the northward, or whether it was an isolated phenomenon.

All the previous attempts to cross the ice cap farther south had been made from the Argentine side; and all of them, of course, had had to provide for the necessity of returning by the same route. To cross from the Pacific side, on the other hand, would involve no such necessity, as we would be travelling towards inhabited country. There was also the advantage that we would be going more or less with the prevailing wind, an extremely important factor.

The vital problem, however, was how to reach a suitable starting point on the Pacific coast. So far as I knew, this coast was uninhabited for several hundred miles in either direction. The nearest ports were Puerto Natales to the south and Puerto Montt to the north, both more than 500 miles away; and it would be extremely expensive to charter a suitable vessel from either to carry an expedition to its base. There is a fairly regular coastal traffic between Puerto Montt and Punta Arenas, and all the ships of less than 10,000 tons follow a route through the channels of the archipelago. It might be possible to arrange to be dropped by one of these ships at the entrance of one of the many fjords leading to the foot of the main range, and to complete the journey in a Zodiac boat. There were, however, several serious objections to this plan: in the first place it would be a hazardous operation unless we were lucky enough to strike a spell of fine weather at exactly the right moment, which was most unlikely; secondly, we would be severely limited in the amount of stores and equipment that we could take, and thirdly, it would mean that we would have to abandon the Zodiac and the outboard motors which could not possibly be carried across the ice cap. There was also the difficult problem of arranging for our evacuation from our base should we fail to get across.

On my way home in April 1960 I went to Santiago to discuss things with Jack. He was as enthusiastic as ever, but inclined to think that we should have a rest from Patagonia for a season, and spend his next long vacation exploring the volcanoes west of the Atacama desert instead. However, we discussed the question of landing an expedition at the head of one of the Pacific fjords with the President's Naval A.D.C., who seemed confident that the Chilean Navy would co-operate in such a project. I had plenty of time to consider the plan on the voyage home, and the more I thought about it the more exciting it seemed; so that by the time I reached England I was determined to attempt it the following season.

The choice of a starting point on the Pacific coast was one of fundamental importance. The Admiralty Chart showed no fewer than six fjords leading from the main north-south channel to the glaciers flowing down from the northern part of the ice cap, each offering a possible line of approach. Though they had all been charted at some time during the last 100 years, there appeared to be no recent data to show how far they were navigable. The ice cap could also be approached southward from the Canal Baker. This channel, which is more than 100 miles long, is the deepest inlet in the whole of that tortuous coastline. It has several branches; the most southerly of these, the Calun Fjord, contains the mouth of the Rio Pascua, which drains Lago O'Higgins. A few miles west of this affluent, the Jorge Monte Glacier, one of the largest in Patagonia, thrusts its massive front far out into the waters of the fjord.

After a careful study of the available data, I decided to approach the ice cap from this direction, a choice which offered several apparent advantages. In the first place the branches of the Canal Baker were far better charted than were the fjords to the south, and there was no doubt that a ship could safely reach a point within a few miles of the Jorge Montt Glacier. Secondly, the enormous size of this glacier suggested that it had an uninterrupted flow from the ice cap, which probably meant that the slopes leading up to the plateau were comparatively gentle on the northern side. Thirdly, there was evidence that the glacier had shrunk considerably in recent decades, and in doing so it had probably left a strip of country free from forest, which might be a great help on the first stage of the journey. This argument would not apply to a glacier flowing through a less open valley.

The choice of the approach suggested an exciting extension to my original plan. Instead of merely crossing the northern section of the plateau, I now envisaged a journey over the entire length of the ice cap to its southern extremity in the Cordon Darwin (a chain of mountains in the Cordillera Darwin) above Lago Argentino. The distance to be covered would be about 150 miles, twice that of the original plan and many times as long as any journey hitherto attempted in that part of the world. Certainly, the second half of it would be over ground previously covered and it was arguable that the extra time would be better spent in the unexplored northern sector; but as a large part of my object was to overcome the tyranny of wind and weather and the old bugbear of restricted travel, the idea of covering the whole region in one magnificent sweep had an irresistible appeal.

Jack agreed that the party should be composed of four members. It was important that we should all be competent mountaineers, and that at least one of the party should be a geologist. It was also most desirable that we should all have had some experience of the unpleasant conditions that we were likely to encounter, so that everyone would be well aware of what they were in for. After much deliberation we decided to invite two Chilean mountaineers, Eduardo García and Cedomir Marangunic, to join us. García (30) was the leader of the expedition that we had met on Lago O'Higgins. He had also been a member of the Japanese expedition to the mountains north of the Rio Baker in 1958, and of a Chilean expedition to Cerro Paine in 1959. With this experience he certainly knew what to expect. Marangunic (23) was a geologist, and he had been with García on Cerro O'Higgins. A Yugoslav by birth, his family had emigrated to Punta Arenas where they had adopted Chilean nationality; so he, too, was well acquainted with local conditions.

The key to the success of the venture lay in the choice of equipment. My previous experience had shown that the type of equipment used on mountaineering expeditions in the Himalayas was entirely inadequate against the rigours of the Patagonian climate. For example lightweight tents of the kind used for the high camps on Everest were quite incapable of withstanding torrential rain driven against them for hours on end by gale-force winds; and I was far from sure that they would not be destroyed by some of the more powerful gusts I had experienced in Patagonia. It was essential that we should have a tent with very high water-repellent qualities, that was capable of being pitched in the most violent wind, and strong enough and stable enough to withstand a prolonged battering from the most savage storms; otherwise, not only would life become quite intolerable, but we might find ourselves in a very precarious situation.

Jack urged that we should resort to the old-fashioned pyramid tent used on the classic Antarctic sledge journeys, and still by no means obsolete. It is a double-skinned tent and its chief virtue is stability, for which, unlike most mountain tents, it does not rely upon its guys. Because of its shape the pressure of the wind tends to hold it down instead of lifting it up, and at the same time its poles are subjected to the minimum strain. With plenty of snow or other weights piled upon its skirts, or snow flaps, it can withstand an enormous force of wind. For its normal use on sledge journeys the ten-foot poles are made in single lengths, and are kept in place inside the canvas; it is then the easiest of all tents to pitch. But for mountaineers the pyramid has several disadvantages, which account for the fact that they hardly ever use it. In the first place, it is very heavy; secondly, even when the poles are made in three sections, it packs into a very awkward load, and it is difficult to reassemble; finally, it requires a very wide platform on which to stand.

However, after listening to a great deal of conflicting advice on the subject from polar explorers (much of it discouraging) I came round to Jack's view that the pyramid was the only satisfactory solution to our tent problem. I ordered the standard model made by Camtors for the Falkland Islands Dependencies Survey. It was designed to accommodate three men, and was only just large enough to take the four of us. To increase the ground space appreciably would have meant adding considerably to the height of the tent, which would have made it harder to pitch and easier to blow down. The outer 'skin' was made of Ventile 19, and the inner of a lighter fabric. Instead of a detachable groundsheet normally used, I had the tent made with a sewn-in groundsheet. The chief advantage of the former is that when the loads and the groundsheet have been packed up before striking camp, the tent can then be used as a latrine. I considered that we should forgo this luxury to secure greater protection from the wet; though, later, there were many moments when I questioned the wisdom of this choice. The tent weighed sixty pounds; about twice as much as two two-man mountain tents.

The question of clothing presented a difficult problem. At high altitudes, or indeed in any conditions of dry cold, however severe, it is a simple matter to provide complete protection: sufficient woollen, or better still, down under-garments, covered with a light windproof material are all that is required. But ordinary windproof cloth such as we had used on Everest is useless against hard-driven rain. I spent a great deal of time searching for a waterproof fabric that could be worn while doing hard physical work without becoming saturated with inside condensation. At length I came to the conclusion that no such material had yet been invented. 'Gannex' cloth, which we had used the previous season, is devised to retard condensation so that if the garments can be ventilated at frequent intervals, they can be kept reasonably dry inside. Unfortunately, it is not possible to do this completely while carrying loads with the result that condensation is bound to occur locally (around the shoulders for example). However, the cloth had provided at least a partial solution to the problem, and I decided to use it again.

As the major part of the journey would be over the relatively flat surface of the ice cap, a sledge was one of the most important items of our equipment. Sledge-hauling was a subject about which I knew almost nothing, and again I consulted the experts. The trouble was that none of the standard designs used in polar regions was suitable for our purpose. Before we could use it, we expected to have to carry our sledge a very long way, through bogs and dense forest, over rough ground and shattered icefalls, probably involving difficult mountaineering, and often exposed to a high wind. It was essential therefore that it should be collapsible, light, compact, easily portable and fairly tough. The advice of experts is usually conflicting, and I found that of polar explorers to be no exception. Some told me, for example, that the Swedish 'Pulka' sledge would be ideal for our purpose, others that it would be useless. Then there was the vexing problem of finding someone to make the sledge. I was still in the throes of indecision about six weeks before our baggage was due to be shipped to Punta Arenas, when I received a letter from John Bull, a young man who had been to the Antarctic with F.I.D.S. He told me that on hearing of my problem from Sir Vivien Fuchs, he had designed a collapsible sledge which could be made of fibreglass. He had consulted the Fibreglass Company of St Helens who had agreed to make the sledge for nothing if he would provide them with a mould. I sent him a telegram and he spent the following weekend making the mould out of three-ply. The sledge arrived in London a few days before our baggage had to be sent to the docks. It was a strange-looking object, orange coloured and shaped like a shallow punt; it weighed thirty-five pounds and could be taken apart into four sections which fitted into each other like eggshells. On the bottom it had two narrow wooden slats to prevent it from slipping sideways.

Another question which I found hard to decide was whether or not to take skis. There could be no doubt about their value on the ice cap, where they would certainly save us a lot of hard work. But they are very awkward things to carry, particularly in thick forest and in a high wind. Jack, who has no half-hearted opinions, was strongly in favour of taking snowshoes instead. He had had some experience of using them in the Antarctic and considered that they were almost as good as skis for sledge-hauling. Though I discovered that very few of the experts shared this view, I decided to accept his judgement. It transpired, however, that there were no snowshoes available in Britain. Hillary told me that he had intended to get some for his expedition to the Himalaya and had scoured the country for them without success. In the end I approached Slazengers and asked if they would construct four pairs to my (or rather Jack's) specification. Their response was splendid; it seemed as though the entire staff took a personal interest in the matter; frequent discussions took place on the telephone between the works in Leeds and the London office and specimen snowshoes were sent to me by special messengers for my comment on various points.

Expedition food is always a fruitful topic for acrimonious discussion. There is a curious difference between Himalayan mountaineers and polar explorers in their approach to this subject. While the latter have always been ready to accept a spartan ration for even their longest sledge journeys, a simple unvaried diet based entirely upon the nutritional value of the food, mountaineers usually insist that expedition food should be varied and palatable, and that their daily provisions should include a number of luxuries. This, I believe, is due to the tradition started by the early Everest expeditions and followed by most of the other classic expeditions to the great peaks of the Himalaya. It was thought that the climbers' appetites would be impaired by altitude and that everything possible must be done to tempt them to eat enough. The argument had some basis in fact; but the custom of lavish provisioning also arose from the fact that on these expeditions, transport was no real problem. We used to go to Everest, for example, with a cavalcade of 350 pack-animals, most of them carrying supplies that were far from essential. On the mountain itself there were innumerable porters available to carry our baggage; our advance was necessarily slow because of the need for acclimatisation, so that a few days spent in carrying up extra food was a matter of little importance.

Like most traditions this one has been hard to break, and even today the idea of a basic food ration has not been widely accepted by mountaineers in the Himalaya. When, in the thirties, Tilman and I started our campaign to promote lightweight expeditions in that field, we were regarded as cranks in the matter of food. But our meagre diet was in the first place dictated by sheer necessity; then we discovered that, once we had got used to it, we were much better off with our simple fare. In fact we were only following the long established practice of polar explorers.

Besides its primary value in saving weight, the basic ration makes it far easier to control the caloric intake of the party, and to ensure the maintenance of a balanced diet. Oddly enough it also seems to make people much more contented with their food, providing of course that the ration is sufficient for their needs. In my experience, which covers a very wide range of catering arrangements, I have always found that the more lavishly an expedition is victualled, the greater the variety of choice supplied, the more people complain about the food. I will not attempt to account for this curious psychological paradox.

I adopted the following ration scale (per man per day):

Sugar	8 ounces
Quaker oats	5 ounces
Wholemeal biscuit	4 ounces
Dehydrated meat	4 ounces
Butter	2 ounces
Cheese	2 ounces
Milk powder	4 ounces
Rum fudge	2 ounces
Soup powder	1 ounce
Potato powder	½ ounce
Total	**32½ ounces**

This provided about 4,500 calories. A supplementary supply of vitamins was taken in tablets. The exceptionally large amount of sugar allowed was, in a sense, a luxury; for sugar has a relatively low calorie/weight ratio; but I have found that it is always in very great demand on an expedition, even among people who do not normally consume much of it; presumably because it is so rapidly converted into energy.

While I was engaged in procuring our food supplies, I had a great piece of luck. A firm of packers, Felber, Jucker and Co., was concerned with a process of vacuum packing food in a new plastic material called 'Ralsin', which is extremely strong and almost as light as tissue paper. The head of the firm, Adrian Jucker, who happened by chance of hear of my plans, very kindly volunteered to pack our food in this way. When he explained the process to me I realised that it would provide the ideal solution to an old problem. Hitherto when calculating the logistics of a mountain journey at least twenty per cent had to be added to the weight of food carried to allow for packing; and on a long journey this amounted to a very considerable extra burden. But Ralsin was so light that its weight could be virtually ignored; moreover it was so strong that it could stand any amount of rough handling, and so impervious that it could be soaked in water indefinitely and still afford complete protection to the food inside.

A four-man/day ration of each food item was weighed into a Ralsin bag, which was then treated by the vacuum-sealing machine. The effect of this on the food inside was to compress it into a hard, flat slab; though as soon as the bag was opened and the vacuum released, the food would expand again into its normal consistency. One of each item was put into a larger bag, which was also sealed and formed a day-pack for the party. The only items that were not dealt with in this way were the butter and the cheese which were shipped out in cold storage.

It was obviously impossible to make a precise estimate of how long the journey over the ice cap would take. The most important unknown factors were the difficulties we would encounter in reaching the plateau and the extent to which our progress there would be impeded by the weather. The previous season it had taken us more than two weeks to carry all our baggage to the head of the O'Higgins Glacier, despite the fact that we had followed a known route and had been able to use pack transport through the forest. With neither of these two great advantages, it might easily take us twice as long to make our way up the Jorge Montt Glacier. I was well aware that we would be lucky if we got more than ten per cent of reasonably fine weather during the journey; it was quite likely that we would get none at all. Before reaching the ice cap I reckoned that we would be able to press on regardless of the weather; but on the plateau it would be a different matter, and there we might be held up for long periods, unable to move. However, the fact that the prevailing wind is from the north-west while we would be travelling on a southerly course, was very much in our favour.

In view of these unknown factors, it seemed best to base our estimates largely upon our carrying powers and to make our timetable fit in with this. Carrying 60-pound loads we would be able to shift 720 pounds in three relays. The estimated weight of our equipment (tent, sledge, etc.) was 208 pounds; the balance of 512 pounds would provide enough food and fuel for fifty-five days. Assuming that it would take us three weeks to reach the head of the Jorge

Montt Glacier, we would arrive on the ice cap with enough provisions for another thirty-four days, and a total weight of baggage of 525 pounds, which was probably the maximum load that we could drag on the sledge. Thus a supply of food and fuel for fifty-five days was a convenient amount to start with. Unless the difficulties were very much greater than expected, eight weeks seemed a reasonable allowance of time in which to complete the crossing, and even this could be safely protracted for a week or so by cutting down our rations towards the end of the journey. I had sixty day-loads prepared, and took some additional food in bulk for dumping at our starting point in case we should fail to make the crossing and be forced to retreat.

The Chilean Navy offered to take the expedition from Punta Arenas to our chosen base on the southern shore of the Canal Baker, in a small vessel, *Micalvi*, used for servicing the navigation lights and maintaining contact with the few scattered settlements along the coasts. As my companions all worked at the University of Chile, their available time was restricted to the period of the long vacation, which in Chile is between mid-December and the beginning of March; so we had originally planned to start shortly before Christmas. Later it appeared that *Micalvi* would not be available then, and the time of our departure from Punta Arenas was put forward to about 10 December; but they managed to get special permission to leave before the end of term.

I arranged for our stores and equipment to be shipped out on the Pacific Steam Navigation Company's M.V. *Salaverry*, which was due to sail from London at the end of October and to reach Punta Arenas on 18 November. Everything was packed in two large crates which were ready to be taken to the docks on 26 September, when I was notified that owing to a strike of tally clerks there was such congestion on the wharves, that no more cargo could be received. At first I was not greatly concerned, as there seemed to be plenty of time in hand. But as the strike dragged on, and there seemed little hope of a settlement, I became seriously alarmed that our baggage would arrive too late for our rendezvous in Punta Arenas. I heard that there was another ship sailing from Antwerp about 20 October for the same destination, and had almost decided to send the crates, which together weighed more than half a ton, over to catch it, when, on the 12th, I was told that *Salaverry* had gone to Glasgow to load, and that the baggage must be there to be put aboard not later than 14th. The crates were dispatched north by express delivery, though how the bulk of the ship's cargo could be sent all the way from London to Glasgow at such short notice I could not imagine. Then on 14th I heard that the Glasgow dockers were refusing to handle *Salaverry*'s cargo and the ship was being sent to Liverpool. However, at the last moment the strike ended, and a few days later I learnt, with enormous relief, that *Salaverry* had sailed with my precious crates on board. She was now expected to arrive at Punta Arenas on 4 December, which still allowed a few days to spare for further delays.

9 Crisis in Punta Arenas

It was a dismal winter evening, with a raw wind and light rain, when I left London for Buenos Aires. Three days later, on 30 November, having flown nearly halfway round the world, I arrived at Punta Arenas to find myself in similar conditions, except that the wind was more biting and the rain heavier. I was met at the airfield by William Booth, of the British Consulate and Cyril Jervis, who drove me to the town. A hotel room had been booked for me: but it seemed almost as cheerless as the weather outside and did nothing to dispel the impression that I was in a very remote corner of the world.

After lunch, clad in climbing boots, two heavy sweaters and an anorak, I summoned up the necessary resolution to go for a walk. Picking my way through a morass of mud and puddles which threatened to engulf my ankles, buffeted at each street corner by a piercing blast, I was not inclined, on that summer afternoon, to form a very favourable first impression of Punta Arenas ('Sandy Point'). Like all Patagonian towns that I had seen, it had an air of impermanence, as though it had been thrown together in a haphazard fashion for the temporary accommodation of a nomadic population. Certainly, unlike Rio Gallegos or Santa Cruz, it had some large and solid buildings that looked as though they had been built to stay, but for the rest one was reminded of a film version of a Klondyke gold-rush town, emerging from the grip of the long Arctic winter. It is only fair to add that when I saw it in the sunshine, and with my spirits warmed by the delightful hospitality of the inhabitants, this first jaundiced view was considerably modified.

I climbed up into the hills to the west and was soon out of sight of the town. Summer arrives late in these southern latitudes; the season was equivalent to the end of May in the northern hemisphere, and yet here, in latitude 53° S., corresponding to that of Northern England, it seemed as though spring had scarcely begun. The country had the wild, bleak look of the Yorkshire moors on a stormy day in midwinter, snow lay still on the higher ground, and no flowers had yet ventured to bloom among the coarse grass tussocks. Some dead trees were scattered here and there, their skeleton branches bearded with lichen, and the harsh cries of the plovers overhead enhanced the melancholy of the scene. Out over the Straits of Magellan a few shafts of sunlight pierced the racing clouds and lit the grey sea with a lurid glow.

The next morning I called on Admiral Balaresque, Commander of the 3rd Naval Zone based on Punta Arenas. He had some very bad news to tell me. Apparently *Micalvi*, the ship that was to have taken us to the Canal Baker, had recently been driven ashore in a storm and so severely damaged that even if she were not a total loss, it would certainly be a very long time before she was in commission again. Moreover all the available ships in the area were heavily engaged in salvage operations, and the Admiral could see no prospect of being able to provide us with an alternative means of transport for at least a month or six weeks when, even if it were then forthcoming, it would probably be too late for my companions to embark on the expedition. He told me, however, that the main fleet was due to arrive at Punta Arenas that day from Valparaiso and was returning north about 10 December; he thought it possible that the commander-in-chief might allow us to be taken to the Canal Baker in one of the smaller ships which could rejoin the fleet farther north. Naturally he could not promise anything but he generously offered to do anything he could for us.

I had lunch with Mr and Mrs Sven Robson at their house at Rio Seco, twelve kilometres along the coast from Punta Arenas. Their garden was a riot of colour such as I have rarely seen even in the best-tended gardens in England. Robson was the manager of the South American Export Company which operated a large meat-freezing plant at Rio Seco, and he also held the honorary post of British Consul. He very kindly invited me to stay at the staff guest house of the 'Freezer'. I moved to these comfortable quarters that afternoon, and spent most of the next few days walking in the hills and having long discussions with Cyril Jervis, the Chief Engineer of the 'Freezer', who lived at the guest house.

Jervis was a man of decided views and a wide variety of interests. He spent much of his spare time operating his amateur radio, with which he communicated with other Hams in all parts of the world. One of his most regular contacts was Herbert Masters at Estancia La Cristina, at the head of the north-western branch of Lago Argentina, with whom he was on familiar terms despite the fact that they had never met. At that time Herbert was away in Rio Gallegos, and so 'off the air'; but Jervis promised that when they next spoke to each other, he would tell him that we hoped to reach La Cristina from the ice cap during the first half of February. Less than a week later Jervis' radio was to play a decisive part in the shaping of our fortunes.

The latest news of *Salaverry* was that she was expected in Punta Arenas on 6 December, and she was now so near the end of her voyage that there seemed to be no reason to fear a further delay. If we were to be taken north in a ship of the main fleet, it seemed that we would not be leaving before the 10th, which would allow plenty of time for unloading our baggage from *Salaverry* and checking over the stores and equipment. Meanwhile a letter from Jack informed me that he and the other two were extremely busy winding up their professional affairs in Santiago and had arranged to fly to Punta Arenas in a military plane on the 8th. It seemed to be cutting things a bit fine, but I assumed that they knew what they were about. With nothing to do but await events and keep my fingers crossed, I decided to go over to Tierra del Fuego to spend the weekend with my friends the Bridges; so I took a plane to Rio Grande on Saturday morning, the 3rd, having booked a passage on the next return flight on Tuesday the 6th, so as to be back in Punta Arenas in time for *Salaverry*'s arrival.

I was met at Rio Grande by Oliver and Betsy Bridges, who drove me to their *estancia*, Viamonte, on the Atlantic coast, forty miles farther south. On Sunday we went to lunch with their friend George, the manager of the Tennessee Valley Oil Company's concession near Rio Grande. It was a most convivial party and I was feeling distinctly mellow when we started back at 3.30. On our way through the town, Oliver stopped at his agent's office to pick up his mail. Among this was an urgent telegram for me from Robson, sent an hour or so after I had left Punta Arenas the day before. It told me that arrangements had been made for the expedition to be taken to the Canal Baker on a frigate, which was under orders to sail at noon on Wednesday, the 7th; and that this was the last opportunity we would get. Robson also told me that he had informed Jack by telegram, and he advised me to return immediately.

That I must do so was obvious; but the next plane back (on which I was booked) was on Tuesday the 6th, and was not due to reach Punta Arenas until the late afternoon. This would allow me very little time to get the baggage off *Salaverry* (if she had arrived), deal with the customs formalities, which are apparently necessary even in a 'free port', sort out the equipment, and have our fuel containers filled with paraffin. Moreover, in that part of the world, flight schedules are even less reliable than in Europe, and planes are often delayed by as much as twenty-four hours. Actually I was quite unaware of the real nature of the crisis until much later; which was a good thing for it saved me a very unpleasant thirty-six hours.

After discussing the matter at some length, Betsy suggested that we should go back to George and ask him to help me out. I was reluctant to ask such a favour from a comparative stranger, but there seemed to be no alternative. When we returned to the oil camp, George was sleeping off the effects of his own lavish hospitality; he was, however, generous enough not only to excuse our rude interruption of his siesta, but to offer very practical help. He said that if I returned at nine o'clock the following morning he would arrange to have me flown in the company's plane to a place called Sombrero, an oil town about 300 kilometres away. From there I would almost certainly be able to get a lift to Puerto Porvenir on the Magellan Straits, whence a ship sailed over to Punta Arenas every afternoon starting at about four o'clock. This appeared to solve my problem and I went back to enjoy another night at Viamonte with an easy mind.

The main island of Tierra del Fuego is divided between Chile and Argentina; the frontier runs from north to south roughly through the middle, with Rio Grande in Argentina and Sombrero in Chile. When I arrived at the oil camp on Monday morning, I found that a complication had arisen. Apparently international regulations stipulated that no plane was allowed to cross the frontier without at least twenty-four hours' notice; which meant that I could not be taken to Sombrero by air. However George very kindly supplied me with a car and a driver instead. This alternative arrangement took some time to make, and it was eleven o'clock before we set out, which meant that we would have to average at least 40 mph if I were to catch the ship. Much, of course, depended upon the condition of the road, which turned out to be far from good. Moreover the driver, who was obviously not at all pleased to have been given the job, was quite out of sympathy with my sense of urgency; and gradually my hopes sank as we bumped over the endless flat expanse of country.

At one o'clock we reached the Argentine frontier post, where I hoped that the formalities would not be unduly protracted. After examining our papers, the gendarme in charge informed us that no vehicle was allowed to leave the country without a special permit, which apparently we did not possess. He was quite unmoved by my entreaties, which were probably unintelligible anyway, and there was nothing for it but to turn back; a decision which the driver accepted with irritating complacency. We had covered about fifteen kilometres on the way back, travelling a great deal faster than before, when we met a large lorry bound for Sombrero. I decided to cadge a lift on it, for although I realised that there was no chance of catching the ship from Puerto Porvenir, I still hoped that there might be some alternative means of reaching Punta Arenas that day. I was squeezed in between the lorry driver and his mate, who were most friendly; and when I had made them understand that I was in a hurry, the huge vehicle began to travel at an incredible speed. At 4.30 we thundered into Sombrero. The whole town looked almost as if it had sprung up overnight.

Oliver had given me a letter of introduction to an Anglo-Chilean friend, Mr Sutherland, an executive of the oil company in Sombrero. The driver knew where he lived and presently we stopped in front of a pleasant modern bungalow, which might have been one of a garden suburb in England. It stood near a church made of gaily painted wood and of a most unconventional design, which rather reminded me of a Walt Disney cartoon. Mr Sutherland was away on the mainland, but his wife invited me in and sat me at a table spread for a very English tea. She spoke even less English than I Spanish; but Oliver's letter explained my problem, and having read it she started to make a series of telephone calls while I was charmingly entertained by her nine-year-old daughter.

After tea Mrs Sutherland appeared to have matters under control; indeed she seemed so confident that all would be well that I was quite content to leave myself in her capable hands without even bothering to find out what was happening.

At six o'clock a small bus, or *collectivo* arrived, and in this, the only passenger, I departed for my still unknown destination. An hour or so later, having covered some sixty kilometres, we reached a cluster of corrugated iron sheds near the shore of a wide lagoon; there was also a jetty with a tiny freighter alongside. The water of the lagoon and the gentle, arid hills surrounding it, reflected the golden light of the evening sun. This, I discovered, was Puerto Percy, used by the oil company for bringing equipment and supplies over from the mainland. I also learnt that the freighter was due to sail for Punta Arenas at ten o'clock that night.

The little ship arrived at Punta Arenas at two o'clock in the morning and one of the crew escorted me to the Hotel de France where I was given a bed in a double room. At 3.30, just as I was dropping off to sleep, my room mate came in, still obviously enjoying the effects of his evening's entertainment, and in no way abashed to find that he had company. I rose at 6.30, dressed, shaved and swallowed some coffee; then I waited impatiently until eight o'clock, which I felt was the earliest that I could decently telephone to Robson. It was then that I heard the shattering news.

Salaverry had been further delayed and was now expected to arrive on the 8th, twenty-four hours after the time fixed for the departure of the frigate *Covadonga* which was to take the expedition to the Canal Baker. Robson had been in consultation with the admiral who had regretfully told him that *Covadonga*'s sailing could not possibly be delayed as this would affect the scheduled movements of the whole fleet. It seemed, in that sickening moment, as though our whole enterprise was on the verge of collapse.

There was, however, one chance that all was not yet lost. The admiral had suggested that if we could get into contact with the commander of *Salaverry*, Captain Thomas, and persuade him to co-operate, it might be possible either to transfer our baggage from *Salaverry* to *Covadonga*, when the two ships passed each other somewhere in the channels, or for our baggage to be put ashore on one of the islands, where it could be picked up by the frigate on her way north. It appeared that the commander-in-chief had agreed to this proposal; but would Captain Thomas? It seemed a great deal to ask of any commander, particularly one whose ship was already several weeks late, to undertake, without the authority of his company, an operation which would certainly delay him still further and might involve some risk in those difficult and usually stormy waters; to say nothing of the extra work imposed upon himself and his crew. I imagine that there are very few who would not refuse such a request. Then there was the purely practical matter of whether such a manoeuvre were possible. But the most intractable question of all was this: would Captain Thomas be able to locate our two crates and get them out? They had been loaded in Glasgow as ordinary freight, he still had about 2,000 tons of cargo in his holds, most of which had been taken on during the voyage, so that it seemed more than probable that our baggage was somewhere near the bottom of its particular hold; and it would obviously be impossible to shift even 100 tons of cargo while still at sea. The more I pondered the situation, the more hopeless it seemed.

Meanwhile, however, one important obstacle had been removed. South American customs officials are not as a rule the easiest of people to persuade to deviate from their regulations (at least not by words alone); their bureaucratic instincts are usually well developed. To discharge cargo before it reached the port to which it was consigned, at some unspecified point on the coast, is a highly irregular procedure; and yet Robson had managed to obtain permission from the customs authorities in Punta Arenas for it to be done. This certainly was encouraging. Also, at Robson's request, Jervis had succeeded the previous evening in making contact with *Salaverry*, and had arranged for us to speak to Captain Thomas at 1.30 that afternoon.

I spent most of the morning at Naval Headquarters. The admiral and his staff were extremely kind and went to a great deal of trouble considering the various aspects of the problem and working out alternative plans to submit to Captain Thomas should he be willing and able to co-operate. *Salaverry*'s position when Jervis had contacted her at 6 p.m. on Monday was in the northern part of the Gulf of Penas. Assuming a speed of fifteen knots she should have passed through the English Narrows by noon that day. Situated at the southern end of this channel there is a small meteorological station called Puerto Eden, the only inhabited locality for several hundred miles in either direction. It was also calculated that *Salaverry* and *Covadonga* would in all probability pass each other in the dark during the night of the 7th, when it would be extremely difficult to transfer the baggage, even in the unlikely event of fine weather. It was therefore thought that we would probably have to resort to the alternative plan whereby Captain Thomas would put our baggage ashore at an agreed point on the coast for us to pick up. After a careful study of the charts it was decided that the best place for this would be Fortescue Bay, an uninhabited inlet on the south-west coast of the Brunswick Peninsula which offered a protected anchorage and a sandy beach. I became so absorbed in these fascinating plans, that I almost forgot how very unlikely it was that they would be put into operation.

There was another important matter that I discussed with the admiral. When it was arranged for the expedition to be taken to the Canal Baker in *Micalvi*, it had been agreed that the ship should pay a second visit to our landing place about five weeks later, so that in the event of our failing to reach the ice cap, we could return there to be evacuated. Now, with the new arrangement, this plan had to be reconsidered, and it was evidently a problem that was causing the Admiral some concern. In view of the great courtesy shown us by the Navy, and the lengths to which they had gone to help us, I was most reluctant to press for a relief to be sent. On the other hand I was not quite happy at the prospect of starting the journey with no line of retreat. However, an unexpected solution presented itself.

For some years the Chilean Government had been working on a project to establish settlements at suitable points along the vast stretch of the country's southern coastline. I now discovered that comparatively recently one such settlement, composed of two families, had been established quite close to the point that we had chosen to land. This fact, of course, altered the whole position, for it meant that if we should fail to cross the ice cap, instead of being stranded in uninhabited country we would be able to fall back upon the settlement where at least we would find the means of survival for an indefinite period. So I told the Admiral not to bother to send a relief at least until the end of February, when it would be clear that we had failed to make the crossing, and that even then there would be no particular hurry.

Robson drove me out to Rio Seco for lunch. With the fate of the expedition about to be settled I felt slightly sick and had little appetite. After lunch we assembled in Jervis' room, and at 1.30 precisely he switched on his transmitter and began the rigmarole of repeating call signs. Presently, with some relief, I heard the voice of *Salaverry*'s radio operator, and Jervis and he began what seemed an interminable exchange of technical information about reception conditions. Then Jervis asked if Robson might speak to the captain, and there was a long pause while the latter was brought from the bridge. After a further interchange of call signs, Captain Thomas came on the air addressing Robson. He had no idea, of course, what was afoot, and began by asking a number of questions about arrangements for the discharge of his cargo, which had then to be answered. I tried hard to judge the character of the man from his voice, and derived a good deal of comfort from its calm, good-humoured tone.

Then at last Robson broached the crucial issue. Briefly and clearly he explained the situation, outlining our project and emphasising the vital part the Chilean Navy were playing in our plans. I could not have had a better advocate. I added my personal plea, and then waited, holding my breath, while the transmission was switched over. Captain Thomas began by saying that he was delighted to make my acquaintance even if it were only on the air, and that he had always been keenly interested in the expeditions to Everest. He did not seem in the least put out by our extraordinary request, and without any hesitation went on to say that he would 'do his damnedest' to help us out. But he warned me that he could promise nothing; he had no idea where our crates were, and it was quite probable that they were in a part of the hold which could not be reached. He told us to contact him again at 4.30, by which time he would be able give us the answer. I did my best to thank him, and then told him of the Navy's proposal that he should put the baggage ashore at Fortescue Bay. He replied that he had never heard of the place, but that he would look into the matter and discuss it later if he had succeeded in extracting the crates; and with that the conversation closed. For the first time that day, despite the captain's warning, I felt that there was a reasonable chance of the expedition starting. In my excitement I had quite forgotten to inquire about *Salaverry*'s position.

Meanwhile there was another question to worry about. Would the others arrive in time? On Saturday, Robson had sent a message to Jack through the British Embassy in Santiago telling him that they must reach Punta Arenas before noon on Wednesday; on Monday he received word from the Embassy, that the party had left that afternoon for Buenos Aires, presumably because there was no plane direct to Punta Arenas. There was an Argentine Airlines plane due to leave Buenos Aires at midnight on Tuesday and to reach Punta Arenas at 11 on Wednesday morning. It was the one I had come by the week before, and then it had arrived at noon. I could only hope that they would manage to get seats on this flight (not always an easy matter at short notice), and that the plane would be on time.

However, a pleasant surprise was in store for me: at four o'clock came the news that the others had arrived on the plane from Rio Grande. Speaking to Jack on the telephone I heard enough about their adventures to realise that it had been a very close call. He had not received Robson's message until late on Monday morning. There was a plane from Santiago to Punta Arenas on Tuesday, but on this there were no seats available. The Argentine Airlines Comet was due to leave for Buenos Aires in two hours' time and he decided to try to catch it in the hope of being able to take Tuesday night's plane to Punta Arenas. But there was a great deal to be done in that time: Garcia and Marangunic had to be located and alerted; money for the long journey to be obtained from the bank; an Argentine visa to be secured; and a number of other matters to be seen to including his packing. They caught the Comet with no time to spare. When they reached Buenos Aires they found that there were no seats available on Tuesday's plane to Punta Arenas. However, they discovered that there was a plane belonging to a privately owned company, 'Austral', leaving for Rio Grande in two hours' time from another airfield, twenty miles away. If this plane was on time it should arrive just in time for them to catch the one on to Punta Arenas. It did.

The unexpected arrival of the rest of the party seemed to be a good omen, Surely, I thought, our luck would not desert us now. All the same I was in a state of considerable nervous tension when we assembled in Jervis' room again at 4.30. Contact with *Salaverry* was established, and again there was a long exchange of technical talk between Jervis and the ship's operator, which I found hard to bear with patience, before Captain Thomas was allowed to speak. But at last he came through with the wonderful news that the crates had been found and brought out of the hold. He said that as they were far too big to be put into his ship's boats, they would have to be opened and the stores and equipment repacked into manageable parcels; to which I readily agreed.

The captain told us that his ship was then approaching the northern entrance to the English Narrows, in thick weather. I immediately saw that yet another piece of good fortune had come our way; for this meant that *Salaverry* had not yet passed Puerto Eden, which seemed to be the perfect place to put our baggage ashore. The captain agreed to my suggestion and while we discussed further details, Robson telephoned to the admiral and secured his consent to the new arrangement. My somewhat inarticulate expression of thanks to Captain Thomas was cut short by his obvious desire to return to his bridge to supervise the difficult piece of navigation ahead of him.

A sense of enormous relief flooded over me, and with it a feeling of profound gratitude to all the kind people whose generous co-operation had overcome what had seemed, a few hours before, an impossible situation.

10   Voyage Through the Channels

There were several matters still to be dealt with on Wednesday morning. We had visited *Covadonga* the evening before to pay our respects to her commander, Captain Roebke, who had asked us to come aboard at 12.30. We divided the chores between us, and having arranged to meet at 12.15 at Cedomir Marangunic's parents' home, a few minutes' walk from the quay, we spent a busy morning obtaining a supply of paraffin and hunting for temporary containers to put it in, making a number of small purchases and getting Argentine money from the bank against our eventual arrival in that country. Having also said my goodbyes, I arrived at the Marangunics' house at 12.18 to collect the others.

To my dismay I found that a luncheon party had been arranged in honour of the departing son of the house, to which we were invited together with several other friends and relations. I said that we could not possibly stop for lunch, as we were due on board the frigate in ten minutes. But my protests were cheerfully brushed aside, not only by our hosts but also by my companions. They mockingly suggested that I must have forgotten that I was now in Chile, where punctuality was not regarded with the same reverence as in England. Also, I was told that our host was acquainted with Captain Roebke, and that he was a very good chap, though this argument seemed a bit irrelevant. Chile or no Chile, it seemed to be a gross breach of manners to fail to comply with the Captain's request, to say nothing of the possibility of jeopardising the whole expedition. On the other hand it seemed rather churlish to insist upon wrecking the family's farewell party, and not a very good beginning to my relationship with my Chilean companions. So, having been assured that it would not take more than a few minutes to consume the meal, I quickly capitulated.

As I feared, the luncheon proved to be an elaborate affair of many courses, slowly and formally served. Once having allowed it to begin, it was impossible for me to cut it short without being downright rude; and I had to curb my impatience as well as I could. It was 1.30 before we departed. When we reached the quay I saw to my horror that the frigate had gone, and was already some miles out to sea. For a ghastly moment I thought that she had sailed without us. However, there was a launch manned by naval ratings alongside the quay, and we were informed by a petty officer in charge, that *Covadonga* had merely gone out to box the compass.

It was a protracted operation, and when it was completed she returned to within a quarter of a mile of the quay, and we were taken out to her in the launch. We went forward to report to the captain, who spoke perfect English and greeted me with these words:

'It's a pity, Mr Shipton, that you couldn't keep the timetable we'd arranged. We may have a small navy but we take it seriously.'

I would have been very glad if a trapdoor had opened and swallowed me up. There was no possible reply to that withering reprimand. In the first place it was thoroughly deserved, and to have attempted an explanation would have made matters far worse. However, having delivered his broadside, Captain Roebke waved aside my muttered apologies and went on to make a charming little speech of welcome. He told us that he was honoured to have us in his ship, that he and his ship's company were entirely at our service and that he hoped we would make ourselves at home and consider ourselves free to visit his bridge whenever we wished to do so. Certainly these were no idle words, for throughout the voyage we were treated with delightful courtesy and everything possible was done to make us comfortable.

Covadonga headed due south into a stiff breeze and a choppy sea. To the west, the coast of the Brunswick Peninsula, the southernmost promontory of the American Continent, looked wild and bleak with the ragged clouds racing over its low hills. As I looked out over this stormy scene, I felt a great sense of joyous excitement. I could wish for nothing better than to be here on this warship at the start of a 600-mile voyage through the narrow channels of one of the most fantastic archipelagos on earth, bound for the best of all mountaineering adventures, a journey through an unexplored range. Life occasionally provides moments of complete happiness; this, for me, was one.

We had come aboard with a minimum of clothing, as we intended to abandon most of it as soon as we got the expedition equipment. As the others had brought practically no warm garments, they were provided with padded anoraks from the ship's stores. Jack and I were given berths in the ship's dispensary and the others occupied a cabin nearby. We had our meals with the officers, most of whom spoke good English. After dinner that evening, I was handed a signal from Captain Thomas which said that our baggage had been repacked into twenty-seven parcels which had been put ashore at Puerto Eden. I drafted a message of thanks which Captain Roebke kindly undertook to signal to *Salaverry* as we passed her at about two o'clock in the morning. We went to bed early, and rocked by the gentle heaving of the ship, I went to sleep with a feeling of profound contentment.

When we came out on deck the next morning we were greeted by a biting wind. The scene had changed. Although we were still in the Straits of Magellan, we had rounded the southernmost cape and were heading north-west through a narrow channel between the mainland and the island of Santa Ines. On both sides the land rose precipitously from a belt of forest along the shore, and disappeared into the clouds some 2,000 feet above. Freshly fallen snow lay nearly down to the water's edge, which made it difficult to believe that we were within a fortnight of Midsummer Day.

For many hundreds of miles, the shores along this labyrinth of channels are uninhabited, and the interior of most of the islands is either completely unexplored, or very imperfectly known. Santa Ines is no exception. One of the largest islands of the archipelago, it is some eighty-miles long and fifty-miles wide and, though none of its mountains are more than 4,000 feet high, the central part of it appears to be covered by an extensive ice-sheet. Two expeditions have attempted to explore the interior of the island; they both failed to penetrate more than a few miles inland, partly because of the appalling weather conditions that they encountered, and partly because of the difficulty of the terrain.

During the morning we had a long discussion about our plans for the journey. We found that we were in agreement about most matters: but there was one most important exception. Eduardo and Cedomir approved of my choice of a landing place, but Jack was most strongly of the opinion that we should land some fifteen miles farther east, near the mouth of the Rio Pascua. He reckoned that we were likely to run into considerable difficulties in the upper part of the Jorge Montt Glacier, which we could avoid by taking a more easterly route. We on the other hand considered that by following his route we were likely to be faced with weeks of hard work forcing our way through forest and over a subsidiary range of mountains. We debated the matter for a long time but in the end Jack, though he held to his basic contentions, agreed that the proximity of the settlement might perhaps be a decisive factor.

Meanwhile I was trying to get the measure of my two Chilean companions, and they, presumably, of me. To embark upon an undertaking of this sort with complete strangers may seem rash. But the choice of companions for an exploration is in any case something of a lottery, and my experience has taught me to mistrust my judgement in the matter. Normal acquaintance with a man, however close, is a very poor guide to whether or not he will be a suitable or even a tolerable companion on an expedition. Faults that may normally seem utterly trivial, often become nagging irritations in the enforced intimacy of an expedition; characteristics that may never appear in ordinary life can be distressingly or splendidly revealed in conditions of hardship, danger and physical or nervous strain. Some men who will rise magnificently to a crisis, may yet wilt under the stress of enforced inactivity. Then there is the diverse interplay of characters upon one another. A man may find himself with two companions, both of whom he likes very much, but who cannot tolerate each other. One of my most successful and delightful expedition partnerships was with a man who, I had been warned, was generally regarded as quite impossible to travel with. The argument of those who believe that an 'arranged' marriage has at least as much chance of success as one based upon a love affair, seems to be applicable here.

I had taken an immediate liking to García and Marangunic when I met them in Punta Arenas, and for once my first impressions were confirmed and, on the whole, remained unaltered. García was thick-set, dark and fairly short. Though he seemed reserved at first, I soon discovered that he was a voluble talker, that he had a lively wit and was always ready with an amusing crack about the current situation. He had plenty of self-confidence, and although this was never unpleasantly obtrusive, he was not inclined to take advice. By profession he was an instructor in physical education, though his training had included the study of psychology. Marangunic was tall and spare. In build and to some extent in appearance he resembled Ed Hillary. His chief facial characteristic was his massive underhung jaw giving him the appearance of great determination, which indeed he had. He was quiet, slow of speech, but though he lacked the sparkling humour of García, he was by no means dour, and his face was always ready to light up with a broad grin which caused his huge jaw to stick out even more. Like many determined people he was apt to be stubborn, though his obstinacy was tempered by a logical judgement; he never took up a position without careful thought, and he was generally right.

Jack had told me that neither of them could speak English, which had made me a bit apprehensive. However, I found that he was wrong. García spoke it fairly fluently, though quite ungrammatically; but he had a good deal of difficulty in understanding. Marangunic on the other hand could speak very little, but seemed to understand everything that was said. Thus with one speaking and the other understanding we got along splendidly. Following the modern English custom, Jack and I called them by their Christian names from the start; but though invited to follow suit they persisted throughout the expedition in calling us Mr Ewer and Mr Shipton.

We spent most of the day on the bridge, watching the frigate being steered along her tortuous course, past innumerable islets and an endless succession of passages, some in the form of narrow canyons, some wider than the main channel. Many of the features bore English names, such as Duke of York's Bay, Carrington Island, Smyth Channel and Cochrane Bight, evidence of the part played by British navigators in the monumental work of charting the vast maze of waterways. About noon we reached the western end of the Straits of Magellan, crossed a wide bay opening out to the Pacific Ocean, and then plunged into the still more intricate channels to the north. For most of the day it was stormy, and often we were hit by squalls of rain or sleet, which reduced visibility almost to zero. But towards evening the weather improved; the clouds lifted and the sun broke through, creating the complete arch of a brilliant rainbow against a distant squall, while far away to the east we caught glimpses of some ice-crested peaks framed by the dark green walls of a wide channel. This was the entrance to the Calvo Fjord, up which Tilman's *Mischief* had sailed to the foot of the main range.

I awoke early the next morning to find that the engines had stopped, and going out on deck I saw that the frigate was riding at anchor. We appeared to be in a lake, and not a very large lake either, for there was land close on every side. Though it was still only 6.30, the sun was already high and warm. It was a brilliantly fine morning; the air had a limpid clarity that is found only in those parts of the world subject to long spells of rain; the light and dark greens of the *Nothofagus* forest, splashed here and there with clumps of white magnolias, the glacier-capped peaks of Wellington Island and the cloudless sky were mirrored in the still water about the ship. The contrast to the cold, tempestuous scene of the previous day was astonishing; it was as though we had sailed during the night into a new world of light and colour and peace.

On the westward shore, about half a mile away, there was a single concrete building with a wireless mast; this was the meteorological station of Puerto Eden. Three or four small boats had put out from the shore and were approaching the frigate. When they came alongside I saw that they were very flimsy craft, very roughly constructed. The occupants, two or three in each boat, were savage-looking people, men, women and children, clad in skin or ragged cloth garments, some with long, matted hair falling over their faces and shoulders. These were the Alacaluf Indians, of which there was a small number at Puerto Eden. They squatted motionless in their boats, gazing up at the frigate with expressionless mongoloid faces. Some of the boats contained piles of enormous mussels.

Our twenty-seven bundles of equipment and stores were brought on board, and we made a rough check of the contents before breakfast. The captain had told us that we would stay at Puerto Eden for most of that day, to avoid reaching the upper part of Canal Baker in the dark; so, after breakfast the four of us were taken ashore in one of the ship's lifeboats, driven by an outboard motor. The meteorological station had a staff of three men who showed us over their sparsely furnished quarters. They were obviously delighted to have visitors, which in the circumstances was hardly surprising. They told us that their term of duty in this lonely post was two years. Though on that particular morning it was difficult to imagine a more lovely spot, their usual environment was very different. For months on end in the summer, rain and mist were their daily portion and this was the first time they had seen the sun for more than three weeks. In winter it was bitterly cold, and the nights were long. Apart from their routine duties, there was little for them to do; a certain amount of fishing in the channels, and occasionally a short hunting expedition, though the difficulty of the terrain prevented them going far from the station. However, they did not seem to be unduly depressed by their lot.

Accompanied by one of them, we went for a walk inland. There was no path, and we had not gone more than twenty yards from the station when we found ourselves floundering in a bog, sinking halfway to our knees in mud at every step. Beyond this we started climbing the steep, forested mountainside, and here we had to force our way through dense, tough undergrowth, clutched by thorny brambles and tripped by moss-hidden roots. This and the bog below provided us with a salutary reminder of the kind of country that we might have to penetrate in the early stages of our journey. Even without loads it was exhausting work, and the thought of doing it with sixty pounds on our backs was not a happy one. I began to wonder whether my estimate of three weeks to reach the ice cap would not prove to be wildly optimistic.

Sweating profusely we scrambled up 600 feet or so, and sat basking in the hot sun. Although from there the channels were now open to our view they still looked like a number of narrow, interconnected lakes, divided by scores of wooded islands and promontories, and it was hard to believe that they were a part of the Pacific Ocean, and that they would allow the passage of 10,000 ton vessels on a much frequented shipping route.

Returning to the station we visited some huts belonging to the Alacaluf, scattered along the shore. These people have from time immemorial inhabited the shores of the archipelago from the Gulf of Penas in the north to the western entrance to the Straits of Magellan, a distance of more than 500 miles. Though there is no evidence to show that they ever numbered more than a few thousand, since they were first encountered by western travellers their tribe has dwindled to pathetic proportions. It is estimated that there are now less than 200 scattered over the whole vast area. Some observers, however, say that these numbers are being held, and that there is no likelihood of the tribe becoming extinct in the foreseeable future.

Like other Patagonian Indians, such as the Ona and Yagan, they are exceedingly primitive and, as they have had little contact with civilised people, their way of life still remains almost unaltered. In 1888 the Salesians started a mission for the Alacaluf on Dawson Island at the southern extremity of the area; but it was not successful, mainly because any form of community life conflicted with their nomadic habits. Also it was found that when they congregated together for any length of time they were rapidly decimated by contagious diseases. Indeed, it is said that one of the main causes of the terrible decline of their population was measles, for them apparently a lethal disease. The people of the northern channels, around Wellington Island, had no regular contact with white men until the establishment of a lighthouse on San Pedro Island in 1932, and the meteorological station at Puerto Eden in 1936.

There can be few tribes in the world so completely lacking in organised community life. They have no clan system or chieftainship and they never attempt any form of agriculture or animal husbandry. They wander about the channels in small family units searching for food, and never stop long enough in one place to exhaust the supply. Sometimes, however, they will come together when a whale is found, either dead or trapped in land-locked waters. Then smoke signals are sent up to attract the attention of everyone who happens to be in the locality and the company thus assembled will remain together only so long as the meat lasts. Sometimes too, they will join in a combined raid on a sea-lion rookery when the creatures are whelping. It is only on these haphazard occasions that they unite to practise such tribal customs as initiation ceremonies.

Though nowadays they occasionally beg food from passing steamers, the Alacaluf still subsist almost entirely upon the natural products of their wild habitat. Their staple diet consists of shellfish, the meat of sea lions and marine birds and a small quantity of berries and wild vegetables, such as fuchsia seed-pods; but they also catch other sea creatures such as fish, porpoise and otter, and occasionally deer from the forest. Their food supply is inexhaustible and the most primitive methods of obtaining it are sufficient to meet their needs. This may partly account for the backward state of their development. Nor do they ever bother to store food for any length of time. They do not partake of regular meals, but eat whenever it is convenient and they feel so inclined. They cook all their food (except for sea-urchins which they eat raw) by roasting it on an open fire, and no utensils are used either for cooking or eating.

The smaller varieties of shellfish can be collected along the shore, but the large mussels, which seem to be their favourite form of food, are only found on the sea bottom. To procure these and giant barnacles from a depth of some fourteen feet or less they use spears, but in deeper water, up to about thirty feet, they dive to the bottom and collect the shellfish with their hands. This occupation is generally reserved for the women, who are considered to be better able to withstand the cold. After three or four dives these heroines hurry back to the shore and virtually sit on the fire.

Sea lions are either harpooned or clubbed as they come ashore, but they are also caught in rawhide nets placed across the entrance of half-submerged caves where they are sheltering. Seabirds, particularly cormorants, are mostly caught at night on rocky islets where they congregate to roost. The Indians blacken their faces and hands with charcoal, and hide close by until the birds have assembled and settled themselves for the night. Then they creep out and catch one bird after another, killing them by crushing their skulls with their teeth. Otters and deer are hunted with dogs, their only domestic animals.

The Alacaluf live in oval huts, about twelve feet by eight feet in plan and some six feet high. To make them, a number of saplings are stuck into the ground around the perimeter, bent over and intertwined so as to form a dome-shaped framework; this is usually covered over with sea-lion skins, though if the supply is inadequate, bark, grass or ferns are used instead. The hut is like a primitive version of the *yort*, a dome-shaped tent used by Central Asian nomads. As in the *yort*, a fire is made in the middle of the floor and the smoke is supposed to escape through an aperture in the roof, though usually much of it remains inside; often the whole hut appears to be smouldering. The interior of the huts is kept warm and dry, and the people sleep on a soft litter of twigs. They have no idea of sanitation, and excrement may be found anywhere in the vicinity and even inside the huts.

They used to ignite fires with pyrite and flint, and although now most of them seem to have acquired matches, these are in such short supply that they still try to keep a fire burning continuously and even carry it with them on their journeys. All their travelling is done by water and land journeys are limited to short hunting trips; they never venture into the interior of the larger islands or the mainland. Formerly, despite the cold and damp, they used to go about naked except for a small skin mantle; now, though many of the children are still naked, most of the adults have cloth garments of some sort. As may be expected of people leading such unorganised lives, they have little awareness of time. Apart from day and night, summer and winter, units of time such as hours, weeks and months have no meaning for them. This is perhaps partly due to their inability to count beyond five; their word for 'five' being synonymous with 'many'.

Despite the low level of their intellectual development and their lack of community life, the Alacaluf, in common with all primitive people, have a number of established customs, tribal rites and religious or superstitious practices. There appear to be no sexual taboos prior to marriage, and there is no form of marriage ceremony; when a man and a woman decide to live together the man simply joins the girl's family. Polygamy is not forbidden, but is not generally practised, except in cases of a man marrying two sisters or a widow and her daughter. During childbirth all the men leave the hut, and the husband, having put red paint on his face and right shoulder, a string of white feathers around his head and a white kelp goose skin across his breast, stands guard outside. Infants receive a good deal of affection but little sympathy when they hurt themselves. As soon as they are able to walk children are left largely to fend for themselves, and at the age of four they are expected to handle a shellfish spear and to cook for themselves.

When a death occurs, everyone at the encampment blackens his face with charcoal. The body is either buried or, more commonly, placed in a small cave under a cliff or sometimes just hidden in the undergrowth. Meat and shellfish are placed beside the body, and live coals are put in a miniature hut built near by. This practice seems to indicate a belief in some form of life after death. There is evidence, too, of a belief in a creator-god who causes a soul to enter the body of a newborn baby and to whom the soul returns after death; but it is doubtful whether this concept was derived from their original culture of whether it was acquired by contact with white men.

With their livelihood so dependent upon the elements, their search for food constantly impeded by storms and gales, it is not surprising that the Alacaluf have a great many superstitions concerning the weather. They believe, for example, that bad weather is caused by throwing sand or small pebbles at a hut or into the water; by killing a parrot or even looking at a flock flying overhead and when shellfish are eaten during a voyage, the shells must be kept until they can be deposited on land, well above high-water mark. Fine weather, on the other hand, is likely to be produced by throwing ashes on the water, and when a storm overtakes a canoe party they try to subdue it by throwing eggs into the sea; or if there are no eggs available an old basket is burned instead. To ensure a good season they will bury a large sea lion tooth with a small white stone, and dig them up the following year.

It seemed odd to think of these people with their utterly primitive mode of life, their strange beliefs and customs, so little changed by the twentieth-century world outside, yet living in a comparatively accessible region and accustomed to the frequent passage of ships from Europe through the very heart of their homeland. I wondered if they would benefit, in terms of happiness, by civilisation; but our contact with them was too brief to suggest an answer.

We returned to the frigate for lunch, at which we were served with a dish of the huge mussels we had seen in the Alacaluf boats. They were quite succulent and not as tough as they looked, though I found their taste rather nondescript. We spent the hot afternoon checking our stores and equipment, which we found complete, filling our plastic fuel containers with ten gallons of paraffin and fixing webbing bindings on to the snowshoes, while the crew took a keen interest in our activities. At the last job we showed ourselves most inept, and the Bo'sun came to our rescue with a variety of drilling and riveting tools.

Covadonga weighed anchor at six o'clock and, after a great shudder as her screws churned the water, she began to glide across the lagoon, through a narrow passage between two wooded islands and out into the channels beyond. The sky was still almost cloudless and the air so calm that no ripple disturbed the perfect reflections of mountain and forest whose colours were now beginning to deepen in the soft evening light.

After supper, at about eight o'clock, we returned to the bridge to watch the vessel being steered through the English Narrows. By now the sun had sunk below the lofty crests of Wellington Island and all the land to the west was in deep shadow; but eastward, parts of the mainland shore and all the peaks beyond were still alight with its warm glow. At times it looked as though the ship were heading into a completely land-locked fjord; then suddenly she would swing through an angle of ninety degrees and glide into another passage that had opened unexpectedly on one side or the other. A cunning system of beacons had been arranged at various points, some on the shores, some high up on the mountainsides; the moment and direction of any turn was indicated by a pair of beacons coming into line. Even for a landsman watching the operation in such rare fine weather, it was easy to imagine what a difficult piece of navigation it must be in the usual stormy conditions, with the wind deflected by the mountains into sudden hurricane gusts from any direction, with blinding squalls and with currents sent racing through the channels by the Pacific tides.

Having written half a dozen letters which were to be posted when the frigate reached Valparaiso, I went to bed at about midnight, tingling with excitement at the thought of what the next day would bring.

11 The Landing

10 December. I awoke at 6.15 and, with no inclination to linger in bed, I dressed and went up to the bridge. Captain Roebke was there, muffled in a greatcoat and a thick woolen scarf and wearing a long-peaked, light blue baseball cap which seemed to be his regular headgear when at sea. The frigate, now steering due east, was already far up Canal Baker, and I could distinguish the point of land which marked the place where the wide channel divided into its two upper fjord systems, one leading north-east to the mouth of the Rio Baker the other south-east to the Rio Pascua. We were less than three hours from our destination.

The weather had changed. There was a fresh northerly breeze, and though the sun was shining, a large part of the sky was covered by sultry-looking clouds. The captain told me that he was expecting a storm within the next twenty-four hours, and that he was anxious to get through the Gulf of Penas, which was notorious for its rough seas, before it began to blow really hard. But it looked as though our luck, which had miraculously steered us through the various crises of the last week, was still holding. My enjoyment of the voyage had been slightly marred by a nagging worry that when we reached our destination, stormy weather might prevent our landing; for in this event we obviously could not expect the frigate to wait for better conditions. Now it was virtually certain that we had escaped this final hazard, though once again, it seemed, by a narrow margin.

After breakfast we carried our baggage to the port side of the ship and stacked it there, ready for disembarking; then we returned to the bridge to wait for the exciting moment when we would catch our first glimpse of the country which we would have to penetrate on the first stage of our journey. We had now entered the Calvo Fjord, which was similar to most of the channels through which we had been sailing for the last few days. Isla Francisca was close on the starboard side, ten miles long and densely forested, screening our view to the south. Then, as we rounded the eastern end of the island, the Jorge Montt Glacier suddenly appeared, curving upward in a mighty sweep from the gleaming peninsular of its shattered front, past a line of ice-peaks and vanishing over the far southern horizon. Twenty minutes later *Covadonga* dropped anchor off the northern shore of Isla Faro, which lay across the entrance of a deep bay.

While one of the boats was lowered and loaded with our baggage, we said goodbye to our hosts. I had been deeply touched by their friendliness and by their keen interest in every detail of our plans; now they seemed genuinely sorry to see us go, and they gave us an impressive send-off. We climbed down into the boat which was manned by a lieutenant and three sailors, the outboard motor was started and we were soon running at five knots before a gentle swell. We rounded the western corner of Isla Faro and the frigate disappeared from view. At that moment we heard three farewell blasts from her siren.

Only about forty years ago, the bay we were now in was almost entirely occupied by the Jorge Montt Glacier. Since then the ice had retreated about six miles, and although still extended far out into the water in the south-eastern corner, it had left a long strip of sandy shore at the southern extremity of the bay, which we could now see. This shore seemed to be the ideal place for our landing, and I was tempted to ask the lieutenant to take us there. But it was important that we should establish contact with the settlers on whose goodwill we might be forced to rely in case of an emergency; and it would obviously be a good thing to do so while we were still guests of the Chilean Navy. We did not know exactly where the settlement was, but we thought it was located somewhere on the north-west shore of the bay. While we were discussing the matter, we caught sight of a rowing boat nearly a mile astern in the direction of Isla Faro; so we turned about and made for it.

Its sole occupant was a middle-aged man, with an expression of infinite serenity on his handsome weatherbeaten face. He reminded me very much of a Scottish crofter. Without evincing any surprise or curiosity, he calmly and efficiently lashed his boat to ours as we came alongside, still travelling so fast that the resulting jerk on his rope very nearly pulled him overboard. He guided us past a promontory to an inlet on the western side of the bay, and thence about half a mile up a creek. There, in a sheltered forest clearing, we came upon the settlement. It appeared to consist of two solidly built log houses; but our visit was so brief that we never discovered whether there were more buildings behind.

The launch was run ashore on a small shingle beach, where we were greeted by two younger men, obviously very excited by our arrival which was also watched from the houses by two women and several small children. We offloaded our baggage and stacked it on the beach, while the Lieutenant walked up to the houses accompanied by two of the *pobladores* (settlers). We inquired of the third whether he could lend us some horses to transport our baggage to the southern shore of the bay, for this was six miles away and it would take us several days of hard work to carry the loads there ourselves. The answer was that there were no horses available, that in any case it was very difficult to reach the end of the bay overland, but that we could be taken by boat the following day if the weather remained fine.

When the Lieutenant returned, however, he offered to take us in the launch before returning to the frigate. I was surprised by this generous offer, for it was already eleven o'clock, and I remembered that the Captain had told me he was anxious to get out of the Canal Baker and across the Gulf of Penas without delay. But I accepted without hesitation and our baggage was reloaded on to the launch. Meanwhile we distributed three jackets, three pairs of trousers and my old overcoat among the *pobladores*. They were delighted and evidently found it hard to believe that these valuable articles, most of them brand new, were really gifts. We also offered to supply them with sugar and coffee and a number of other luxuries if they would visit our base, which they said they would do in the course of the next day or two. With that we parted on excellent terms.

By then the tide had ebbed so far that we had considerable difficulty in heaving the launch off the beach. This done by the aid of levers, we set off down the creek. We had not gone more than 300 yards, when the motor stopped. It was soon discovered that the engine had seized, presumably from lack of oil, and that it was no further use. The launch was rowed to the shore, where our baggage was again offloaded while a sailor ran back to the settlement. After a while he reappeared, coming down the creek with our friends, the *pobladores*, in two rowing boats. Then the lieutenant, who must have been feeling somewhat harassed but was too polite to show it, and the three sailors bid us a warm farewell and addressed their task of rowing the heavy launch five miles back to the frigate, where no doubt they would meet with a less friendly reception from their captain.

We distributed ourselves and our baggage, which with packing-cases and surplus stores must have weighed nearly half a ton, between the two rowing-boats, and started down the creek once more. When we rounded the headland into the bay, we were met by a stiff head-wind and a choppy sea. It was disappointing to find that the breeze had gone round to the south, but I was consoled by the thought that it would help the unfortunate crew of the launch. Jack and I were together with one of the *pobladores*. Our boat was a cumbersome affair and none too seaworthy. Little fountains of water gushed up between her timbers, and the rising tide in her bottom could only be kept at bay by fairly continuous baling. There was one pair of oars, and only room for one man to pull on them. The other boat, carrying our companions and the other two *pobladores*, had two pairs of oars, but it was evidently more cumbersome to row for we managed to haul ahead.

As we butted into the waves, an occasional shower of icy spray sweeping over us, it seemed to me that the wind was increasing; our progress appeared to be so slow that I began to wonder if we could cover the six miles to the southern shore of the bay. But our *pobladore* was quite unmoved and said cheerfully that it was fortunate that we had such a fine afternoon for the trip. All the same I was not sorry that we kept fairly close along the shore. He rowed solidly for the first hour, and then Jack and I took it in turns to relieve him. At first I was glad of the exercise for I felt very cold; but I was a great deal more glad when my spells came to an end and I had a chance to rest my aching forearms.

Gradually, as we came under the lee of some high cliffs at the south-western corner of the bay, the wind dropped and the water became calmer. Jack, who had a good command of Spanish, questioned the *pobladore* about his life in this remote place. He was formerly a merchant seaman, and he and his wife had come there from Puerto Natales with two other families three years before. With the assistance of the Chilean Government they had brought with them a couple of dozen sheep and the necessary tools for building their houses and for clearing and tilling the land. Their small flock had already increased to about sixty animals, and with their houses built and a small area of land under cultivation, they considered themselves fairly well established; but they had had a hard and sometimes anxious time. Two or three times a year they were visited by small government vessels which brought them supplies of such things as flour and sugar in exchange for their wool. Of course this was not an economic proposition for the government, whose object was to foster the settlement and development of this vast uninhabited coast. They had no other contact with the outside world.

They certainly did not seem discontented with their lot. Their conditions of life and their problems were probably not so very different from those of the Masters when, at the beginning of the century, they came to settle at La Cristina; but while the latter were strangers in a foreign land and for a time even more dependent upon their own resources, their climate was more agreeable and they could at least get out when they wanted to. As in the case of the Masters, I was deeply impressed by the determination and cheerful courage that had prompted these people to leave their homes to embark upon their lonely and hazardous quest of an independent life. I was sorry that we could not stay with them for a little while to see something of their strange Swiss Family Robinson existence; though I reminded myself that the opportunity to do so might still be forced upon us.

After three hours' rowing we reached the southern end of the bay and we ran the boats ashore near the point where a stream intersected the long sandy beach. The *pobladores* helped us to unload our baggage, and saying they would visit again either the next day or the day after, they departed on their return voyage. In fact, though they kept their promise, this was the last we saw of them.

It was now about 3.30. There was no wind; most of the cloud had vanished and the sun was deliciously warm. We could not have wished for a better afternoon for this long-anticipated moment of arrival at the starting point of our journey, nor for a more beautiful landing-place. The beach ran westward for half a mile to the line of tall cliffs which curved round the south-west corner of the bay, and eastward for nearly a mile to a massive wall of blue ice which, extending far out to sea, formed the end of the Jorge Montt Glacier. From the beach a wide plain extended inland for several miles. As this had only recently been abandoned by the ice (probably within the last hundred years) it was almost devoid of vegetation except for coarse grass and small scrub. From the cliffs at the western end of the beach a ridge ran up to a long mountain spar; the upper part of its steep forested slopes still held masses of winter snow, while lower down they were intersected by gleaming white ribbons of torrents and waterfalls. To the east the plain was bounded by the trunk of the glacier, which from the beach looked like an enormous white whale basking in the sun. Beyond the far end of the plain the glacier disappeared behind a range which, curving away to the right, climbed in a series of rounded steps to some high and distant peaks. It appeared to be separated from the western ridge by a wide valley. We called it 'The Barrier Range'.

Some three hundred yards from the beach we found an ideal camp site; a piece of flat ground of ample dimensions, close to the stream, but ten feet above it, which afforded reasonable protection from flooding, and surrounded on three sides by cliffs and hillocks of gravel and clay. Carrying our baggage over from the shore we became so hot that we took off our shirts, and by the time we had pitched the tents we were more than ready for a brew of tea.

We spent the rest of the afternoon and most of the evening unpacking our stores and equipment, checking them, separating the necessities from the surplus stuff which could be left behind and, as far as possible, making up individual loads to be carried forward. We were well aware of how lucky we were to be doing this in such perfect weather, for had it been pouring with rain or blowing half a gale or both, it would have been a difficult and unpleasant job. As it was, everything was tossed around with happy abandon, to be counted and sorted at leisure. To my relief nothing was found to be missing from my lists, for I had intended to make a final checking of the equipment at Punta Arenas, and having been denied that opportunity, I was slightly apprehensive that some small but vital item, such as prickers for the Primus stoves, or wax for the sledges, had been omitted. The only thing I had forgotten was a maximum-minimum thermometer, and for this oversight I received a stern reprimand from Jack.

The question of whether items of equipment were or were not necessary, or if not strictly necessary whether they might or might not be so useful as to be worth their extra weight, involved us in long and sometimes heated debate.

Indeed, throughout most of the journey it continued to be something of a bone of contention. Remaining true to my deep-rooted prejudice in favour of travelling light, I usually found myself in a minority of one, and I had to fight so hard to uphold my principles that the others came to regard 'Chuck it away' as my guiding precept or as a psychological oddity which must be humoured but at the same time kept under watchful restraint. In the weeks that followed, whenever anything was mislaid, one or other of the Chileans would invariably remark, 'Ah! Mr Sheepton chuck it away my spoon' or 'my glove'.

Jack, for example, had brought a plant press, and while I applauded his zeal for scientific investigation, I thought (or hoped) that there would not be sufficient opportunity for botanical collecting before we got on to the glacier to make it worth while carrying it all the way across the ice cap. After a stubborn struggle he agreed to abandon it on condition that he might retain some small bottles of alcohol which he had brought for collecting insects. Eduardo had brought a considerable weight of what is known to mountaineers as 'ironmongery', including pitons and the like, used in extremely difficult climbing operations, beyond the scope of old-fashioned implements such as ice axes and crampons. I could not imagine that we would attempt anything that would involve the use of these advanced technical appliances, and I pressed him to leave them behind. But Eduardo pointed out that they were the property of his club, and that they were practically irreplaceable in Chile. With this argument he won the day and the useless pieces of iron were carried all the way.

A more unusual gadget bought by the Chileans was a huge saw with villainous teeth. Its purpose was to enable us to cut large blocks of ice or snow from the surface of the glacier, with which to build igloos in case our tent was destroyed by a storm or blown away. Although neither the possibility of this contingency nor its ugly consequences had escaped me, I was very doubtful whether a saw would be of much help to us in building an igloo on the type of surface we were likely to meet. Much has been said and written about the construction of ice caves and houses, but, having never employed the technique myself, I have always supposed that it required special conditions, such as deep, hard snow for building, or a steel slope for tunnelling. However, the others were so sanguine about their ability with the aid of a saw in any conditions to whip up a comfortable residence in a couple of hours or so that, in view of my ignorance, I could hardly insist upon dispensing with this means of our salvation. So the monster remained with us, its jagged teeth a constant embarrassment while carrying loads and packing the sledges and a perpetual menace to the tent, the fuel containers and the ration bags; until one day, five weeks later, after a particularly severe blizzard, I noticed that it was no longer with us. Whether it was because by then my companions had acquired more confidence in the tent or less in their ability to build an igloo, its loss was not mourned; nor was I accused of having 'chucked it away'.

The presence of a considerable supply of surplus food, of course provoked further discussion. Our daily ration had been calculated with great care and it was generally admitted that its calorie and protein content was sufficient for our needs. The surplus food had originally been brought to stock a depot against the possibility of an enforced retreat; but I had now decided to hand it over to the *pobladores*, since if we were forced to return, we would in any case have to rely upon them for our sustenance. Besides such basic commodities as biscuits, sugar and oats, it also included a number of luxury items not in the ration, sweets, hot drink powder, lemonade powder, 'energy tablets' and the like. Also Jack had found time during his brief stay in Punta Arenas to acquire a supply of bully beef and various packets of jelly and 'pudding mix'. He and Cedomir were both of the long, lean type of man that seems to be perpetually hungry, and the idea of leaving all these goodies behind caused them such anguish that in the end I agreed to allow some of them to be taken at least as far as the next camp where we might have a better idea both of our carrying capacity and of the difficulties ahead of us.

Remembering the disastrous failure of our stoves the previous year, I had decided this time to use the ordinary paraffin-burning Primus which, in my opinion, is still by far the best and most reliable kind of stove for light travel. I had brought a large one for regular use and a small one to be kept in reserve. We had been provided with an enormous supply of spare parts from which we made a careful selection, and jettisoned the rest. I have always found it difficult to estimate the consumption of paraffin over a given period; for so much depends upon such factors as how often water will be available and for how much of the time it will be necessary to melt snow, how much draught there will be inside the tent and how much the stove will be used for purposes other than cooking, such as drying clothes and warming the tent. We could safely predict that all these factors would be adversely disposed, and we decided to provide ourselves with a liberal allowance of a gallon per week, or eight gallons in all. This turned out to be almost exactly the right quantity. The fuel was carried in large plastic containers, one of which had been designed for use by the British Army in making parachute landings. We had a number of smaller plastic bottles to hold our current requirements.

Our personal belongings varied with the individual, the only stipulation being that each man should not have more than twenty pounds excluding his boots and Gannex suits. Mine consisted of two sweaters, two shirts, two pairs of pyjama trousers, a string vest, eight pairs of socks and one of gloves, balaclava helmet, sleeping bag and air mattress, camera and twelve rolls of film, one pound of tobacco, two pipes and two paper-backed books (*Madame de Pompadour* and *Cakes and Ale*). Our crampons were carried separately.

Long before we had finished sorting out the stores and equipment to be taken with us, it was clear that four relays would be needed to shift it. However, I was not particularly worried about this; for we were well ahead of our original timetable, and by carrying some extra food with us we could afford to take our time over the initial stages of the journey. If we ran into difficulties during the next ten days, it would be time enough to cut down our loads more ruthlessly. Our main concern was to reach the head of the Jorge Montt Glacier while there was still plenty of snow covering the icefalls and crevassed areas. We had heard that the spring was late in arriving in Southern Patagonia, and that although parts of the country had suffered a drought, this did not apply to the mountainous areas to the west which on the contrary had experienced exceptionally heavy snowfall. These reports were confirmed by the deep deposits of winter snow that still lay in the forest a couple of thousand feet above us. It was most probable, therefore, that we would find good conditions on the upper part of the glacier at least until the end of December.

When everything had been sorted out and the tents pitched, we built an enormous fire of driftwood. It was the only camp fire we were to enjoy during the expedition. Besides the pyramid, I had also sent an old Meade tent with the baggage from London. I had intended to leave this in Punta Arenas for use in my subsequent wanderings. Now, unfortunately, it would have to be abandoned, but at least it provided me with the luxury of a tent to myself during the few days spent at the first camp, and afforded the others a postponement of the cramped conditions to which we would have to accustom ourselves.

After supper I strolled down to the shore to enjoy the evening light and to ponder over our peculiar situation. There was no breeze, and the bay was too enclosed and too remote from the Pacific to allow the ocean swell to disturb its calm. For the most part the only sound was the gentle hiss of tiny waves breaking along the beach; but every now and then the peace was shattered by the thunderous roar of ice calving from the glacier front which, in the gathering dusk had assumed a sinister glow. Though the sky was streaked with cloud it appeared to hold no menace. It seemed that the captain's gloomy prediction of twelve hours before had been wrong, and that we could look forward at least to another day of this holiday weather.

That moment can, I think, be counted among the highlights of my life; for then I was captured by the same surging excitement that I remember when I started for my first Alpine peak, for my first Everest expedition and for the long trek across the Karakoram to Kashgar; or again when Tilman and I reached the upper gorge of the Rishi Ganga, and at our base camp in the Shaksgam Valley. All these were moments of anticipation, and although I have not always found that anticipation is better than fulfilment, it has a special quality (fear, perhaps, is part of it) that seems to make a more lasting impression on the mind.

The prospect of the journey across this strange ice cap was as exciting as any I have known; and to have been landed on this lonely shore and left to our own resources with no immediate means of retreat added a delicious tang to its savour. The fact that the task would be largely a contest, not against mountaineering difficulties, but against the notorious Patagonian weather, and that for most of the time we would be physically miserable, mattered not at all.

It was good to find that advancing years had not blunted my sensitivity to such feelings.

12 The Approach

I awoke at one o'clock to find heavy rain beating against the tent, and the canvas flapping angrily in the wind. It seemed incredible that less than four hours before I had been sitting on the shore enjoying the stillness of a perfect evening. But such unpredictable changes in the weather are only to be expected in Patagonia, so with a curse of resignation I buried my head in my sleeping bag to protect it from the fine spray coming through the roof of the tent. I drifted back to sleep wondering vaguely how far *Covadonga* had progressed across the Gulf of Penas before the storm began. At four o'clock I woke again, to find it raining and blowing still harder. Above the noise of the storm, I could now hear the roar of the stream, which sounded so close and so loud that I wondered if after all the ten foot banks would be sufficient to contain the swollen torrent. I opened the door of the tent and looked out. It was already light, and as there appeared to be no immediate danger of a flood, I went back to bed.

We had intended to be off to an early start that morning, five o'clock I think was the time agreed upon, but now, in these conditions, it seemed a bit pointless, so I dozed on until 6.30 before rousing the others. We lingered over breakfast, vaguely hoping that the weather might moderate, but by eight o'clock we could delude ourselves no longer; the holiday was over and we must turn out to face the harsh reality of our self-inflicted torment. As we splashed about in the mud, our hands numbed by the wind and rain, we realised again how lucky we had been to have had the opportunity of sorting things out in fine weather. Four sacks, each containing four two-day food packs, had been strapped to our Yukon carrying frames, and all we had to do was to shoulder our sixty-pound loads and start marching.

The cloud ceiling was down to about 1,000 feet, but through the driving rain we could still see the base of the mountains at the far end of the plain. Beyond the sand dunes and moraine hillocks grouped around the shore, we reached a stretch of flat country, covered with tussocks of coarse grass. To our great relief the ground was firm, for we had been quite prepared to find here a wide expanse of bog, like the one that we had encountered at Puerto Eden, which would have taken us a very long time to cross. After three-quarters of an hour we found ourselves confronted by some low hills, formed by a series of *roches moutonnes*, or outcrops of rock worn smooth by glacier action, over which we had to climb.

When we reached the highest ridge of the hills, we looked down upon a lake about four miles long and nearly two miles wide, which was damned back from the sea by the trunk of the glacier. Its surface was half-covered with innumerable icebergs, of all shapes and sizes. Two of them were several hundred yards across, and as their surface still showed the original crevasse formation, they must have drifted away from the glacier without much fuss, which indicated that the eastern part of the lake was very deep.

We climbed diagonally across a series of ridges, some of them with deep clefts between, and made our way down to the western shore of the lake, which we followed for a quarter of a mile. Here we found thousands of waterfowl either feeding along the shore or sitting on the water a few yards from it. As we approached they kept rising into the air with a mighty beating of wings, circling overhead and settling again a few hundred yards away. Many of the birds, however, had young families, and remained behind to protect their chicks as they scurried into the water at our approach. The great majority were upland and ashy-headed geese, though there was also a number of steamer duck and several species of smaller birds including teal.

Despite the rain I was beginning to enjoy myself. My load was sitting comfortably on my hips, there was not too much drag on my untrained shoulders, and since the first hour or so I had got my second wind. It was exciting to see each new aspect of the way ahead and the ground was varied and interesting. Moreover this first stage was proving delightfully easy, and with no bog and no forest to impede us, we were making rapid progress inland.

The plain had merged into craggy moorland, intersected by deep gullies containing torrents, one of which was so swollen that we had some difficulty in crossing it. It stopped raining and the cloud ceiling broke and lifted, leaving small wreaths of mist clinging to the steep, forested slopes to our right, where the white ribbons had expanded into impressive cascades. Crossing the moorland, we reached a point where the ground fell away in front of us and we found ourselves looking up a long valley to the south-west. At its exit there was a wide, circular basin which lay between the high ground on which we stood and the base of the mountains to the south. This had once contained a lake which had formed behind a bank of old moraine, some 400-feet high; but the barrier had been breeched and now the river from the valley ambled sluggishly across the floor of the basin and drained through a narrow defile.

When we reached the river we found it to be some twenty yards wide and very deep, and it seemed as though we would have to make a detour into the valley, and possibly a long way up it, before finding a way across. This was not an agreeable prospect for, with all our baggage, the extra distance would have to be covered four times both ways. However, though it was still only 12.30, we decided to leave this problem until another day. We had reached a point from which it would be necessary, in any case, to make a thorough reconnaissance of the mountains ahead of us, before deciding upon our next line of advance. From a camp hereabouts, two of us could swim across the river and tackle this task, while the other two were exploring up-stream for a suitable place for a crossing with the baggage. So we dumped our loads on a high platform overlooking the river, and made our way back to camp, with the intention of bringing up another relay that afternoon.

It was very nearly three o'clock by the time we reached camp. I was feeling distinctly tired and regarded the prospect of carrying another load with abhorrence. Although they did not care to show it, I do not think that the others liked the idea any more than I did. But it was not raining and we had no real excuse for wasting the rest of the day, so after consuming one of Jack's tins of bully beef, we had a short rest and set out again carrying three sacks containing the remaining twelve two-day ration packs and a load of fuel. However, I decided that on this second carry we should go only as far as the torrent that had held us up that morning, a little more than halfway up the river; a decision which my companions were very ready to accept. Even this was more than enough, for when at eight o'clock we got back to camp, I felt very weary indeed, and after a half-hearted attempt to eat some supper I slunk away to my tent. I tried to console myself with the thought that we had made very satisfactory progress that day, but I was not really in a mood to take pleasure in anything, even in lying down.

The second day was a great deal less agreeable than the first. I awoke feeling very old and decrepit; my body ached all over as though it had been beaten with clubs and it required a great deal of resolution to get out of my sleeping bag and into my damp clothes. I elected to carry the two sledges and the infernal saw, a gesture of ostentatious unselfishness which I soon regretted, for although together they weighed rather less than sixty pounds, they made an awkward load which constantly threw me off balance, while the various sections drummed together with a maddening monotony. My packframe, which yesterday had felt reasonably comfortable, now seemed like an instrument of torture. A painful bruise had developed below the small of my back, upon which the frame bumped with merciless persistence, while the straps dragged at my aching shoulders. It was raining hard, mist obscured the view and there was no longer the excitement of treading new ground to counteract my misery.

The only consolation was that there was a calculable time limit set upon this penance, for we knew exactly how many marching hours we had to do. I disciplined myself to refrain from looking at my watch for at least ten minutes at a time, and amused myself by trying to estimate how long it would take to reach various points in view. Each half hour we stopped for an exquisite five minutes of rest which, I was gratified to notice, the others seemed to enjoy as much as I.

The torrent was still more swollen than it had been the day before, and the problem of crossing it with the two relays of loads caused a pleasant diversion. In any case I was beginning to feel better by then; my limbs had lost much of their stiffness, some semblance of vitality had returned to my wretched body, and by the time we reached the river with the second relay, I was even willing to admit to myself that the expedition might after all have some worthwhile purpose. The worst was over, and although I knew that it would be several days yet before I was fit enough to carry a load with any semblance of nonchalance, I could now look forward to a steady improvement in my condition.

However, the day had not yet finished with its quota of woe. On our way back across the *roches moutonnés* that evening, I carelessly stepped in a hole and sprained my right ankle. When we reached our camp we found that the *pobladores* had been there and had very kindly left a leg of mutton hanging from a stake. At first the Chileans were delighted by the prospect of a barbecue, but it was still raining heavily and none of us felt inclined to build a fire with sodden pieces of driftwood, and still less willing to add it to his next day's load, so, alas, the generous gift was left untouched.

The following morning, 13 December, my ankle was still so swollen and painful that Eduardo, who had assumed the role of the expedition's doctor, insisted that I must rest it for a day, and I was forced, with a fair show of reluctance, to agree. By then only four loads remained to be shifted, and it was decided that the other three, taking the pyramid tent with them, should establish Camp 2 by the river, and that Jack and Cedomir should remain there to investigate the problem of the crossing, while Eduardo returned to spend the night with me. It was fortunate that we had the Meade tent to make this manoeuvre possible.

It was extremely irritating to be incapacitated as a result of my carelessness, and it was obvious that it would be some days before my ankle recovered completely. However, for the present I could at least assuage my conscience with the reflection that my companions would have a comparatively easy day; so, settling myself luxuriously against Eduardo's sleeping-bag, I became completely absorbed in Nancy Mitford's fascinating portrayal of court life in eighteenth-century France. At two o'clock Eduardo arrived back, soaking wet but as cheerful as ever. He massaged my foot and then entertained me for the rest of the evening with lively accounts of his various expeditions in the Andes.

My ankle was slightly less swollen the next morning, so after a leisurely breakfast, we strapped it tightly with an elastic bandage and prepared to start. Eduardo left a letter for the *pobladores* telling them to take over everything that we had left behind in the camp. This included some clothing, a pair of boots, the tent and a considerable quantity of sugar, tea, coffee, sweets, biscuits and various tinned foods. They must have been delighted.

Carrying only my personal belongings, I managed to hobble along at a reasonable pace. Though the weather was raw and bleak it was not raining, and with the whole day before us we could make long and frequent halts. Early in the afternoon, as we approached the end of the lake, we were delighted to see the pyramid tent perched on top of the high moraine bank. This meant that the others had found a way of crossing the river, and when we reached the place where the loads had been dumped we found that they had all gone.

After a brief search we caught sight of some of them piled on the far bank near the point where the river entered the defile. On a strip of mud shore below, the fibreglass sledge lay assembled, with a climbing rope tied to either end, one of which, stretching across the river, was attached to an ice-axe driven into the mud on the near bank. This then, was the means by which Jack and Cedomir had made the crossing. I was surprised, because I would not have expected the joints of the sledge to be anything like watertight enough for it to be used as a boat. However, when we had hauled it across, we discovered that the joints had been cunningly sealed with wads of toilet paper.

Even so it was a delicate operation, particularly for the first man, to make the voyage. The sledge, which was shaped like a punt, was eight feet long and only six inches deep. Eduardo sat in it and when I had heaved it gently off the shore we found that it floated with about an inch of freeboard. Fortunately, the river at this point was protected from the wind and very sluggish, so that there was scarcely a ripple on the water. Very gingerly Eduardo started to haul himself across by means of the rope attached to the far bank. He had progressed about four yards, when suddenly the sledge capsized hurling him into the water which was out of his depth. He scrambled out, while I hauled the upturned sledge back to the shore.

When he had recovered his breath and relieved his feelings with some violence, he stripped off his sodden clothes and boots and tried again. This time he lay prone in the sledge with his head forward, using one hand and his teeth to pull in the rope. About halfway across the sledge gave a lurch and shipped some water. For a moment I thought he was over again, but he managed to recover his balance and reached the far shore without further mishap. I then hauled the sledge back across the river, and loaded it with our belongings. I also took the precaution of stripping off all my clothes and my boots, which I sent across with the rest. Meanwhile Eduardo was sprinting up and down a stretch of beach, trying to restore some warmth to his naked body. When my turn came to make the crossing, all I had to do was to lie perfectly still in the sledge, doing my best to control my shivering, which might have been quite enough to upset the frail craft, while Eduardo pulled it across. All the same I was very relieved to reach the other side without a ducking in the icy water.

Having taken the sledge to a safe place well above the reach of the river, we climbed to the crest of the moraine bank. The tent had been pitched at a point a quarter of a mile farther on, near two little ponds which furnished our water supply. It commanded a splendid view north-west across the lake to the coast, and to the south across the basin to the steep, forested slopes of the Barrier Range. The cloud ceiling was down to about 1,000 feet and, although we could see several miles up the valley, its upper part was obscured. The moraine bank ran eastward for a mile or so, rising gently, and joined a prominent northerly spur of the Barrier Range, though it looked as if there might be a deep gap between it and the main massif.

Jack and Cedomir were away, presumably making a reconnaissance, so we settled ourselves into the tent, lit the Primus and brewed tea, which was just about ready when they returned. They had climbed most of the way up the spur but, finding themselves in thick mist, had returned without solving the problem of our next move. However we certainly could not complain, for their ingenious method of crossing the river had probably saved us several days' delay and a lot of hard work.

This was the first time that all four of us had occupied the pyramid tent together, and as it was to be our home for nearly two months we were interested to see just how cramped our quarters were to be. It was originally designed as a three-man tent for use in the Antarctic. The interior floor space was eight feet square, and as our air mattresses were two feet wide there was just enough room for them to fit side by side. To begin with we lay with our heads along the back wall and about six inches from it. The mattresses were six feet long so that there was a corridor some eighteen inches wide along the entrance wall, which was occupied by such things as the Primus, the current ration packs, boots and various other bits of personal gear. The space between the outer and inner entrance walls was used for stowing the cooking pots and flasks of fuel, and also, later, as a reservoir from which to refill the pots with snow.

There were three tapes stretched across the tent seven feet above the floor, which served as clothes lines on which to hang our wet garments. Theoretically the hot air rising from the stove and collecting in the apex of the tent (where there was a small ventilator) should have dried the clothes. I am told that in the Antarctic it does so most efficiently, but with us it never seemed to have the slightest effect, mainly, I suppose, because of the high humidity of the atmosphere even in the coldest weather. Nevertheless we all continued to hang up our clothes and often our boots, in the fond hope that they would dry. At least it provided us with a means of getting them out of the way.

Cedomir and I occupied the places along the side walls of the tent, while the others had the places between. The advantage of the outer berths was that we commanded the corners of the tent and could also dispose of small personal belongings such as pipes, diaries or books along the side walls. But this was outweighed by several serious disadvantages, and often in the weeks that followed I regretted my lack of foresight at the outset in not commandeering one of the inner berths. In very heavy rain the water came through the inner walls and trickled down them on to our sleeping bags; in strong winds the flapping walls beat a constant tattoo upon our recumbent bodies; when drift-snow piled against the side of the tent its icy mass often pressed in upon us, further constricting our meagre living space; finally, we could not sit up without our heads and shoulders pressing hard against the damp and usually heaving walls. But on the whole we were well satisfied with our quarters.

To travel successfully in the mountains of Patagonia one must make up one's mind as far as possible to ignore the weather, and we were resolved to make this our basic principle. But we were now in a situation where it would be useless to advance without a thorough reconnaissance of the way ahead, and to make this we needed reasonable visibility. With the weight of baggage that we were carrying, a bad choice of route might involve us in endless delay and unnecessary toil. Our previous experience of Patagonian glaciers had shown that the ice on their lower reaches was usually extremely broken, and from what we had seen of the Jorge Montt it appeared to be no exception. Our aim therefore was to get on to it as far up as possible, preferably well above the present snow line. To do this it seemed that we would either have to cross the Barrier Range or find a way around its eastern end. If neither way proved feasible it was just possible that from the head of the valley we might find a pass across the western end of the range, which would lead us into the upper basin of the Jorge Montt.

Throughout the 15th it rained steadily, and for most of the day the cloud hung so low that we could barely see the lake, 400 feet below. Obviously nothing could be discovered in such weather, so we remained in our sleeping-bags with clear consciences, and as we still had a good deal of surplus food with us, we spent much of the time eating a variety of snacks. It was then that Eduardo began to develop a keen interest in English limericks and bawdy songs, which he sustained throughout the trip. He wrote them down in his diary and committed them to memory, reciting or singing them each evening, in what he called his English lesson. Misquoted in his Spanish accent, even the old schoolboy chestnuts sounded very funny. He was constantly demanding new material, and in time had compiled such a copious anthology that Jack and I were astonished at our own resourcefulness.

Late in the evening the rain stopped and we emerged from the tent for a breath of fresh air. The clouds had lifted and there was a brightness in the west as though somewhere the sun had succeeded in breaking through. The light was reflected on the floor of the basin in a vivid emerald, while in the opposite direction the livid forms of the icebergs seemed to be floating in a nebulous bowl of navy blue.

The improvement in the weather was maintained and by the morning it was comparatively fine. Though the sky was still overcast the peaks of the Barrier Range were clear and for the first time we could see the whole length of the south-western valley. There seemed to be little chance of finding a southward pass from its head, for it appeared to be flanked on that side by an unbroken wall. Fresh snow lay on the mountains and in the forests well below the 2,000 feet level.

At seven o'clock Jack and Cedomir set off on a reconnaissance. There was no doubt that if the weather held until noon they would be able to reach a point on the Barrier Range high enough to see all that was needed; so Eduardo and I stayed behind and spent the morning bringing the rest of the loads up from the river, and airing the sleeping bags and mattresses. We also weeded out the surplus food, and a few more pieces of unnecessary equipment, so that our baggage could now be shifted in three relays.

The others returned at one o'clock. They had made a thoroughly successful reconnaissance, and the news they brought was excellent. First they had climbed to the crest of the spur, beyond which, as we had already seen, there was a deep canyon, partly occupied by a tongue of ice from the glacier. Following it along they found that the spur led directly on to the eastern ridge of the Barrier Range. All this ground had been under ice so recently, that it was entirely free from the dense forest which covered the northern slopes, only a short distance away. Climbing diagonally up the ridge, they had reached a high point on its crest which commanded a view of the whole of the middle basin of the glacier including its western flank beyond the Barrier Range. Here there was a safe and easy corridor between the ice and the rock which would enable us to travel several miles along the side of the glacier without being forced on to it. But their most encouraging discovery was that only a short way beyond the corner of the range, along a line barely 2,000 feet above sea-level, the broken ice of the lower glacier disappeared beneath a smooth mantle of snow on which we would be able to use the sledges. Moreover their view had extended to the southern horizon where the head of the glacier, sweeping up in a broad icefall, disappeared over the rim of the ice cap. Though they thought that we might have some difficulty in climbing this icefall, there appeared to be no other serious obstacle in view.

After lunch we carried a relay of loads to the top of the spur, about 1,000 feet above. My ankle was still painful and I had to be careful where I trod. Reaching the crest we made our way along a series of terraces between long, whale-backed rocks until we reached a little tarn capped in a grassy hollow. It was a delightful spot, and as it was probably the last we would find before entering the icy world beyond, we decided to place our third camp there.

While the others started back, I went on 100 yards or so to the top of a knoll to get a view of the glacier. A few minutes later I returned to the tarn, and was removing my packframe from the load I had been carrying, when I heard a slight noise behind me. Looking round, I was astonished to see two huemul (a kind of deer about the size of chamois) gazing at me less than four yards away.

These creatures live in most parts of Patagonia where there is forest, but as a rule they are so shy that they are very rarely seen. In all the time that I had spent in the forests around Lago Argentino, Viedma and San Martin, though I had often come across their tracks, I had never set eyes on one of them. Yet these two had not been encountered by accident; they must have heard us arrive at the tarn ten minutes before and had come to see what was going on.

I rose slowly to my feet, expecting to see them turn and bolt; but not only did they hold their ground, they showed not the slightest sign of alarm. I advanced until I was about two yards from them; still there was no reaction. I had intended to see if I could actually touch one of them. I believe I could have done so, but I thought better of it, for I was so enchanted by their complete confidence that I was reluctant to do anything that might destroy it. I tossed them a piece of biscuit that I had in my pocket, and they ignored the friendly gesture. After a few minutes they seemed to grow bored with me, and to my amazement they started to nibble at the grass. Presently one of them came across my piece of biscuit; he sniffed at it and left it alone.

I have often been in places where the wildlife had never before been disturbed by human intrusion, but to find wild animals so completely without fear was a new and delightful experience. I left the huemul to their grazing and made my way back along the spur.

The following day, 17 December, we brought up the rest of the loads in two relays and established Camp 3 by the tarn. That evening we received another visit from the huemul.

13 The Reluctant Sledge

Exactly a week had elapsed since our landing. So far things had gone so much more easily than we had expected that, although a certain amount of time had been wasted, we had reason to be satisfied with our progress. We had been most fortunate in our choice of an approach route, which had proved to be completely lacking in the two obstacles that we had most feared, bog and forest. Moreover, it looked as though the heavy deposits of winter snow still lying at a low altitude would afford us easy access to the upper part of the glacier. All the same it was a somewhat depressing thought that, in spite of our good fortune, we were still only five miles in a direct line from the coast, and little more than 1,000 feet above the sea.

There was a difference of opinion about the route we should follow beyond Camp 3. Jack was in favour of climbing round the end of the Barrier Range at a fairly high level to reach the trough beside the glacier. Cedomir on the other hand thought that we should cross the ravine on the eastern side of the spur, and climb the tongue of ice beyond, which he said, would lead us on to an easy section of the glacier. Eduardo and I, not having seen the ground, could not take part in this dispute; but after listening to both arguments, I exercised my casting vote in favour of the latter route, mainly because the fresh snow, which still lay on the lower slopes of the range, might cause us some trouble.

Intending to make a long carry on the 18th, we got away to an early start. We climbed diagonally down into the ravine so as to lose as little height as possible, and reached the ugly, sweating mass of the glacier tongue. For the most part the ice was deeply undercut, but there was one place where a semicircular ledge protruded like a giant tree fungus towards a convenient boulder, enabling us, with a long stride, to effect a lodgement on to it. The side of the tongue was steep for a couple of hundred feet, but the ice was rough and so encrusted with gravel that we could climb it without crampons. Gradually the slope eased off and before long we reached the crest of the tongue close to its junction with the main glacier.

I suddenly realised that despite my two days of enforced rest, I had already come to terms with my load. No doubt this was partly due to the interest of climbing on ice which held my attention, but it was no longer the loathsome taskmaster it had been, chaining me to a galley plank of unremitting toil. My movements had acquired some degree of balance and rhythm, some semblance of pleasurable control. Load-carrying was never among my favourite pastimes, but like other forms of hard labour, there is some satisfaction to be derived from its mastery.

Cedomir had been right. Though the glacier over to our left was badly shattered, the whale-back ridge of the tongue merged into a long corridor of unbroken ice along which we could now advance rapidly. Only an occasional crevasse crossed our path, and none of them was wide enough to present much difficulty. Moreover, we were climbing steadily and, only two hours after leaving camp, we reached the first patches of snow. Here we put on the rope and proceeded more cautiously, for although the snow was sufficient to conceal most of the crevasses it was thoroughly rotten. However, it deepened as we climbed and when we reached the head of the corridor we saw in front of us an unbroken sweep of solid spring snow disappearing into the mist.

Obviously this was the place to start using the sledges. We had brought neither of them with us, so we dumped our loads and, leaving a red flag fluttering from a tall bamboo staff to mark their position, we raced back down the glacier, reaching camp in time for an early lunch. That afternoon we carried up a second relay, which included the sledges, and returned in the evening in a mood of buoyant optimism, to spend our last night on dry land (relatively speaking).

I always find it something of a wrench to leave a land of growing things for a lengthy sojourn among the harsh monotones of glacier regions, the dead, scentless world of ice and snow. Though next morning it was raining as usual as we packed up the tent, and the grassy hollow where it had stood looked bleak and sad, at least it was green, and the forest in the mist below looked warm and friendly. I felt a sharp pang of nostalgia at the prospect of a long absence from the soft colours and sweet smells of vegetation. But in the early part of an expedition of this kind the outraged senses must make a long series of adjustments to changed conditions of living, and luckily the regret for each lost comfort is quickly forgotten.

The weather began to clear as we climbed on the glacier and, by eleven o'clock when we reached the dump, it was no longer raining. We set about assembling the fiberglass sledge which took us nearly an hour. Having never hauled a sledge before I had been looking forward keenly to this new form of exercise, and I was impatient at the delay. I do not know quite what I had been expecting; I think I had visualised pushing against a gentle restraint of the harness; a little monotonous perhaps and even tiring over a long period, but involving no really strenuous effort. Anyway it would be a delightful change from being weighed down by a load.

We still had some 700 pounds of baggage. It was obvious that we could not move it all at once, but we expected to be able to drag at least half of it quite easily on the fiberglass sledge, keeping Jack's sledge in reserve until the time came when we would be hauling a full 500-pound load. We were in for a rude shock.

At last the sledge was ready and loaded with half the baggage. We strapped on our snowshoes and walked up and down to try them out; they felt fine. Then we climbed into our harnesses, which consisted of nine-inch webbing belly-bands and shoulder straps, and took up our positions; the taller pair, Jack and Cedomir, on the longer traces in front, Eduardo and I behind. The great moment had arrived. The word was given, 'Ready! go!' We took the strain; nothing happened. We heaved; still nothing happened. We might have been chained to a rock wall. Then at last with a mighty effort, our bodies lying on our harnesses at an angle of forty-five degrees, we managed to stagger forward for about five yards, when we came to a dead stop, the front of the sledge having ploughed deep into the soft, sticky snow.

Clearly we could not go on like this; so with one accord we sank down in the snow, panting hard, to consider the matter. The implications of our pathetic failure to haul even 350 pounds over this type of snow were all too obvious; and as they flashed across my mind I felt a sense of desperate frustration, verging on panic. As the snow conditions were not likely to improve and might well become worse, it looked as if we would have to continue this dreary business of relaying for most of the journey. But it was not the dreariness of the prospect that was worrying me. To be forced to continue relaying for the next five or six weeks would completely upset our timetable, and with it our provisioning. Secondly, it was very doubtful if relaying would be possible in the kind of weather that we must expect to meet on the ice cap.

However, it was no use dwelling on these gloomy thoughts, so we removed about 100 pounds from the sledge and tried again. This time, though with a great deal of effort, we managed to drag it along in fits and starts. We kept falling over our snowshoes which made it impossible to maintain the even pull necessary to keep the sledge moving smoothly. The action of walking in snowshoes is a kind of shuffle; lifting the toe and dragging the heel, and to perform this movement satisfactorily, it is necessary to keep the body upright. But to pull hard enough to move even our lightened sledge we still had to lean far forward, and this meant that at each step the toes of the shoes buried themselves in the soft snow. There was nothing for it but to give up using them until we could evolve a better technique. Without them, of course, we sank deeper into the snow, but at least we found that we could maintain a steady movement.

We struggled on for half an hour, in which time we covered about half a mile. Then we stopped, pitched the tent, and returned with the sledge for a second load. All this time we had been in mist, and it was only when we started back along our tracks that we realised that the slope up which we had hauled the sledge was a good deal steeper than we had thought. This at least was some comfort, for it partly accounted for the very great effort that the job had demanded.

The second and third relays were lighter than the first, and with a well-beaten trail to help us we had brought all the loads up to the tent by four o'clock. After that we bedded down and brewed some tea, which helped momentarily to revive our chastened spirits. But an atmosphere of depression hung over us that evening, and even Eduardo found little to laugh at. It was one of the few occasions that he neglected his 'English lesson'; instead, he collaborated with Cedomir in calculating the probable rate of our future progress, the results of which were anything but encouraging. However, Jack's unshakeable confidence did much to dispel the gloom.

In the hope that snow conditions would be better early in the day, we decided to start getting up at 4.30 the next morning. I have acquired the ability to wake whenever I wish, so I had already assumed the unpopular role of morning rouser. It was usually a difficult task, and I am inclined to think that my nagging persistence in its execution was my principal contribution to the success of the expedition.

We found when we emerged from the tent that there had been a very slight frost during the night, and that though the snow was by no means firm, it was much less soggy than it had been the previous day. We had decided to assemble Jack's sledge, and by distributing the load between it and the 'punt', we hoped to be able to drag more than we had managed the day before. It consisted of two runners, each four feet long and six inches wide, with a framework, two feet high and three feet wide, of wooden uprights and cross-slats. It took about two hours to put it together. We also removed the two wooden slats from the bottom of the fiberglass sledge to reduce surface friction. The purpose of these slats was to prevent the sledge from slipping sideways while traversing a slope or in a cross wind. Though, later, we suffered a good deal from this, the slats were never replaced, partly because by then they were in regular use as extra tent pegs.

After applying a lavish coating of ski-wax to the sledges we loaded them with 300 pounds, and attached Jack's to the back of the 'punt'. Then we took up our previous positions in the traces, and pulled. To our great relief the sledges moved forward smoothly, and with rather less effort than it had cost us to drag 250 pounds the previous day.

We marched on a bearing 4° West of South which, though we could not see it, we reckoned to be the direction of the middle of the upper icefall. A moderate north-westerly wind was blowing some sleet across our faces, but the clouds were several hundred feet above us, and visibility extended to about two miles; so we had no difficulty in maintaining our course with only occasional reference to the compass. The glacier at this point must have been at least eight miles wide, and though we could see the base of the mountains flanking it on the west, those on the eastern side were invisible.

It was very hard work, and before we had been going ten minutes my thighs had begun to ache. Also I was panting hard because of my inability to maintain any kind of rhythm, which is so essential to minimise fatigue in any form of physical activity. A practiced climber, for example, should be able to walk up a steep slope, even in soft snow and carrying a heavy load, even when he is not particularly fit, without becoming out of breath, simply by moving with a precise and balanced rhythm. In a combined effort such as sledge-hauling, it is of course much more difficult to establish a good rhythm, particularly in soft snow or on a breakable crust; for the tall members of the team must adjust their natural strides to those of the shorter men, and there must be a quick and sympathetic response by the others when one man is checked by, say, a collapsing foothold. Later we began to improve in this respect, but on that first day we remained hopelessly uncoordinated, floundering along, sometimes pulling far more than our share of the load, sometimes with slack traces behind us. This of course resulted in an enormous waste of effort.

I decided to break the march up into half-hour spells, with five-minute halts between. The hand of my watch moved with maddening slowness, and I tried to keep my eyes off it as much as possible and think of other things. With the improved visibility I could now see that we were climbing steadily. It was difficult to estimate how much of the effort we were expending was due to the gentle upward slope, but it seemed reasonable to hope that when we reached the plateau, unless snow conditions there were very much worse, we might be able to drag 400 pounds This would include about three weeks' food and fuel which, even if further relaying proved impracticable, should be enough to enable us to reach the Viedma Glacier and to make our way down the Rio Tunnel. This at any rate was a comforting thought.

At the third halt someone suggested that we should reduce the length of the spells to twenty minutes; this met with general approval. The change had an excellent effect on morale, and for the next two hours life seemed relatively pleasant. We than had a half-hour halt for lunch, which consisted of biscuits, butter, cheese and fudge. At every second halting place we left a marker flag or a snowshoe stuck upright in the snow to guide us in thick weather, in case our tracks should become obliterated.

We came to a small icefall where we had to alter course and zigzag through lines of crevasses, and up the steep slopes between. Here we had to exert all our energy to haul the sledges up, and in two places we had to detach them and pull them up separately. Every now and then one of us would fall into a crevasse up to his waist; then of course the sledges would stop and the victim, unable to move forward, would have to struggle out backwards. On one occasion, Jack's sledge ploughed its nose into a crevasse and stuck in a precarious position across a black abyss. A few weeks later in the season this little icefall would have caused us a lot of trouble. As it was, though it gave us a good deal of hard work, it presented no serious problem, and above it we emerged once more on to a smooth, gently inclined surface.

We stopped for one of our five-minute halts at about two o'clock. I had decided to do two more spells before dumping the load and returning. I was just about to announce this when Jack said that his legs felt like rubber, and suggested that we should 'call it a day'. I was a little surprised, because I had hardly ever heard Jack admit to being tired. In sledge-hauling it is very difficult to tell how much effort each member of the party is exerting. So long as you are careful to keep your trace taut, you might be pulling hardly at all, and yet escape notice. I expect all of us at one time or another suspected that one of our companions was not pulling his weight, particularly when the sledge seemed to be unusually heavy. But no one would ever suspect Jack of malingering; for he always threw every ounce of his very considerable energy into whatever he was doing. I had thought that he had probably been pulling harder than any of us for most of the time; now I was convinced of it; so I had no hesitation in accepting his suggestion, which had the hearty support of the other two.

As we were stacking the loads we noticed that the four-gallon Army fuel container was missing. It had been riding on Jack's sledge, and must, we thought have fallen off during one of the contretemps we had had on the icefall. We were somewhat alarmed, for as it contained half our fuel supply, its loss would have been serious. On the way back we found it resting on the lip of a crevasse.

We were all very tired, and although the way back was all downhill, and the empty sledges needed virtually no pulling, we sat down to rest several times. It seemed a very long way back to camp, which should, of course, have given me a good deal of satisfaction, but I could think of nothing but the cup of hot, sweet tea that I would be holding to my thirsty lips in the not too distant future.

When we reached the tent, we anchored the sledges against the possibility of a gale, and crawled in through the tunnel entrance. Most of our clothing was fairly wet, but our trouser legs, socks and boots were saturated from contact with the sodden snow; so we stripped off our lower garments before setting about the urgent business of lighting the Primus and brewing the nectar we craved. Snow had first to be melted and then more added until there was sufficient water to fill our three-pint pot, for nothing less would satisfy our needs. The process was exasperatingly slow.

I am something of a purist in the matter of tea-making and always insist that the water be brought fully to the boil before infusion; I believe that I would have to be dying of thirst before I would countenance any slackness in this respect. I do not, however, go to the length of taking a teapot on an expedition; for I find that, by throwing the tea-leaves into a pan of boiling water and then removing it from the fire, the result is quite as satisfactory as that produced by the standard method.

At last the water was bubbling to my satisfaction. The moment of bliss was almost at hand. Cups were held ready to receive the precious liquid, each with its quota of sugar and milk powder. I was about to throw in the tea-leaves, when the stove tilted, the pot slid off and emptied its entire contents over my naked feet.

I had been looking forward so passionately to that drink, that despite the pain, my first reaction was one of bitter disappointment, and it was a little while before the gravity of the disaster began to dawn on me. However, it was not lost on the others; after a moment's horrified silence, they began to express such concern that, though touched by their sympathy, I thought it slightly exaggerated.

Our small supply of medicines contained no specific remedy for burns, but feeling that something should be done, and with Eduardo's approval, I smeared my feet and ankles with Vaseline. Gradually the scalded flesh began to swell, a ring of huge blisters developed round my ankles, and the skin on top of my left foot withered and flaked away, leaving a raw surface like freshly cut meat. It was generally agreed that the wounds must be kept exposed to the air as much as possible.

Meanwhile a fresh supply of snow was melted, but when eventually the tea was ready, I found that my appetite for it had lost its edge. The tea disposed of, the preparation of the stew was put in hand. This constituted our main meal and was generally anticipated with lively enthusiasm. It took about an hour to prepare, which included melting the snow. First a four-ounce packet of soup powder was emptied into the water and boiled for ten minutes. We had three varieties, tomato, ox-tail and mushroom. Then three dehydrated meat bars (sixteen ounces in all) were crumbled into the soup and allowed to boil for a further ten minutes. Finally, potato powder and Quaker Oats were added for thickening. I had brought several packets of various dried herbs, such as thyme, sage and bay leaves, which not only provided some variety of flavour, but completely extinguished that curiously uniform taste that grows more and more monotonous, and even repulsive, when a diet is confined to processed foods. We never grew in the least bit tired of that stew, and had no desire to exchange it for anything else.

We each had two eating utensils: a plastic mug with a capacity of about three-quarters of a pint, and a spoon. Hitherto I had been opposed to the use of plastic mugs on the grounds that they made the tea taste queer; but these, which had been brought from Santiago, were free from this defect. When all the cups had been completely filled with stew, there was always a small amount, half a dozen spoonfuls, left in the pot which was carefully divided between us at the end of the meal. Then one man was allowed to scrape the pot, a privilege always awarded to Jack or Cedomir.

After supper Eduardo bandaged my feet to protect them from contact with the inside of my sleeping bag, and we settled down for the night, postponing any discussion of plans until we saw what the morning would bring. I tried with little success to keep my mind off my stupid accident and its possible consequences, and eventually, with the aid of a large dose of aspirin, fell asleep.

14   A Cheerless Christmas

Soon after it was light I removed the bandages to examine my feet. The right foot was comparatively unscathed, apart from a slight swelling of the flesh and the blisters round the ankle which looked like a kind of elephantiasis; the skin was not broken. The condition of the left foot, however, was not so good. It was very swollen and most of the upper surface of the foot was an open sore.

I could no longer delude myself that perhaps after all I had escaped injury bad enough to hold us up. It was quite obvious that I would be immobilised for several days at least. It was not that my foot would have been too painful to walk. With burns, as with frostbite, there is serious danger of septicemia, an affliction which would have placed, not only me, but all of us in a most unpleasant situation. It was imperative both to keep the wound dry and to avoid friction. Though we were supplied with canvas over-boots, or mutluks, it was impossible to walk even for half a mile through the sodden snow without our feet becoming saturated; and no system of bandaging, however ingenious, could avoid continuous rubbing against the upper surface of the foot. Galling though it was, there was nothing for it but to possess my soul in patience and to hope that the wound would soon heal.

It was pouring with rain and blowing quite hard, so I refrained from disturbing my companions, who woke at about eight o'clock after eleven hours' sleep. While tea was being brewed, we discussed plans to meet the new situation. First it was decided that they should have a day's rest. Then Jack suggested that they should spend the following day in an attempt to reach the upper icefall to find a route through it; but on further consideration he agreed that it was probably too far away for such a reconnaissance to be effective, particularly in bad weather.

Allowing for the food and fuel that would be consumed in the next two days, we estimated that 360 pounds of these still remained to be carried forward from Camp 4. We decided to reduce this by a further twenty-five pounds by abandoning most of our supply of cheese, which was contained in small tins and therefore had little food value relative to its weight. Cedomir lodged a strong protest against this decision, but he was overruled. The point was that if my companions could drag 250 pounds to the dump (Camp 5) the following day, they would then be able to take me along the day after, together with the remaining eighty-five pounds, composed of the tent and our immediate necessities. The process would then be repeated as far as Camp 6, which we hoped would be close enough for work to begin on the icefall.

It was a dismal prospect having to lie like a useless log while the others did all the work, but they were so cheerful about it that the whole thing seemed to become a huge joke. Cedomir remarked that, what with a sprained right ankle and a scalded left foot, I was very lucky not to possess a third leg to invite a final calamity. Eduardo composed a song in Spanish about a man from the Himalaya who had a strange grudge against his feet which he was continually trying to mortify; this was clearly the explanation of the mystery of the prints of naked feet found on Himalayan snows. I was not able to judge the quality of the song, but it sounded fluent enough, and it certainly delighted its author.

The others left at 7.30 the next morning. I watched them from the entrance of the tent until they had gone about half a mile, when they disappeared over an undulation in the glacier. I was relieved to see that they were making fair progress. I settled down to kill time until they returned, regretting that I had not allowed myself a few more books. However I am a very slow reader, and with a system of rationing I managed to spin out my enjoyment of *Cakes and Ale* for several days. Also, Jack had lent me *Bleak House*, so on the whole I was reasonably well supplied. Fortunately I had an ample stock of tobacco, and as normally I would be unable to smoke much during the day, there was little danger of my running short.

At eleven o'clock I set forth on a necessary pilgrimage outside. As it was then not raining I put a mutluk on my right foot and left the other naked. Then, treading down the snow with the former I proceeded with a crab-like move-ment until I had reached a suitable distance from the tent. Later in the journey we suffered a good deal from constipation, this was due partly to the lack of roughage in our diet, but mainly to our reluctance to expose our persons to the wind and driving snow which caused us to discourage our natural inclinations for long periods. Our lesser needs were easily satisfied inside the tent by the use of plastic bottles.

So far we had experienced none of the gales that had been expected. In this we were very lucky indeed, for really rough weather now would have been much more difficult to deal with than it was later, when relaying was no longer necessary.

It rained hard throughout the afternoon, and the thought of the others struggling along in such dreary conditions, made me feel all the worse not to be with them. They arrived back at about 5.30, soaked through and tired, obvi-ously having had a tougher time than before. Our tracks had disappeared and they had had to plough a fresh trail; also they had been pulling eight pounds more per man. However, despite poor visibility, they had located the dump without trouble.

I felt somewhat cheered the next morning at the prospect of a move. There was little change in the condition of my foot, which was depressing, but although the wound was still raw and very sensitive, at least it looked clean and there was no sign of its becoming septic. Also the swelling was slightly reduced, and with my foot covered with a bandage and one sock (I normally wore three pairs of socks), I managed to get my boot on without causing undue pressure on the wound.

By the time we had packed up our bedding and the tent it was nine o'clock. I sat in a comfortable nest of rucksacks prepared for me on the 'punt', while the tent was tied on to Jack's sledge, the apex pointing forward. With the poles left in place it was ten feet long, so that it resembled a large calibre siege gun on a disproportionately small gun carriage. The weight on the sledges was slightly heavier than it had been the day before, and my companions probably did not derive much benefit from their tracks which, though visible, were largely covered by snow that had fallen during the night. However, as they would not have to return, they could afford to take longer rests between spells of pulling. I timed the spells, calling out the passage of five-minute periods for the benefit of Jack and Eduardo who did not possess watches. It made me feel like an Eastern potentate driving a team of slaves.

I tried to help by using my ice axe as a punt pole; I doubt if I did much good but I derived some satisfaction from the gesture, and at least it helped to keep me warm. Even so, after a couple of hours I was thoroughly chilled by the raw wind and driving sleet. When we reached the steep passages on the small icefall, despite Jack's protests, I got off the sledge and, treading very carefully in the tracks, hobbled along behind. The exercise provided a temporary relief to my stiff body; nevertheless I doubt if the others were more glad than I when eventually we reached the dump and established Camp 5.

During the next two days, Christmas Eve and Christmas Day, my morale sank to a low ebb. My foot, if it were healing at all, was doing so with maddening slowness. I am not well endowed with patience in such circumstances and I had become thoroughly exasperated by my role of a useless piece of baggage, by this infernal inactivity to which I could set no term. I was tempted to throw caution to the winds, and take a chance with my wretched foot. I doubt if my mood was improved by the fact that the others were in excellent spirits, and seemed to be thoroughly enjoying themselves. This of course was completely illogical, for obviously my own situation no less than theirs would have been far worse had they been reluctant and pessimistic. All the same I am ashamed to remember that I found it difficult to respond cheerfully to Eduardo's witticisms and good-natured sallies.

On the 24th they succeeded in reaching the foot of the icefall with the first relay, and on the 25th they carried up the second, again leaving only the tent and our immediate necessities and me to be shifted. Both days were long and hard, but they were evidently becoming accustomed to the exercise of sledge hauling, and no doubt their technique was improving, for on both evenings they returned noticeably less tired than before. On both occasions the bad weather had prevented them from seeing much of the icefall, but at least they had seen no serious obstacle to begin with.

On the 26th I had another ride on the sledge. Though I became as cold and cramped as before, it was a very pleasant change from lying alone in the tent. I was eager to catch a glimpse of the icefall, but the visibility remained so restricted that I could see nothing of it. By then, however, having travelled diagonally across the glacier, we were quite close to its eastern side where a series of rock buttresses loomed through the mist. At the end of each spell of pulling, I retrieved the snowshoe or marker flag that had been left there on the first relay. When eventually we reached the last spell, I got off the sledge and walked behind, taking great care always to keep my left foot rigid and to place it on firmly beaten snow.

The possibility that they might climb the icefall the very next day, and so reach the edge of the Plateau, put the others in a particularly exuberant frame of mind that evening. They engaged in a lively discussion of plans, and in making various estimates of times, distances and weights. Jack produced a set of logistics based on the airy assumption that I would remain a passenger for the next three weeks. I thought this hardly tactful, but I was prepared to believe that it was not unkindly meant and refrained from violent comment. In any case the worst of my depression was over, and I was in a more benevolent mood than I had been for several days. This was partly because I was caught up in the general excitement at reaching the last obstacle before the ice cap, but mainly because my foot, far from having suffered by my walk that afternoon, was at last beginning to show signs of healing. I was secretly determined to get up the icefall under my own steam.

Someone suggested that the following day should be devoted to a thorough reconnaissance of the icefall to find the best way through it. After some discussion, however, the majority were in favour of taking some loads at least up the first part, so as to obtain some idea of the effort involved in hauling the sledge up the slopes. Accordingly the others set off at 7.30 with the fiberglass sledge laden with 200 pounds while I lay at the entrance of the tent to watch their progress. The weather was much improved. The sky was completely overcast, but it was not raining and the clouds had lifted to a couple of thousand feet above the glacier. However, I was too close under the icefall to see more than the first 300 or 400 feet of its central section, where a corridor of unbroken snow, running up between lines of crevasses, offered an obvious line of approach. To the east, the buttresses whose dim forms I had seen the previous day, had taken shape as a line of rock peaks flanking that side of the glacier. Beyond the right-hand end of this line I could see a formidable cascade of ice-cliffs, which merged with the main icefall and which I estimated to be about 2,000 feet high.

I watched the others making their way up the corridor. They were obviously finding it very hard work, but they were moving steadily, and after about an hour they reached the top, and disappeared over a ridge beyond. According to our aneroid, Camp 6 was 3,500 feet above sea-level. Assuming that the northern part of the ice cap was the same altitude as the southern (5,000 feet), the height of the icefall would be about 1,500 feet. I had little doubt that there was a way through, but to pass the time I worked out an alternative route up the right-hand buttress over the rock peak and descending to the top of the 'cascade'. It would take the best part of a week to perform the manoeuvre, as of course we would have to carry the sledges, but it seemed to be quite feasible. Then I lit the Primus and started to melt a supply of water for our evening meal.

At 10.30 I heard shouts, and looking out of the tent, I was surprised to see the others sitting on the sledge tobogganing down the corridor. Presently they arrived with the explanation of their early return. Above the place where I had seen them disappearing they had found a broad ramp running diagonally up to the left which, though it had been hard work hauling the sledge up through deep snow, had presented no technical difficulties. Beyond the top of the ramp, which they had reached in little more than two hours from the camp, there was a network of very large crevasses stretching as far as they could see. Though the ground was by no means steep, and though the crevasses seemed to be very well bridged, the snow was so soft that they came to the conclusion that it might be better to place Camp 7 at the top of the ramp, so as to tackle the next section of the icefall in the early morning. So they had decided to return, and after a cup of tea and an early lunch they carried up a second relay.

The next morning I announced my intention of walking up to the next camp. My foot was very much better; a reasonably solid scab had formed over the wound, which no longer hurt, and in fact was now itching exquisitely. With reasonable care I should be able to keep it dry and avoid rubbing off the scab. As I expected, my decision produced a strong protest from Jack who considered that my foot was still far from healed, and that my usual impatience was prompting me to take an unnecessary risk. However, the others were less averse to the idea which of course meant that the rest of the loads could be taken up in a single relay.

While the sledges were being loaded, I started slowly. It was a great joy to be moving again. The clouds had come down once more, but it was not raining or snowing and, though we were shrouded in dense mist, there was a feel of better weather in the air.

When we reached the dump at the top of the ramp, I suggested that, instead of pitching the camp there, we should go on through the icefall, with the tent and personal gear and whatever else could be taken on the fiberglass sledge. For it seemed to me that in view of the great depth of the snow, its condition was not likely to alter except for the worse. It was certainly arguable that a way through should first be found before attempting to take the sledge; but after some discussion my suggestion was adopted.

Cedomir went ahead on a twenty-foot climbing rope, which was attached to the sledge and also lightly held by Jack. This enabled him to do his share of the hauling, and at the same time gave him sufficient freedom of movement to test the snow for hidden crevasses. It also minimised the chances of our standing on the same crevasse; though it could not ensure against it for, as we soon discovered, the crevasses were running in every direction. Jack was harnessed on a long trace, Eduardo on a short one, while I followed behind the sledge on a rope attached to Eduardo. It was not perhaps very sound mountaineering practice, but in the circumstances it was the best arrangement we could devise, and certainly it was less dangerous than carrying heavy loads.

Considering that we were barely 4,000 feet above the sea, and that it was already past midsummer, the amount of snow covering the ice was remarkable. It was obviously the remains of winter and spring falls which should have disappeared long before. We were most fortunate that it had not done so, for the icefall was very broken, and in normal summer conditions it would have been impossible to drag the sledges through it, and even walking might have been difficult. As it was, except for the major ice-cliffs and crevasses, the riven surface was smoothed to gentle undulations. Also, though the snow was soft and each of my companions was continually falling into hidden crevasses, it was sufficiently deep and packed to prevent a massive collapse of the bridges.

All the same it was extremely hard work for the others and often it was as much as they could do to keep the sledge moving. It was very galling not to be able to help them, but at least I was not riding on the sledge, which was something to be thankful for. They had to follow a tortuous course to avoid obstacles and, as visibility was still restricted to a few hundred yards, I kept an eye on the compass to maintain a general southerly direction.

Then suddenly, at two o'clock, the slope eased, no more crevasses were visible, the snow became less deep and presently we found ourselves walking over an almost level surface. It was difficult to believe that we had passed right through the icefall and were actually on the Plateau. For one thing, the aneroid registered our height as 4,500 feet, and we had been expecting to have to climb at least another 500 feet, which in those conditions would have taken a long time. We went on for a quarter of an hour, but met with no further obstacles and the flat, smooth surface continued to stretch away into the mist; so we decided to pitch camp.

At six o'clock, while supper was being prepared, we noticed that it was exceptionally cold, and that the light inside the tent, usually dim, had become uncommonly bright. Eduardo poked his head outside to investigate these phenomena and immediately gave a delighted yell. He then scrambled back, seized his boots and his camera and shot out of the tent, nearly upsetting the stove in his hurry. Peering after him through the tunnel entrance, I saw the cause of his excitement.

The mist had cleared. To the eastward, rising from a level horizon of snow, there was a line of fantastic peaks sparkling in sunlight against a background of pale blue sky. Though their sides appeared to be completely vertical, they were almost entirely sheathed in ice, while their tops were crowned with immense mushroom shaped cornices.

There was no longer any doubt that we had reached the Ice cap, for it was also clear to the southward, and in that direction we could see nothing but gently undulating snow stretching away into the distance. This alone would have been sufficient cause for jubilation. It was 28 December; only eighteen days had elapsed since our landing. Though the rim of the plateau had been farther away than we had expected, the route to it had proved a great deal easier than we had dared to hope, and despite the time wasted as a result of my stupid accident, which had been minimised by the stalwart work of my companions, we were two days ahead of our schedule. Now, at the best possible moment, after weeks of rain and mist, it seemed that we were to be blessed with a spell of fine weather.

For the first time I felt absolutely confident in our ability to complete the journey across the whole length of the ice cap to Lago Argentino. We had food and fuel enough to last us for another thirty-seven days, and it seemed that nothing but a serious accident or the most diabolical weather could stop us now. We had reckoned on spending up to a week in an attempt to climb Lauturo, but that was a secondary project which could be embraced or rejected according to our situation when we arrived at the foot of the volcano.

So far of course we had been incredibly lucky in the matter of wind and we could hardly expect this state of affairs to continue indefinitely. We had yet to discover to what extent we would be immobilised by rough weather. I had always expected that we might be held up for a week at a time, but much would depend upon our ability, not only to travel, but to strike and pitch camp in the kind of wind we were likely to meet. Then there was the question of how long we would have to continue relaying. Obviously this would be impossible in really bad weather; but I was hopeful that we would soon be able to haul all our baggage together, and that in any case, even if we were forced to abandon some of our food, we would still be able to carry enough to see us through.

15 On the Plateau

The clear sky brought a sharp frost for the night, and in the morning the first beams of the rising sun touched the tent at half-past four. Encouraged by this delightful novelty, and spurred by the prospect of a few hours of hard-frozen snow, my companions made an exceptionally rapid departure. Their task was to bring the rest of the loads through the icefall from the top of the ramp. I expected them to take the whole day to complete it.

I took the bedding outside to give it a much-needed airing, and then sat down to study the view and to give my foot a dose of sunlight which I supposed might do it good. The air was still and the sky completely free from cloud. The deep trough of the Canal Baker was still visible over the northern rim of the plateau, and beyond it I could now see the great peaks flanking the *Hielo Patagonico del Norte* ('North Patagonian Ice'). To the west, there was a range of rounded mountains which formed a low rim to the brimful basin of the plateau ice. There were several gaps in it where the ice spilt over giving rise to the various glaciers flowing down to the fjords of the Pacific coast.

To the south, my view was limited by the slightly concave surface of the plateau, but above it I could just see the ice crest of a far distant peak. It almost certainly belonged to the group of mountains we had seen from Nuntak the previous year, and a compass-bearing to it gave me the general direction we would be following.

The peaks to the east, now part of a vast sunlit landscape, looked less unearthly than they had appeared before. Then, as brilliant objects floating in the evening sky, they might have been twenty, thirty or forty miles away. I could see now that they were not more than eight miles distant and that they stood only about 2,000 feet above the plateau; but they were still magnificent. The limpid air and the steep rays of the sun revealed more clearly the floral patterns of the ice draping their sheer sides.

This most lovely feature of the mountains of Southern Patagonia is caused by the winds, heavily charged with moisture, striking against exposed surfaces to form a coating of rime. It clings to vertical and even overhanging precipices as readily as it forms on gentler slopes, and its tensile strength is such that there seems to be no limit to its development. The steeper the slope the more it is exposed to the force of the wind, which results in the creation of wildly improbable shapes on the faces of the peaks and of immense cornices along the *windward* side of their summit ridges.

At eleven o'clock, while I was in the tent melting snow on the Primus, the others arrived. I was astonished when they told me that they had brought everything with them. The frozen snow had made their task a great deal easier than we had expected. The sun had been late in reaching the icefall, and they had managed to relay the loads through it before the surface had begun to melt. At the top, they had piled them all on to the two sledges and, Jack pulling his own and the other two the 'punt', they had arrived triumphantly with some 400 pounds of baggage.

I made tea and handed it out to the others, and we all had lunch sitting on the sledges in our shirt-sleeves. The peace of the meal was disturbed by a final passage of arms with Jack about my foot. It had suffered little from my activity of the day before, and now looked and felt so much better that I had decided the next day to resume hauling, or at least to give it a trial. The announcement of my intention produced a strong reaction, including a discourse, couched I thought in somewhat patronizing terms, about my habitual impatience. I retorted with some heat, that I was the best judge of the situation, and that in any case it was my foot. On the latter point Jack rightly observed that we all had an equal stake in its welfare. He appealed to Eduardo as our medical adviser to use his restraining influence, but Eduardo tactfully changed the subject.

After lunch the others decided to take advantage of the fine weather and transport half the baggage forward for a couple of hours that afternoon. By then, of course, the snow had melted and the surface had reverted to its usual soft condition; but it was a great deal pleasanter to work in good visibility, and it seemed a pity to waste the opportunity. They set off at one o'clock. Two hours later the camp was enveloped in cloud, and by five o'clock when they returned, it was snowing. Our precious spell of fine weather had lasted less than twenty-four hours.

The next morning it was as thick as ever. Some sleet was falling, but there was still not much wind. We packed up the camp and started at about eight o'clock. Jack hauled his own sledge, and the rest of us pulled the 'punt'. Formerly we had marched in pairs abreast, now we did so in line, with Cedomir out in front on a climbing rope and Eduardo and I behind on a long and short trace respectively. It was a much better arrangement, for only one set of tracks was needed, and we could pull more evenly. My foot gave me no trouble, a relief equalled only by the satisfaction I felt at being able at last to do my share of the work. Despite my enforced rest I found the hauling a great deal less laborious than it had been ten days before.

The tracks of the previous day were barely visible, but the others had taken the precaution of marking the route with snowshoes, and in well under two hours we reached their dump. We added a couple of sacks of food, about 120 pounds, to our load and went on, I held the compass and shouted directions to Cedomir, 'left a bit' – 'right a bit', to keep him on our chosen course of 4° west of south. We rested for five minutes after every half hour of pulling.

At the third halt after the dump, Cedomir complained that he could not see properly. He was evidently suffering from a mild attack of migraine; so I took over the lead and Eduardo the compass. After a bit, Jack, who was following behind, pointed out that we were steering a very erratic course. We stopped to investigate the matter and discovered that the cause was Eduardo's ice axe which was deflecting the compass needle; so he gave me the offending weapon to carry.

After two or three spells, I came to the conclusion that the climbing-rope made a very unsatisfactory towing line; partly because the elasticity of the nylon made it impossible to maintain an even strain, and partly because the waist loop was unsuited to the purpose. Now that we were on the plateau the risk of falling into a crevasse was negligible, and it was therefore quite unnecessary for the leader to be on a climbing rope; so I exchanged it for the harness and a long trace.

We decided to pitch camp at two o'clock to allow time to bring up the rest of the loads from the dump. This proved a wise precaution. Cedomir said that he was quite recovered and insisted upon going back with the others while I remained behind to perform the various camp chores, such as inflating the air-mattresses and melting snow. At about four o'clock the wind began to rise. Snow was falling and the mist was still dense; I became slightly apprehensive that, despite the markers, the others might have difficulty in finding the tent. They arrived before six, but even so the tracks had been almost obliterated.

Throughout the evening the force of the wind increased, and that night we were treated to a full-blooded Patagonian storm. For the first time I began fully to appreciate the qualities of the pyramid tent, and I was devoutly thankful that I had followed Jack's suggestion to bring it. It gave a wonderful sense of security compared with the various types of mountain tent I had used hitherto. Its rigidity depended hardly at all upon its guy ropes; its shape ensured that the force of the wind, from whatever direction, was converted into a downward rather than a lateral pressure; the drift-snow piling up against its sides tended to perfect its streamlining, and the four poles, by meeting at the apex, had the maximum strength to support its weight.

Though by the morning the storm had abated, it was still fairly violent, and we were faced with a problem that had long been pending. It was obvious that we could not afford to be prevented from travelling by any but the most savage weather. But even in a comparatively mild blizzard relaying would be a hazardous procedure. In the first place our tracks would be erased almost immediately; with visibility restricted to, say, fifty yards, it would be very difficult to steer a return compass course with sufficient precision to ensure picking up our markers, unless they were placed at impossibly short intervals; and to lose our way would almost certainly be disastrous. Then there was the possibility of the dumps becoming drifted over and lost; and although perhaps this was not likely to happen within twenty-four hours, there was no guarantee that worsening weather would not prevent the second relay from being made for several days. But the most important factor was the direction of the prevailing wind which, particularly in bad weather, was from the north-west. One can often march, even in reasonable comfort, so long as the wind is coming more or less from behind when it is impossible to move in the opposite direction, facing the blinding drift. Thus it might happen that we would carry a relay forward, and find ourselves unable to return. In fact, as it turned out, in the weeks that followed there were few days when we could have travelled in a northerly direction.

Theoretically we now had about 550 pounds of baggage, not counting the weight of the sledges. In practice we had to drag more than this, for it was impossible to remove all the snow from the tent and the various sacks, which in any case were soaking wet; so that the total weight to be dragged must have been well over 600 pounds The question was whether we could manage such a load; this could only be answered by trial, and we decided to conduct some experiments before packing up the camp.

We emerged from the tent at nine o'clock, to face the harsh world outside. Everything except the upper part of the tent was buried in snow, and our first task was to dig out the sledges with ice axes and aluminium shovels. The snow was so wet that in ten minutes, our gloves were soaked. The most difficult job was extricating the traces. To prevent these from becoming entangled we had made a practice of leaving them stretched out in front of the sledges. They were now buried under two feet of snow which was so compact and heavy that they could not be freed by pulling, and we had to dig trenches along their whole length.

When, after nearly one hour and a half, in a strong wind and driving sleet, we had succeeded in extricating the sledges and the various loads, we scraped the bottom of the 'punt', and applied a coat of ski-wax. Then we loaded it with the sacks of food, and Jack lay on top to act as a 200 pounds weight. After several trials, we found that three of us could just pull it with a load of 400 pounds. In the existing conditions, however, Jack's sledge, in relation to its size, was more efficient; partly because the deep snow offered less frontal resistance to its runners. Laden with 150 pounds he was able to pull it without too much effort.

By the time we had concluded these experiments, it was nearly midday, and we were wet and cold. With the tent still to dig out and pack, it was obvious that there would not be time for more than a few hours sledging that day. We decided, therefore, to take a half holiday, and crawled back into the tent where, with the Primus giving full blast, we soon succeeded in creating an agreeable fug. It was comforting to know that we could now shift all our baggage together, and that we had finished with the monotonous back and forth business of relaying. Undoubtedly for the next week or so it would be extremely hard work, but our load would become lighter by about ten pounds each day, and however slowly we went at first, our progress would surely be faster than it had been hitherto.

The next morning I roused the party at 3.30, when the first light of dawn was seeping faintly through the walls of the tent. The stove was lit in morose silence (verbal silence, that is, for the word was certainly not otherwise applicable in the roar of the wind and hammering of the tent canvas); after which most of the party dozed off again, until clouds of steam issuing from the pot gave the signal for further reluctant action.

Our breakfast invariably consisted of 'brose' followed by tea. For the preparation of 'brose' each man put six heaped tablespoons of oats, two of milk powder and two of sugar into his mug, mixed them together and added boiling water. For tea each man was allowed two heaped tablespoons of sugar. If anyone took more than his share, which occasionally happened in the early stages of the journey, his crime was discovered at the end of the day; and although the culprit could not then be detected, one hoped that his conscience was troubled enough to prevent a recurrence.

A few days later we had one of those contretemps, which in retrospect appear so incredibly petty that one is ashamed to recall them, but which seem to be inevitable when people are confined together at close quarters and in circumstances of some discomfort. A surprising amount of emotion is usually involved, and the difficulty at the time is to make an objective assessment of the importance of the issue, and to see clearly the extent to which one is actuated by sheer cussedness.

On this occasion the dispute arose over the position to be occupied by the stove during the preparation of breakfast. Hitherto a space was created for it between Jack and Eduardo in the middle of the tent. The point of this arrangement was that the heat from the stove would more effectively reach the clothes which were supposed to be drying aloft. I objected to it on three grounds: in the first place the creation of a space in the middle meant that Cedomir and I were squeezed even harder against our respective walls, which were usually wet and often pressed inwards by a cold mass of drift-snow, secondly the tendency of people to fall asleep again after the stove had been lit obviously increased the danger of fire and flood; thirdly, I could not get at the stove in that position, and as the party rouser it was a great deal easier for me to light the stove myself than to induce a reluctant response from my companions by shouting. My remedy was to place the stove in the corridor by the entrance, and for Cedomir and me to reverse our lying positions, so that we could easily reach it. This plan had the additional advantage that we could also reach the space between two walls of the tent for fresh supplies of snow which were constantly required for replenishing the pots.

For some reason Jack was bitterly opposed to this innovation, and for a while I refrained from pressing the matter; but with the worsening of the weather and the institution of earlier breakfasts, my sense of frustration got the better of me, and I decided to act. At the outset of the new regime Jack signified his disapproval by making full use of his considerable length to occupy as much of the corridor as possible with his feet, so that I had to lie across them to get at the stove (which I did as heavily as I could!). Primus stoves, like horses, are peculiarly sensitive to emotional atmosphere, and to succeed with them one must be thoroughly relaxed. I made three unsuccessful attempts to light the stove, each resulting in a conflagration. Jack's caustic comments suggested that he nursed a secret hope that I would set the tent on fire; but this was not gratified until some weeks later, when I burnt a hole in the inner entrance flap, and by then my system had won general approval.

On the whole, however, considering our constricted living quarters, there were remarkably few of these quarrels, and I have rarely travelled with a set of more congenial companions. Eduardo's good humour was indefatigable; he was a tireless raconteur, and if occasionally I found his stories a bit tedious, it was only because the language difficulty made it hard to detect their point. Cedomir maintained an unruffled calm. He spoke little, but his obvious delight in Eduardo's jokes (and even Jack's and mine) was very touching.

When we emerged from the tent that morning the weather was still pretty rough, although the force of the wind showed signs of slackening. Visibility was very bad: ten yards away in any direction the white mist was indistinguishable from the snow. After thirty-six hours there was a great accumulation of drift-snow to dig away, so that it took us a long time to get the tent down and the sledges packed. Jack, with his usual insistence on doing more than his fair share of the work, loaded 170 pounds of baggage on to his sledge, leaving 380 pounds for the rest of us to drag on the 'punt'. I harnessed myself to the leading trace, with Cedomir behind me and then Eduardo; Jack followed behind the 'punt'. From now on the man on the leading trace acted as 'helmsman'. With a mighty heave we started.

I had been expecting to have to work hard; but the effort involved in keeping the sledge moving was a great deal more than I had bargained for, and I soon began to wonder how long I would be able to maintain it. I sank into the snow almost up to my knees, and the necessity of lifting my feet so high at each step while leaning forward at a steep angle was exhausting enough in itself without having to do my share of the pulling. I had to watch the compass constantly, for I found that if I took my eyes off it even for a few seconds, I was liable to swing as much as ten degrees off course. This meant that I could never look at the snow in front of me, with the result that I frequently stumbled. Before long the sweat was pouring down my face and (despite my shaggy eyebrows) into my eyes. With the combination of sweat and sleet my goggles became fogged, which made it difficult to see the compass. Every ten minutes I stopped for a rest, gasping for breath, with my head on my knees.

After an hour and ten minutes I handed over the lead to Cedomir. I was very relieved to find how much easier it was to follow behind him; to have the solid foundation of his tracks to step on, to see where I was putting my feet and to be able to concentrate my whole attention upon maintaining a steady pull on my trace. It seemed like a sinecure by comparison. For the rest of the day's march we worked in regular ten-minute spells of hauling, followed by a brief rest. The work of leading was divided between the three of us, each doing three consecutive spells in front.

At eleven o'clock we ate our day's ration of rum fudge, two ounces each, and at one o'clock we stopped for half an hour for lunch, which consisted of a four-ounce packet of biscuits each with butter. We sat under the lee of the sledges, but our underclothes were soaked with sweat, and although by then the wind had dropped to a stiff breeze, we soon became so chilled that there was no temptation to prolong the halt. We also had a small supply of glucose sweets (six a day each) which we sucked as we went along; they helped to keep thirst at bay. I used to try to preserve most of mine until after lunch to boost my flagging morale. Soon after three o'clock we all agreed that we had had enough for the day, so we offloaded the sledges and set about the chilly task of making camp.

When the wind was very strong there was a considerable risk of the tent being blown away while we were pitching it. If this had happened it would probably have travelled a great deal faster than we could have followed, and there would have been nothing to stop its flight until it reached the eastern side of the ice cap. To prevent this disagreeable occurrence we followed a carefully prepared drill. First the tent was laid on the ground with the apex pointing into the wind, and the entrance uppermost. Then the near guy was securely fastened to an ice axe which had been driven deep into the snow. While I sat on the apex to hold it down, the others spread the front 'skirts', or snow-flaps, which were two feet wide, pegged them down with long aluminium spikes and weighted them with ration sacks. The next stage of the operation was the most critical. I held the rear guy and paid it out round the ice axe as required, while Jack took charge of the apex and allowed it to rise until the others could crawl beneath the madly flapping canvas, grasp the rear corners of the 'skirt', haul them back and peg them down. Then each took hold of one of the front poles and, as Jack allowed the apex to rise to the extent of his reach and let go, they planted them firmly in position.

When the tent had been trimmed, we shovelled snow on to the skirts and secured the five guys, which usually meant digging deep holes to reach snow compact enough to hold the pegs. To minimise the accumulation of drift-snow we built a barricade of snowshoes and Jack's sledge a few feet from the back, or windward side of the tent. Most of the baggage not required for the night was distributed along the skirts to supply added weight; the rest was stowed under the upturned 'punt', which was secured to two ice axes. In moderate weather the whole operation took about an hour to complete, but in really bad conditions it took considerably longer.

Chaos reigned inside the tent as we struggled to remove our sodden mutluks and boots, stripped off our clothes, inflated our mattresses and unpacked our bedding; but it was such a relief to be in out of the wind that no one minded. Then at last came the blissful moment when we were in our sleeping-bags clasping our mugs of tea. As soon as this had been disposed of we set about the preparation of the stew; and that in turn was followed by a final brew of 'brose'. Thus it was nearly eight o'clock before we were ready to settle down for the night. Though it was still fully light, we had no difficulty in falling asleep; for we were all very tired but by no means dissatisfied with the day's work.

16 Familiar Landmarks

From now on, the pattern of our daily routine remained unaltered. Though gradually the dawn came later, I continued to rouse my companions at 3.30 each morning. The reason for this spartan procedure was that we always took such an infernal time to get started, and a late start was demoralising. Jack always held firmly to the belief that the snow was in better condition before noon than after. Though I never disputed this theory, I was inclined to think that it was largely an illusion induced by fatigue towards the end of a day's march.

Each morning we aimed at being ready to start by seven o'clock, but we rarely achieved this. Our reluctance to exchange the cosy warmth of our sleeping bags for the chilly hospitality of our wet clothes was, of course, part of the reason. We tended to linger over breakfast and to grasp at any excuse to postpone the evil moment, such as polishing goggles or mending a mutluk. When our personal gear had been packed, three of us would crawl out of the tent, leaving Eduardo to deflate the mattresses, pack them and the pots, stoves and ration bags, and to clean the inside of the tent.

What really took the time was digging away the snow that had half buried the tent during the night and extricating the sledges and gear, a job which sometimes cost us more than three hours. Except on rare occasions drift-snow was always sweeping across the plateau, stinging our faces and clogging our goggles so that it was difficult to see what we were doing; though we tried to work with our backs to the wind as much as possible. With temperatures hovering around freezing point, the drift often melted and froze again, with the result that the skirts of the tent became encased in solid blocks of ice which had to be chipped away with ice axes. We had to be very careful not to damage the tent. At some time during the first few days, someone put a shovel through the outer wall, but fortunately this accident was not repeated. The snowflap, however, came in for a severe battering, and before long it was torn across in several places.

The most unpleasant conditions for working were when the temperature was above freezing point, for then the drift was wet, and our gloves, boots and trouser legs were soon saturated, and our hands and feet became unpleasantly cold. Dry drift was a comparative luxury. It was, of course, almost impossible to distinguish between real drift on the one hand and sleet or falling snow on the other; they all came at us more or less horizontally.

Once the digging operations had been completed, the task of packing up the tent and loading the sledges were comparatively simple; and the first few spells of hauling provided a welcome change, particularly as we then got warm. Our performance soon improved; on the very next march we lengthened our spells of hauling to fifteen minutes, and after a few days we were able to resume our old practice of twenty-minute spells.

We looked forward keenly to 'elevenses', which I always announced with the cry of 'fudge up', and usually to the lunch halt; but when the wind was particularly severe we postponed our lunch until after we had camped. By then, of course, we were ravenous and the task of pitching the tent became specially tedious. We never went on much later than three o'clock, and we sometimes stopped even earlier.

It might be supposed that this rigidly circumscribed routine was monotonous, but I do not think that any of us found it so. This was partly because of our constant preoccupation with chores that were both varied and of some immediate urgency, partly because we were so often in a state of looking forward with an almost passionate zest to the satisfaction of some bodily need such as food or rest or tea or warmth, and partly because of our absorption in the job in hand and our desire to improve our performance. Despite the loathsome prospect of getting up in the early morning, I remember looking forward keenly to the next day's march, hoping that snow conditions would be better, wondering how far we would get and what we might see. I certainly experienced none of the boredom and frustration I remember during the attempts to climb Everest, the endless coming and going over the same piece of ground, the long period of lying in a tent, too weak from oxygen lack to enjoy physical activity or even food. Here we had no altitude to weaken us, and we became steadily fitter and more able to contend with our environment.

An important factor was our mental attitude to the weather. We had embarked upon the journey with the full realisation that it would be the main hazard, the chief obstacle to be overcome. The numerous stories we had heard of travellers being storm-bound, unable to move for weeks at a time, had prepared us for the worst. For my part, I had been definitely scared of the wind, and had often tried to visualise what it would be like trying to pitch a tent in the kind of storm Geoff and I had experienced in the 'Vulcan Viedma' two years before. But now that we were here, actually coping with the problems of the weather, we soon gained confidence in our ability not only to survive the worst it could do, but to travel in almost any conditions. This confidence enabled us to derive a positive pleasure, by no means masochistic, from the violence of the elements.

In some respects the weather was different from what we had expected. Unlike my previous experience of the ice cap, snowstorms were heavy and continuous, and rain was correspondingly rare. Though this resulted in a far greater density of drift which was tiresome on the march and caused us such a lot of hard work in the mornings, it had the advantage that the crevassed areas remained well covered. It was also a great deal colder; as a rule this did nothing to improve snow conditions, but at least we did not get so completely soaked as we had before. The previous year we used to regard a snowstorm followed by a frost as a sure herald of fine weather; this time, however, it was never the case.

A less welcome novelty was the dense mist which often persisted for days at a time and rendered navigation difficult. Most of the time on the northern part of the ice cap we had only a vague idea of our position, and were never quite sure of the course we should steer. But the most irritating thing about it was that we saw so little of our surroundings. Even this had its compensations, for when the mist did clear the scenic effect was dramatic and very moving.

On the afternoon of 2 January we made a landfall. The mist was less dense than usual; suddenly a dark mass loomed ahead of us and gradually assumed the form of a long line of cliffs. We altered course a few degrees to the westward, which appeared to take us nearly parallel to it, for when we camped an hour later it was still about the same distance away.

During the night the wind dropped, and with it the temperature. When I awoke in the morning it was so calm that there was not even a breeze to rustle the frost-encrusted tent canvas. After breakfast Jack and Cedomir set off to collect samples from the rock wall, the base of which was only just visible through the mist, leaving Eduardo and me to pack up the camp and load the sledges. It was an easy job that morning as very little drift had accumulated. As we worked the mist about us began to vanish, and the long, serrated crest of the wall slowly emerged, first as a shifting phantom, then in form so sharp that it still seemed to have no substance. The sun did not appear, but to the northwest there was a great expanse of pale-blue sky set in a golden frame, and a million crystals of frosted snow sparkled in the reflected light. There was nothing else in the scene, just the sky and the mist and that lonely rock standing in the midst of a vast expanse of snow, but its very simplicity gave me a sense of profound peace which alone would have made the whole journey worthwhile.

Jack and Cedomir were away for an hour and a half. They brought back specimens of granitic rock known as 'Tonalite', of which the wall was composed. It was mainly white, but mottled with large black crystals of hornblend.

Our camp had been almost at the western end of the wall, from which extended a long snow hump. To get around the corner without making a long detour we had to haul the sledges over this, which involved us in a mile of uphill work. But the snow was good, and we had been so stimulated by the enjoyment of the morning and our hope of a spell of fine weather, that we were bursting with energy and high spirits. The hope, however, was short lived; and before we had been going a couple of hours it had started to blow again, the temperature rose with lamentable effect on the snow, and heavy clouds raced low overhead.

For two days we passed through an archipelago of scattered rock peaks, rising like lofty islands out of the plateau. We rarely saw their summits, but when they did appear, sheathed in glistening rime, looming out of the mist and swirling drift, they had the ethereal quality of a Chinese painting. This resemblance reminded me of the Chinese practice of displaying their pictures individually and not together in galleries, which they consider a barbarous custom calculated to spoil the effect of any masterpiece. Certainly with mountains their splendour and their beauty are enormously enhanced by visual isolation from their neighbours, and for this reason I have little liking for panoramas.

Cedomir came to the conclusion that all these peaks were composed of the same granite rock as the wall, which he had also found occurring in the vicinity of Cerro O'Higgins, and that it formed a massive intrusion extending right across this part of the range. The peaks undoubtedly formed part of the group where we had expected that we might find further evidence of volcanic activity, either recent or extinct. Though, of course, our observations were far too cursory to come to any definite conclusion, the presence of all this granite seemed to make it very improbable that any part of these mountains was of volcanic origin, and to suggest that Lautaro was after all an isolated phenomenon.

The patchy visibility, though greatly preferable to the perpetual blanket of dense fog we had had before, was sometimes confusing. On one occasion when I was in front with my eyes on the compass, I looked up and I had the distinct impression that the mist had cleared and that I saw a range of mountains very far ahead. I was quite convinced, not only of the reality of what I saw, but that I recognised the shape of the distant peaks. I let out an exultant shout, 'Look! Lautaro'. I was very puzzled by the lack of response from my companions to this exciting announcement. Then, a few minutes later, my eyes suddenly snapped into true focus, and I realised that my distant range of mountains was in fact a line of crevasses about 100 yards away.

According to our aneroid we were now 5,600 feet high. One morning we suddenly found that the sledges had become very light, and we realised that we were going downhill. The incline was not perceptible to the eye, but it made a remarkable difference to the running of the sledges, and for two hours we scampered along at a fine speed. We reckoned that we must have reached the wide trough in the ice cap which we had seen the previous year running from east to west to the north of the Nunatak. It was an encouraging thought, for it meant that we were approaching the end of the first half of the journey.

The weather had become steadily worse. On the 7th, after a particularly heavy storm, we ran into bad *sastrugi*, a snow formation caused by the wind, rather like giant sand ripples, though instead of being smooth and firm, the ridges were usually crested with small ice cornices with soft snow beneath. It was exhausting work hauling the sledges over this rough terrain, for every few yards they buried their noses in soft banks of snow, and we had to go back to dig them out. For hours on end we seemed to make hardly any progress. Visibility was almost nil, and the leader, intent upon holding the course, kept stumbling over unseen obstacles. Jack's sledge suffered severely; it was not really built for such rough treatment, and by ten o'clock, it was on the verge of collapse. It was one of the days when we did not indulge in a lunch halt, and we were certainly not inclined to stop to effect the necessary repairs; so we piled Jack's load on to the 'punt', tied his sledge on behind and all pulled together for the rest of the march. Jack was somewhat crestfallen. He was very proud of his sledge and though its performance both before and later provided ample justification for his pride, this setback was a sad blow.

This was the third consecutive day on which we had seen nothing but the snow immediately around us. We had supposed that the almost constant mist in which we had been travelling might be a phenomenon peculiar to the northern part of the ice cap, and that once we had crossed it, even if the weather was no more agreeable we might at least have better visibility. We could no longer cling to this comforting theory.

According to our reckoning we should now be very close to the northern buttresses and glaciers of the Cordon Pio XI, and we were most anxious to avoid blundering into them; for had we done so we might find ourselves amongst a complicated system of ridges and passages from which, in thick weather, we might have some difficulty in extricating ourselves. None of us had ever marched on a compass course for so long, through such featureless country and in such persistently bad visibility, and we had to admit the unpleasant possibility that we might have gone wildly astray. We were aiming for our old friend the Nunatak, with the intention of passing between it and the volcano, though it would be almost as convenient to pass to the east of it. In any case it would be far better to err to the left than to the right. Since passing the 'Wall' we had been marching on a course 8° east of south, but two days before, with this in mind, we had altered it to 14°. There was an atmosphere of expectancy in camp that evening which did much to compensate for the toil and disappointment of a frustrating day.

The morning of the 8th was comparatively calm and Jack decided to repair his sledge, while the rest of us were packing up the camp. It was Cedomir who drew our attention to a dark form which could just be discerned through the blank whiteness of the mist. He and I both took a compass-bearing to it and we agreed that it lay 13° east of south, almost exactly on our line of march. Could it be the Nunatak? It was low on the horizon, which was encouraging, for I remembered that all the rock buttresses which we had seen on the northern side of Lautaro stood high above the plateau. Yet it seemed almost incredible that, after weeks of almost blind travel, we had hit our target with such precision.

We loaded the sledges with unusual alacrity and started hauling, our suppressed excitement translated into redoubled effort. The mist was clearing and before long the rock began to take shape: two spurs rising steeply out of the snow plain to converge on the crest of a level skyline ridge. Suddenly I was convinced, beyond all shadow of doubt, that it was the Nunatak.

The party was in high spirits. We had reason to be well satisfied both with our performance and with our situation. It was four weeks and a day since we had landed. We had completed the crossing of the whole of the northern half of the ice cap, no part of which had been visited before; and we had done so in better time than our most optimistic estimate. Except for one brief spell, the weather had been continuously bad and, although we had been very lucky to escape the wind on the Jorge Montt Glacier when we were most vulnerable to it, we had been able to travel in the worst of the storms so far. And now, despite the difficulties of navigation and our persistent uncertainty as to our whereabouts, we had hit off the Nunatak as accurately as though we had been following a well-marked path. There was, of course, a considerable measure of luck about this achievement; all the same, it was gratifying. Our only regret, a big one at that, was that we had seen so little on the way. From now on it was 'money for old rope' as Jack put it. We would be travelling through known country, so that whatever the weather we should have no trouble in finding the way, and with lightening loads we would be able to travel increasingly fast.

The thoughts of my companions turned to the dump of food at our old camp on the Nunatak, and at each brief halt it was discussed, until somehow it was built up to a vision of gastronomic plenty. Jack and I had no clear recollection of what we had left there. I thought there were some meat bars, biscuits, sugar, oats and possibly some chocolate. Personally I had no interest in any of it except the sugar, and was secretly opposed to adding to our loads, but I was reluctant to damp the general enthusiasm and so held my peace.

We headed for the eastern side of the corridor. The Nunatak was a good deal farther away than it had appeared, and we were now pulling uphill, so it was noon before we reached a point abreast of its northern end. There we left the sledges and walked over to the familiar gully leading to our old camp. Remembering the network of crevasses guarding the base of the rock, we roped together, but this time there were none visible. Despite the unhappy memories that it evoked, Jack and I both confessed to feelings of nostalgia when we reached the old site.

It was buried under several feet of snow, and almost unrecognisable; so much so that we had great difficulty in locating the spot where we had left the dump. We dug in several places without success. As we had neglected to bring shovels with us, the digging had to be done with ice axes, and it was laborious work. The mood of *bonhomie* that had prevailed in the morning gradually evaporated. Eduardo, with unwonted asperity, remarked that in Chile when people left dumps of food they always built cairns over them to mark the spot. A bitter wind was blowing over the ridge; I had left my sweaters on the sledge, and despite the digging I became miserably cold. Not having had my heart in the enterprise from the first, I was now thoroughly sick of the futile quest for food we did not need. But the look of angry disappointment on Cedomir's face, the strongest emotion I had ever seen it display, caused me to hold my tongue and redouble my efforts. At last, when even Cedomir's energy was beginning to flag, somebody's ice axe struck a metallic response. It was a four-gallon paraffin tin lying in a rock crevice encased in ice. We wrenched it out and found another below. One of them contained twenty meat bars and a two-pound tin of butter, very rusty but apparently intact; the other was half full of an evil-smelling, glutinous substance which might once have been sugar, or oats or milk powder or a mixture of all three. The only other thing we found was a two-gallon fuel container from which the petrol had drained away. It seemed rather a meagre haul after all the build-up, but Jack and Cedomir were evidently delighted with the prospect of extra rations of butter and meat, Eduardo forgave our technical oversight and I was thankful to get away with the addition of only a few pounds of extra weight. So as we returned to the sledges to pitch our camp, our holiday mood was revived.

It was further enhanced by the prospect of fine weather, perfectly timed, we thought, for an attempt to climb Lautaro. The clouds lifted and shafts of sunlight broke through; to the north-east the peaks of Cerro O'Higgins appeared and the whole familiar scene was bathed in the soft colours of evening. Except for the lower buttresses, the volcano remained obscured, but it was evident that no major eruption had taken place during the past twelve months, and that this lonely vent had had no part in the cataclysm which had occurred in Central Chile, 500 miles farther north.

The following day we made our way through the corridor and camped near the spur coming down from the south ridge of Lautaro. We had intended to go far up into the great south-east combe enclosed by the south and east ridges; but the promise of fine weather proved illusory once more, and before we had travelled the length of the Nunatak, the clouds were right down again and a powerful wind was driving the snow at us from behind. We knew that parts of the combe were menaced by ice avalanches from hanging glaciers on the surrounding ridges, and to have camped inside it without being able to see where we were would have been unwise.

We had twenty-seven days' food left, so that we could afford to spend at least a week waiting for a chance to climb Lautaro, and still allow ourselves nearly three weeks to complete the journey, which should be ample. We were now 6,500 feet above sea level, and the summit of the mountain was about 5,500 feet above us. As the corridor was on the leeward side, an enormous quantity of drift-snow was constantly pouring into it from across the south ridge, so that we could hardly expect to find good conditions. Our snowshoes would help us in the lower part of the combe, but the major part of the climb would be up the steep flank of the east ridge where there might be considerable risk of snow avalanches. Once on the crest of the south ridge, which was joined by the east ridge half a mile from the summit, we would be exposed to the full force of the wind. It would certainly be a long climb, probably very laborious, and possibly difficult; to attempt it we would need at least a day of settled weather, reasonable visibility and little wind.

We settled down to wait. As usual Jack was full of optimism, though I must confess that I saw little ground for it in view of our experience during the past month. The wind continued with unabated fury. Though it was probably no stronger than before, it was deflected by the mountain ridges into intermittent gusts, which came at us from all directions and seemed to lash the tent with increased venom. For the first two days we remained in our sleeping bags, content to have an excuse to rest. With the stove going continuously we managed to get our clothes and boots reasonably dry. After that we took to making sorties in search of accessible rock outcrops from which to collect geological specimens. There was no risk of losing ourselves so long as we kept on a compass course from the foot of the spur. Sometimes we could see the steep snow slopes and hanging glaciers flanking the east ridge; with clouds of wind-driven snow racing across them in a series of sweeping spirals, they were an impressive sight. We never saw the upper part of the mountain, but a strong smell of sulphur which reached us from time to time suggested that the volcano was still mildly active.

On the evening of the fourth day, I suggested that we should abandon the attempt on the mountain and continue on our way.[1] There was no sign of an improvement in the weather, and it seemed most unlikely that the next three or four days would bring one. It would be better, I thought, to travel during the bad weather, and if during the next three weeks we were lucky enough to have a fine spell we would have time to use it; for anywhere along the route there would be plenty of opportunities for climbing and minor exploratory journeys. Eduardo and Cedomir agreed; but Jack had set his heart on Lautaro and

---

1 The peak was eventually climbed in 1964 by an Argentinian expedition. An Anglo-Argentinian group (Eric Jones, Mick Coffrey, Ernesto O'Reilly and Leo Dickinson) made the second ascent in 1973. This party also discovered and climbed another volcano, ten miles north of the Lautaro, which they named Cerro Mimosa.

was most reluctant to turn his back on it once more. For a man of his boundless energy, normally so impatient of delay, he had an admirable capacity for 'sitting it out'; like Frank Smythe, he could retire within a cocoon of stoicism which rendered him impervious to the static endurance of unpleasant conditions.

After some discussion we agreed to a compromise: we would wait for another two days, and if by then there was still no improvement in the weather, we would resume our march.

17 Cordon Darwin

I was very glad when the morning of 16 January arrived. The weather was still atrocious, and I think that even Jack was resigned to the decision to abandon our hopes of climbing Lautaro. We steered a south-westerly course, heading for the upper basin of the Viedma Glacier. For the first couple of miles we were going down a gentle slope and, despite the soft snow, we raced along at a fine speed. By now the weight of our baggage was reduced to about 400 pounds, so that even on the level the exertion of hauling was very much less than it had been.

Before we had been going more than an hour, to our surprise we suddenly ran out of the mist into perfect visibility. To the north and east, Cerro Pyramid, the Cordon Gaea and even Cerro Gorra-Blanca, twenty-five miles away, were clearly in view. For a while we thought that the weather was changing, and we considered turning back. But although the clouds were high, the sky was heavily overcast, and the dark bank of fog from which we had emerged remained solid and immovable behind us. It was obvious that the storm was still raging on Lautaro, for although the main part of the mountain was completely hidden, we could see, towering above us, the end of the south ridge from which long streamers of snow were blowing.

The good visibility remained throughout the morning and early afternoon. It was a delightful change to have something to look at as we marched. To the east we could see through the gap leading into the valley of the Rio Electrico to gentle, russet hills far away beyond our world of ice and snow. But it was a fleeting respite; by the end of the march, we were beset once more by mist and driving sleet, and during the next two or three days, the weather became steadily worse, culminating in the most violent storm we experienced in the whole journey.

On the morning of the 18th, after a rough night, I was dressed before the others and emerged from a tent to start the usual digging operations. I could scarcely stand and had to crawl round to the back of the tent where, kneeling with my back to the wind, I began to work with the shovel. The snow was dry and powdery, and it whipped up into my face with such force and in such volume that I could not see what I was doing. After digging blindly for a quarter of an hour, I realised that I was achieving nothing, so I crawled back inside the tent. We waited until 9.30 and then decided to lie up for the day.

In the early afternoon the wind moderated, but it was then too late to start. In any case it was only a temporary lull, and towards evening the storm was renewed with even greater ferocity. The noise was shattering, and we had to yell at each other to make ourselves heard above the roar of the wind. Accustomed though I was by then to rough weather, I began to be uneasy, wondering if even the half-buried pyramid could stand up to such a battering; I was quite sure that any other tent would have been destroyed.

While supper was being prepared, two of the walls of the tent suddenly sagged, and then started to flap madly. Jack and Cedomir dressed hastily, and crawled outside. It took them more than half an hour to refix the guys which had been wrenched from their moorings. When darkness had fallen, the same thing happened again, and this time Jack and I went out to deal with the situation. It was much warmer than it had been in the morning and the drift-snow had changed to drenching sleet. This was the main reason for the guys working loose, for the snow had thawed several feet below the surface. Soon afterwards, however, it began to freeze again and we had no further trouble.

I was awakened once in the night by a particularly violent gust, and lay for a while listening to the crazy racket with a certain amount of enjoyment. However, when I awoke again at the accustomed hour of 3.30, the wind appeared to have moderated, and we prepared to start. Conditions outside were little, if any, better than they had been the previous morning, but this time we persisted. The lower part of the tent was completely encased in ice, and it took so long to cut it away that it was nine o'clock before we had finished loading the sledges.

We had gone about 100 yards when the surface suddenly changed to ice, as hard and smooth as a skating rink, from which all vestige of snow had been swept away. I was in the lead with my eyes fixed on the compass so that I had no warning, with the result that my feet shot from under me and I fell heavily, dropping the compass which went sliding away like a curling stone. I got up, and forgetting I was in harness, tried to chase it, with the result that I crashed again. After that I crawled on all fours until I had recovered the compass which fortunately had come to rest against a patch of snow. I learnt later that my antics looked extremely funny and, by his repeated reference to the incident, Eduardo evidently came to regard it as one of the highlights of the trip.

The wind was swirling across our line of advance, and as soon as the 'punt' was on the ice it was blown sideways and dragged all three of us over. After that Eduardo hitched his trace to the back of the sledge and pulled to windward. Even so it was very difficult to keep a straight course, and we went along in a crab-like fashion, with repeated falls, for a couple of hours, after which we found ourselves on snow again.

The wind was too strong for us to stop for lunch, and in the early afternoon it increased to such violence that, at 2.15, I decided that we had better pitch the tent while it was still possible. As it was, our drill came in for a severe testing. Fortunately, before we reached the most delicate part of the operation, it began to moderate. We thought that this was just a lull in the storm and worked as fast as possible to get the job done before it started up again. But the wind continued to diminish and by the time we had settled into the tent, it was no more than a gentle breeze. By five o'clock there was absolute calm.

As with the sudden cessation of an artillery barrage, the silence was uncanny, almost oppressive. It took some time to become accustomed to the strange tranquility, and even when I awoke the next morning I had a sense of unreality, as if a fundamental part of life were missing.

The mist around us was clearing rapidly as we left the tent, and by the time we started we were in a sunlit corridor between two huge banks of cloud. Two miles away there was a rock buttress, the end of the north-easterly spurs of the Cordon Mariano Moreno. When we reached it we stopped for an hour while Cedomir collected samples. Across the corridor the cathedral spire of Fitzroy appeared through a gap in the eastern cloud-bank, surrounded by its glittering retinue of minarets.

At noon we reached the western end of the 'Vulcan Viedma' where we were faced with a long slope up to a saddle between it and the Mariano Moreno. By then it was so hot that we decided to leave the toil up the slope until the cool of the morning. So we pitched the tent, leaving all our gear out to dry, and spent the afternoon basking in the sun; a delicious contrast to our situation twenty-four hours before. The great ice ramparts of the Mariano Moreno were clear; these and the vast combes between reminded me of the south side of Mont Blanc. Over the long summit ridge there was the same closely fitting blanket of cloud that I had seen almost exactly two years before. Again it was flowing swiftly towards us like the crest of an enormous Niagara, plunging down the eastern precipices and vanishing in the clear air below; and yet the gale that was driving it did not disturb the stillness around us. When the sun sank behind it, the cloud-blanket was fringed with a flaming corona.

Cedomir said that he would like to spend a day examining the rocks of the 'Vulcan', and as the rest of us were not averse to a spell of pottering about on dry land, I decided to grant his request, but with the proviso that we should first cross the saddle.

The morning of the 21st was very cold, but even on the hard-frozen snow it took an hour of very hard work to drag the sledges up the slope. At the crest of the saddle there was another of those remarkable chasms, 100 feet deep, scoured out of the solid glacier ice by wind action, which I had seen before at various points around the perimeter of the 'Vulcan'. Nowhere else have I encountered such spectacular examples of this phenomenon, and it seems that the wind in this particular locality must often attain exceptional force.

We could now look across the southern half of the Viedma glacier basin to the wide pass leading over to the Upsala. In the far distance beyond we saw the summit of one of the peaks of the Cordon Darwin standing above a dark mass of cloud. To the west of this range there is a high plateau which had been discovered by de Agostini, who named it 'Altiplano Italia'. We had already decided that, instead of going straight down the Upsala Glacier as we had originally intended, we would make our way on to this plateau, and from it attempt to climb one of the peaks of the range. With this in view we made a note of the bearing to the peak.

From the saddle we ran down the gentle slope beyond, and in half an hour reached a patch of moraine near a gap in the main ridge of the 'Vulcan', where we pitched the tent. Then we glissaded 1,000 feet down into the circular hollow that Dr Lliboutry had mistaken for the crater of a volcano. It was almost empty of water as it had been two years before, but the icebergs stranded at various levels around the basin showed that this was a seasonal state. Similar glacier-dammed lakes that I have met with in the Karakoram are full in the spring and drained in the summer, and it appeared that this one followed the same routine.

Cedomir spent the rest of the day examining the geology of the area, and Jack made a collection of plants and insects, while Eduardo and I wandered lazily about the basin, enjoying the hot sun and the perfect stillness about us. It was like being in a vast Greek amphitheatre with its concentric terraces, formed by a series of shore-lines, facing a high platform of glacier ice. Beyond the topmost shore-line, 400 feet above the bottom of the basin, there were flowers growing in protected crevices among the rocks.

It was still clear when we left the 'Vulcan' the next morning and headed southward for the pass; but the weather was deteriorating rapidly, and before the morning was far advanced we were enveloped once more in mist and driving sleet. A great deal of the surface snow had melted during the past two days, and before long we began to have trouble with thinly covered crevasses. To prevent ourselves from falling into them, we put on our snowshoes for the first time since our abortive attempt to use them on the Jorge Montt Glacier. Although the sledges were still more heavily laden than they had been on that occasion, we had become so accustomed to hauling, that we now found no difficulty in manipulating the snowshoes.

On the 23rd we travelled through a severe storm, with almost no visibility all day, but were feeling full of energy after our sunny respite, and appeared to make excellent progress. That evening we discussed the question of how far we could go on in those conditions without the risk of blundering into the ridges and hanging glaciers of the Cordon Darwin. We decided to do so for another day, and then to wait for better visibility.

To our delighted surprise the very next day dawned brilliantly fine. For once we did not dally over breakfast, and we came out of the tent into the early sunlight to find ourselves surrounded by a stupendous view. There was not a cloud to be seen anywhere, and the storm-washed air was so clear that even the most distant mountains were sharply defined. To the east there was a slender spire rising from a beautifully symmetrical base; being so much closer, it looked almost as impressive as Fitzroy itself. To the west another range, immaculately white, rose out of the plateau like a gigantic wave.

I was strongly tempted to head towards those nameless mountains and I still harbour some regret that I did not obey the impulse; for even one of their minor summits would command a fascinating view into the unseen country beyond. But they were a long way off in the wrong direction, and my companions had set their hearts on the Altiplano and the peaks of the Cordon Darwin, which stood in compelling grandeur to the south.

There had been a heavy frost and for once the surface of the snow was both hard and smooth. There was no need to wear snowshoes, and the sledges ran so easily that no effort was required to drag them. We made for a col between two nunataks, and strode along exulting in the cold air and the gentle, caressing warmth of the early sun, in the vast mountain world about us and in the sensuous awareness of our own physical well-being.

The slope on the far side of the col was comparatively steep and quite unbroken by crevasses, so we sat on the sledges and sped along at a fine speed for about half a mile to the bottom. By this time the sun had melted the surface of the snow, the dragging weight of the sledges increased, and the rest of the march to the northern end of the Cordon Darwin was hot and thirsty.

We camped in a glacier combe enclosed by two ridges coming down from Cerro Don Bosco, the northernmost peak of the range. Immediately to the west there was a steep snow ramp running up between two icefalls to the northern end of the Altiplano. We decided that if the weather held we would climb Cerro Don Bosco early the next morning before dragging the sledges up the ramp. The peak had been climbed from the Upsala Glacier three years before by a Polish expedition; indeed it was the only summit in the Cordon Darwin to have been reached; but as we were so well aware that the fine spell might end at any moment, we were determined to seize any opportunity for climbing that offered. For the same reason we were careful to site the camp exactly between two rock buttresses at the entrance to the combe, so that by keeping a constant check on compass bearings during the climb we would be able to find our way back even in a blizzard.

I woke the party at 2.30 the next morning and we were ready to start by four o'clock. Dawn was breaking, but many of the larger stars were still shining in a cloudless sky. There had been another sharp frost, and we walked rapidly over hard snow to the head of the combe, keeping well out of the range of possible avalanches from a hanging glacier suspended high up on the western wall. Crossing a well-bridged bergschrund, we climbed an easy gully and over a rock spur, where we paused to put on our crampons. The rising sun found us threading our way through the séracs and cliffs of a small icefall. Beyond this, once more in frozen shadow, we made our way up a steep couloir between two overhanging ice buttresses, to the crest of the western ridge of the mountain.

After weeks of sledge-hauling, the varied rhythm, and balanced movements of mountaineering were sheer delight, and we climbed very fast, with complete disregard for economy of effort. The broad ridge was composed of a series of turrets of crystalline ice, which looked like giant fungi. They were steep but easy to climb and, at seven o'clock, three hours after leaving camp we were on the summit of the mountain.

There was a strong westerly wind, but otherwise the weather was still fine and perfectly clear in every direction. To the southeast, across the wide valley of the Upsala Glacier, we saw the twisting channels of Lago Argentino and the golden pampas hills beyond. We greeted this first view of our objective with an excited cheer. In the opposite direction the view extended across the whole of the southern part of the ice cap, over which we had been travelling during the past week, to the distant ranges beyond. Westward was the Altiplano Italia and a score of peaks standing above it, brilliant against a dark background where the forested valleys of the Pacific lay in a vast well of shadow.

It was, however, our immediate surroundings that lent magic to the scene; for all about us there was an exotic statuary of ice, huge mushrooms and jutting gargoyles, sculptured in rime by the wind, each object composed of a delicate pattern of crystal flowers. Across a deep gap to the south was Cerro Murallon, a great square block of granite, 500 feet higher than the Don Bosco; its smooth, vertical sides festooned with a fantastic ice drapery like massive lace curtains; its flat summit ridge, perhaps 600 yards long, crowned by a line of ice minarets, sparkling in the sun.

Despite the wind, which was unusually cold, we stayed on the summit for nearly an hour before we began to descend the west ridge which offered an easy way down to the Altiplano. We had intended to go straight back to the camp, and to spend the afternoon hauling the sledges up the ramp. But it seemed a pity to waste such wonderful weather over such a dull task. A day like this was extremely rare; there was no knowing what the next day would bring, and it was more than probable that we would not have another opportunity to explore the Altiplano in good visibility. We still had more than twelve hours of daylight before us.

I suggested that we should cross the Altiplano while the snow was still hard, and climb a beautiful snow peak on the other side, which would give us a splendid view of the country to the west, but Cedomir was fired with an ambition to climb Cerro Murallon, and as the others seemed to favour this alternative, I decided to adopt it. The mountain appeared to be almost inaccessible from the north, but traversing round the western side we found a snow corridor running up under the vertical curtains of ice to the south-west face which was considerably less steep.

It was nearly midday when we reached the foot of the corridor, and we stopped there for lunch. Across the Altiplano we could now see through a wide gap to the left of the snow peak, to the vast tract of festooned country beyond. In the midst of this there was a wide channel westward into the far distance, sprinkled with icebergs which looked like tiny white dots on the surface of the water. It was the upper reaches of the Falcon Fjord. The weather was still fine, but clouds had begun to form over the forest far below.

As we climbed, the view to the south gradually expanded, until at last we could see the whole of the Altiplano and a magnificent semicircle of ice peaks enclosing it in that direction. The climbing was laborious because by then the snow was soft, but it was not difficult, and late in the afternoon we reached the summit ridge and looked down the sheer north face of the mountain. Immediately to our right was one of the ice towers, about fifty-feet high which we had seen that morning from the Don Bosco. We reached the top of it without much difficulty and saw several more along the ridge to the east, one of which was higher than ours. But so far as we could judge, the true summit of the Murallon stood at the western end of the ridge about 300 yards away.

We had just decided to make our way back towards it, when suddenly we found ourselves enveloped in thick mist which had blown up from below. It was totally unexpected, for a moment before we had been under a clear sky and we had not seen any cloud in our vicinity. At first we thought that it was a small patch which had formed round the peak, and that it would soon clear again; so we climbed westward along the ridge as fast as we could against the stiff wind.

We gained height rapidly and when after a quarter of an hour the ridge levelled off and then began to fall away. I thought we had reached the summit. But suddenly a shape loomed a few yards ahead of us. It was an ice buttress about twenty-five feet high and almost vertical. Hoping to find an easy way from the back, we tried to pass it on the right, but were stopped by a bulge jutting out over a sheer drop into a cauldron of swirling mist. A similar obstacle stopped us on the left.

It would have been possible to climb the buttress direct in reasonable conditions, though even so it would have taken a long time. By then it had started to snow; it was obvious that the weather had turned bad, and we realised that we might well find ourselves in an ugly situation. It was nearly five o'clock. With visibility limited to a few yards it would be by no means easy to find the route down the mountain. The way back to camp was long and complicated, and if a severe storm developed it might be impossible to find it. Galvanised by these unpleasant thoughts we turned and ran back down the ridge.

We had some difficulty in finding the point at which we had reached it, for our tracks had already been obliterated. Then we plunged diagonally down the steep snow slopes on a south-westerly bearing. Below us to the left we knew that there was a sheer precipice falling to one of the tributaries of the Upsala Glacier and it was necessary to keep more and more to the right to reach the top of the corridor. But with the snow whipping up into our faces it was very hard to keep a sense either of direction or of distance. I was in front and was far from confident that I was going the right way. Fortunately at the critical moment we ran out beneath the cloud and saw the corridor below us. We raced down it and reached our lunch place where we paused for a brief rest.

We had a fleeting glimpse of the Altiplano and of the clouds pouring over the range before they enveloped us once more. From the lunch place we had previously taken a compass-bearing to the saddle between Don Bosco and Murallon so we had no difficulty in reaching it; but the way beyond was more complicated. In such weather it was impossible to retrace the route we had followed in the morning for it would have meant climbing most of the way up the west ridge of Don Bosco. The alternative was to make our way down to the Altiplano and circle round a series of buttresses which we could not see. It was a long, weary plod through soft snow, with sleet driving across our faces; but once again we were lucky, for another clearing of the mist enabled us to find the ramp leading down to the entrance of the combe. There was still plenty of daylight when we reached camp, very tired and thoroughly wet.

Despite our failure, by a narrow margin of some twenty-five feet, to reach the summit of Cerro Murallon, it had been a wonderful day. Nevertheless I felt somewhat ashamed to have taken such a chance with the weather, for had it turned really bad our plight would have been serious. We had gone too far from our camp and the route back was much too complicated for us to be sure of being able to return to it in bad conditions.

18   The Journey's End

The fine spell, which had lasted more than thirty-six hours, was over and the normal regime of wind and mist and driving sleet was re-established. The wind was uncommonly warm, always a bad weather portent, and the snow around us melted so rapidly that the following morning we found that the tent was perched on a pedestal almost two feet high.

We spent the 26th resting after our strenuous exertions of the previous day, and discussing our next move. Our plan to travel over the length of the Altiplano and to descend to the Upsala by way of the Bertachi Glacier, which had been explored by de Agostini, had lost much of its appeal. For we had already seen the whole of the Altiplano and all the mountains surrounding it, and there seemed little point in struggling over it in a blizzard. Jack was in favour of doing so on the slender chance that in the next two or three days the weather might improve enough to allow us to climb another of the peaks of the range; but the rest of us did not share his optimism. Perhaps the smell of the fleshpots was already in our nostrils, sapping our resolution and blunting our appetite for further punishment. At any rate we decided, on a three to one vote, to descend direct to the Upsala Glacier and head for home. We agreed, however, that if the weather should improve, we would use our remaining five days' surplus food by making an excursion into the Darwin Range from the east.

There was a small glacier flowing eastward from the combe and we made our way down it on the 27th. It was fairly steep and we hoped to be able to toboggan down on the sledges; but the surface was composed of a soggy morass of melting snow into which we sank almost to our hips, and we had to pull hard the whole way. On the 28th we made our way diagonally across the Upsala Glacier. The snow became thinner as we went, and we had to follow a tortuous course to avoid crevassed areas. About mid-morning we ran out on to bare ice which was so smooth that the sledges slid over it as if they were on ballbearings, and we often had to run to prevent them from overtaking us.

On leaving the Cordon Darwin, we had crossed a sharply-defined weather frontier. Although the wind was strong and there were some sleet squalls, we had left the mist behind, an occasional gleam of sun broke through the clouds and conditions were altogether much more agreeable. The change of climate showed clearly on the eastern side of the Upsala Glacier, where all the rock walls and ridges were bare, and even the peaks of the Cerro Norte group, which were higher than many of those in the main range, held scarcely any snow or ice.

Gradually the surface of the glacier became more and more broken, and we knew that the time was fast approaching when we would have to abandon the sledges and continue with the loads on our backs; but we were determined to postpone that evil moment as long as possible. Throughout the afternoon the 'punt' came in for a merciless bashing, for we leapt over wide crevasses at a run so that the sledge had sufficient momentum to carry it across and land on the other side with a crash. To prevent it from slipping into a chasm Eduardo hitched his trace to the back so that he could haul it sideways in either direction. Jack had to be more circumspect with his sledge, for although it was a great deal easier to control, it was nothing like so robust; and it was remarkable that he managed to keep up with us. Twice we had to offload both sledges and carry them and the baggage in relays through a particularly bad area.

We were now heading straight down the glacier, close to its left-hand side and immediately above a deep ravine which separated the ice from its containing wall of red rock. At 6.30 we halted and, leaving the sledges, carried the loads down to the bottom of the ravine, where we pitched the tent on a little ice platform between two crevasses.

Early the next morning Cedomir and I set off on a geological excursion into the mountains to the east. After climbing 2,000 feet, we reached the crest of a ridge from which we looked down a sheer precipice into the valley of La Cristina. There was Lago Pearson, its near end surrounded by dark-green forest, and beyond we saw the river ambling through the wide, sunlit valley to the shore of Lago Argentino. To the east the walls of Cerro Norte, black and sinister, towered above us into the mist. Westward across the Upsala the Cordon Darwin was hidden by a monstrous wall of cloud. We got back to camp at eleven o'clock.

The fleshpots were now so near that their call was irresistible; and as the weather on the main range showed no sign of improving, we all agreed to jettison our surplus provisions and take with us only sufficient for three more days. It was also decided to abandon the small sledge, which caused Jack obvious pain. We started at one o'clock, all four of us harnessed to the 'punt'. But the surface of the glacier was so broken that we made slow progress, and we would probably have done better carrying the loads.

We had worked over towards the middle of the glacier to avoid a mass of ice pinnacles on the left, and were making our way along a shallow trough between two pressure ridges. At 3.30 we reached a crevasse far too wide to jump, which extended right across the trough. It was obvious that we could take the sledge no farther, for the ice on either side was far too broken. By then snow was falling heavily, and as it would have taken us a long time to dismantle the tent and repack the baggage into portable loads, we decided to stop there for the night. Pitching the tent on the bare ice was a long job, for we had first to cut a large quantity of ice chips with which to weight it down.

We awoke on the morning of the 30th, to find the glacier covered with nine inches of fresh snow. It was still snowing and the bleak landscape was shrouded in mist. When we came to divide up the loads we found that we still had a distressing amount to carry; this was partly accounted for by Cedomir's geological collection, but it was also due to the Chileans' refusal to discard surplus items of equipment such as the spare rope and Primus and the empty fuel containers. We shouldered our heavy packs and bid a reluctant farewell to the 'punt', which had played such a vital part in the success of the journey.

To the left of the trough there was a series of sharp ridges like waves about to break, running in a south-eastern direction. We climbed along one of these, which I had previously reconnoitred, and reached another trough close to the side of the glacier. In less than a quarter of a mile, however, we were confronted by a chaotic mass of séracs and ice-cliffs which we could not penetrate. The only way of passing it was to climb along another of the ice ridges which led us back up the glacier, with the result that after two hours of hard going we found ourselves close to the place from which we had started.

The rest of the morning followed a similar exasperating pattern. Each advance down the glacier was followed by long detours, often in the opposite direction, cutting steps down into a ravine and up the other side, or balancing along a slender crest of ice, unable to see where we were going. The fresh snow did not improve matters, for in the hollows deep drifts had collected, which hid the crevasses and blurred the outline of the ice bridges. At one point things looked so unpromising that, having dumped our loads, Cedomir and I went off in one direction and Eduardo and Jack in another to find a way through the maze. Our line proved hopeless and before long we found ourselves on an isolated spur from which we could not proceed in any direction. However, the others were more successful, and an hour later we were reunited at the dump with the prospect of better going ahead.

By the middle of the afternoon we had reached a stretch of comparatively smooth ice, and when, at four o'clock, we stopped to pitch the tent, we had reason to hope that we were through the worst, and that it would be our last camp on the glacier. In the evening the wind rose and by nightfall it was blowing very hard indeed. I was thankful that we were not in the Altiplano, where conditions must have been considerably worse. However, the tempest was short-lived and in the early morning the wind died away.

The mist, too, had gone and we could see far down the glacier to the col leading over to La Cristina. We were in a broad trough which ran gently down, smooth and straight, between pressure ridges of shattered ice, a mile or so from the left side of the glacier. No obstacle impeded us as we strode rapidly down the trough until, in a couple of hours, we had reached a point nearly opposite the col. Then we turned left on to the pressure ridges; but as we were following along the line of the crevasses we had little trouble in making our way through the forest of séracs, and by eleven o'clock we were glissading down the flank of the glacier into an ablation valley at the foot of the col.

The journey was virtually over. We were in no hurry to get anywhere. It was warm and a heavy lethargy crept into our bodies. Cedomir found that the rocks were full of fossils, and we spent a long time collecting them before we could summon the resolution to shoulder our loads again and start scrambling up the steep rocks to the pass. Two condors sailed overhead, the first creatures that we had seen since leaving the Jorge Montt, seven weeks before.

An hour later we were on a broad path, walking through enchanting woodland, our world alive again with the song of birds and the smell of growing things. We stopped frequently to lie on soft beds of moss and leaves, gazing up into the trees and taking deep gulps of sweet-scented air. The change of our environment was so sudden, the contrast so complete, that I sank into a kind of opiate trance, from which happy state I did not emerge for several days.

After stopping for an hour by a forest tarn to make tea, we left the path and scrambled down a steep grass slope to the shore of the bay where the old steam launch was riding at anchor. The sun was shining, and the warm, still air was heavy with the fragrance of herbs. Rounding a small headland we disturbed a flock of wild geese; and once across the river on the flat ground beyond, our ears were filled with the sound which, more than anything else, I shall always associate with Patagonia: the shrill, protesting cry of the plovers.

It was six o'clock when we reached the *estancia*. Mr and Mrs Masters were in the sitting room and we tapped on the window to attract their attention. It must have given them something of a shock to see four bearded faces looking in at them, for I very much doubt if they recognised me at first; however they hurried out to greet us with apparent pleasure. It was wonderful to see the old couple again, looking as active as ever despite their eighty-four years. Mr Masters ran off to fetch Herbert, while the old lady began immediately to prepare our supper. I suggested that we should feed ourselves and pitch our tent in the garden, but she vetoed the idea in a tone that permitted no argument. With no help in the house and no labour-saving devices, she accepted the extra task of providing for four hungry men with complete serenity, as no doubt, sixty years before, she had faced the job of building a home in this remote valley.

When Herbert arrived we gave him an account of the trip, while his parents were busy cooking and preparing our rooms. He had always taken a great interest in expeditions to the area, and he knew a great deal about the previous attempts that had been made to cross the ice cap. Cyril Jervis had told him over the radio that we had been landed on the shores of the Canal Baker and hoped to reach La Cristina, but he said that he had not thought for a moment that we would succeed; particularly as the weather had been exceptionally bad since the spring. Indeed, according to Mr and Mrs Masters, it had been by far the worst summer they remembered in the sixty years that they had been there; a piece of news that we found highly gratifying.

At 7.30 we sat down to dinner, served by the old couple who refused to allow us to do anything to help. It consisted of soup and a deliciously roasted joint of lamb, with potatoes and vegetables; and then, of all things, strawberries and cream. A couple of hours later came the final touch of perfection when we slid between clean sheets and turned out the electric light. Twenty-four hours before we had been in a blizzard in a wilderness of ice and snow.

The journey over the ice cap had taken fifty-two days. It had been an experience as completely satisfying as any I have known. Even the vileness of the weather was a source of some satisfaction, for it had been part of our purpose to accept its challenge and to prove our ability to travel securely even in its most savage moods. Above all, I now felt myself to be on terms of intimacy with this wild region which, to my mind, is the highest reward of any mountaineering venture.

19   Land of Fire

Patagonia had proved a field of mountain adventure, far more fruitful than I had originally expected. As in the ranges of Central Asia, the horizon of 'the untravelled world' was constantly expanding; the more, it seemed, one did the more there was left to do. Fresh projects kept occurring to my mind, each more compelling than the last. The potion of the calafate berry had certainly proved effective.

There was, however, a still more powerful lodestone farther south. For as long as I can remember I have been fascinated by Tierra del Fuego. Perhaps the intriguing name had something to do with it; or the remoteness of the place; or Darwin's description of the 'savage magnificence' of the scene, the 'mysterious grandeur' in the mountains. Whatever the main influence, I had long cherished an entrancing vision of lonely, storm-swept peaks, swathed in bands of cloud, protected from all intruders by massive, primeval forest, where exotic plants flourished as though in a tropical rather than a subantarctic environment. When I came to examine the situation more closely, I was astonished to find how much of the mountain country was in fact still virgin ground, and the vision was quickly translated into a consuming desire to get there. Thus, emboldened by my experiences, in Patagonia where, I thought, conditions could not be so very different, I decided to take an expedition there in 1962 to explore and climb the highest ranges.

When Ferdinand Magellan was passing through the Straits which bear his name, he saw a large number of fires burning along the southern shore. They had probably been lit as rallying signals by the natives, who were no doubt astonished and terrified by the sudden appearance of his ships. This apparently was the origin of the name 'Land of Fire'. Magellan thought that it was part of a great southern continent stretching away into the Antarctic, and it was not until half a century later, when Drake, having passed through the Straits, was blown by north-westerly gales round Cape Horn back into the Atlantic, that it was realised that it was in fact an island.

A large part of Tierra del Fuego is flat or gently undulating, with open pampas in the north and well-forested land farther south. As in Patagonia it supports a flourishing sheep industry. The long southern coastline, however, is dominated by rugged mountainous country, which is really the final spur of the great chain of the Andes. Almost all the high mountains are situated on a large, uninhabited peninsula running westward from the main island for more than 100 miles between the Beagle Channel and Admiralty Sound.

At its western end stands Mount Sarmiento, which was climbed, after several abortive attempts, by an expedition led by de Agostini; but most of the Peninsula is occupied by the Cordillera Darwin which contains the highest peaks of Tierra del Fuego. This range covers an area that would easily accommodate the whole of the Mont Blanc and Pennine ranges of the Alps and most of the Bernese Oberland as well, while the extent of its glaciers must be far greater than those of the entire Alpine chain. Moreover, though the highest peaks are only some 8,500 feet they rise straight from sea level, so that from the climber's point of view the mountains are equivalent in size to most of their Alpine rivals.

Yet, until 1962 almost the whole of this great range, with its scores of unnamed peaks, was untrodden ground. De Agostini had landed at several points along the northern coast and had climbed two peaks, 'Italia' and 'Frances' above the Beagle Channel on its southern side; but no one had penetrated to the interior. It was an alluring prospect for any mountaineer prepared to accept rough conditions.

For the Peninsula has a most evil reputation for weather. It is lashed by the same westerly gales that rage around Cape Horn, savage storms that bring long spells of fog and rain and snow. But, as with the sea, part of the fascination of mountains lies in combating the elements that surround them. We accepted the challenge of the Himalayan giants partly because of the problems presented by the rarified atmosphere at great altitudes. Nor is the mountaineer a stranger to disappointment and frustration. How often, for example, did we set out to climb Mount Everest, repeated all the tedious preparations, made the long approach, only to find that a few feet of powder snow on the summit rocks had made our goal inaccessible? Yet we never thought the effort unrewarded. Certainly when I decided to go to the Darwin Range, I was well aware that we might spend nearly all our allotted time immobilised by foul weather, achieving nothing.

My companions on the ice cap had proved so good a team that I hoped that they would all join me in the new venture. Unfortunately Jack was unable to do so. To take his place Eduardo and Cedomir brought another Chilean mountaineer, Francisco Vivanco, known to his friends as 'Pancho'.

I equipped and provisioned the party in much the same way as before. Short skis, however, replaced the snowshoes and we took no sledge. Messrs. Burberry kindly provided our outer garments, and we had some light Terylene smocks, or 'ponchos' as well. We also took a lightweight tent for high camps.

It was believed that the chief obstacle to gaining access to the interior of the Darwin Range would be the almost impenetrable barrier of bog and forest. We had found in Patagonia, however, that this kind of obstacle could often be overcome by careful choice of route, and by taking advantage of clear, firm ground left by retreating glaciers. The entire Peninsula is uninhabited. Though it is possible to approach it by land from the eastern end, it would take many weeks of difficult mountaineering to reach the highest peaks from that direction, so that the only practicable approach to these is by sea. Again the Chilean Navy kindly undertook to provide us with the necessary transport.

Like the whole coastline of Southern Chile the Peninsula is penetrated by a remarkable network of fjords. Many of them have been charted, and the outlines of the remainder have been plotted by aerial photographs. Cedomir and Eduardo made a careful study of these photographs, which proved invaluable in selecting a landing place and a route to the interior. We chose a spot near the head of a fjord running twenty miles southward from an inlet known as Broken Bay in Admiralty Sound, the wide channel separating the north coast of the Peninsula from the mainland of Tierra del Fuego. The fjord had not been charted and, so far as I know, no one had been up it except perhaps the Yagan canoe Indians who used to inhabit these waters. In case it should prove impossible for a ship to reach the head of the fjord, and also to provide us with some degree of independent mobility at sea, I decided to take another Zodiac, similar to the one we had used on Lago San Martin two years before, and a ten horse power Evinrude motor. Both the boat and the motor were very kindly lent to me by the makers.

I reached Punta Arenas on 13 January 1962. My three companions were there to meet me, and we spent the next few days sorting out our stores and equipment which had just arrived from England, and which included a small wireless set. It is not my usual practice to take a radio on these expeditions. I grudge the weight and have always thought that in most emergencies a few pounds of extra food would be a greater asset. Also, in the event of the instrument failing to work, unnecessary alarm would be caused. On this occasion, however, I had been persuaded to take, at least as far as our landing-place, a small transmitter designed for sea rescue. With the help of the Naval signals officers in Punta Arenas we tested the machine and it was arranged that we should communicate with the Naval station on Dawson Island, halfway between Punta Arenas and Broken Bay, at 5.30 each evening while we were at our base. After that they would continue to listen for us at the same time each evening until we returned.

Admiral Balaresque had arranged for us to be taken to Broken Bay in the Naval Patrol Ship *Lientur*, and we set sail in the evening of 18 January. The admiral and his wife, whose son, Paul, was coming with us for the voyage, were at the quay to see us off.

By dawn the following day we were steaming up Admiralty Sound. A dismal scene greeted me as I came out on deck; mist hung low over the water, and the southern shore of the channel, though only half a mile away, was only just visible through the cold rain that was falling. Never at my best at 4 a.m., I felt profoundly depressed at the prospect of being left in this inhospitable land where, for all I knew, it might continue raining for the next six weeks. I returned below to cherish my last precious hours of warmth and comfort.

At seven o'clock *Lientur* entered Broken Bay. Her speed was reduced and soundings taken. The water became steadily shallower, and five miles from the entrance of the bay it was found to be only two fathoms deep. The captain could not risk going any further up the uncharted fjord, particularly in such poor visibility; so it was decided to put us ashore on the western side of the bay. We discovered later that the shallow water was caused by a reef of glacial moraine, and that the fjord beyond was very deep.

While our 800 pounds of baggage was being taken ashore in a lifeboat, we inflated and launched the Zodiac. Watched by most of the ship's company, I struggled for ten minutes to start the motor, until Paul Balaresque quietly drew my attention to the fact that I had connected the petrol feed pipe the wrong way round. After this convincing display of my inefficiency, we set off at high speed and overtook the ship's boat as it was entering the mouth of a small river which emerged from the dense forest along the shore. I had requested the admiral to have us picked up on 5 March and it was now arranged that his place (which we called Ship Creek) should be our rendezvous.

We were still fifteen miles from our destination at the head of the fjord. Though it was still raining, there was no wind, and we decided to take advantage of the calm water and start immediately. As we were loading our stores and equipment into the Zodiac we heard three farewell hoots from *Lientur*, and watched her disappear into the mist, leaving us alone in the silent world.

At ten o'clock we pushed the heavily laden Zodiac out of the creek and headed on up the fjord. As we started the motor, a sea lion popped his whiskered head out of the water a few yards from the shore, looking like an old man of the sea, and gave a hoarse, irritable grunt. Negotiating the reef, we had to be careful to avoid dense masses of seaweed marking the submerged rocks which seemed to extend right across the fjord; but in the clear water beyond we cruised at a steady four knots.

Presently it stopped raining and the mist cleared, forming horizontal strands of cloud which lent an enchanting aura of mystery to the scene. To starboard, at the far end of a wide gulf, a vast glacier, also swathed in cloud-banks, swept down to the water on a wide front. Above it there was a silvery glint which came from the unseen snow peaks. It was thrilling to find my lifelong imaginings of this fabulous land so closely reproduced in reality.

Hundreds of black and white ducks rose from the water at our approach; apart from some steamer ducks and an occasional cormorant they were the only kind of waterfowl we saw. We encountered several pairs of dolphins, which played about us with the enormous zest of their kind. Though they came within inches of the boat, they never touched it.

The weather continued to clear; soon the sun came out, and one by one the great peaks appeared, floating incredibly high above the mist which still clung to the sombre forest on either shore. By 2.30, as we were approaching the head of the fjord, the last vestige of cloud had vanished. We landed at a point where the channel made a sharp turn to the west into an almost landlocked lagoon surrounded by a cirque of glaciers and mountains rising abruptly to 7,500 feet. The glass-smooth water of the lagoon was sprinkled with blocks of floating ice, calved from three great glacier fronts along its shore.

What an incredible contrast it was from the dreary scene of a few hours before! Standing on the shore gazing across at that glorious cirque, the warm sun caressing my naked shoulders, I felt that whatever the Darwin Range had in store for us this introduction was enough to make the whole venture worth while.

We spent the hot afternoon lazily sorting out the food and equipment to be taken with us, and stowing the boat and surplus gear in the forest. We had brought supplies to last for forty-five days; three days' food was left in the dump, and the rest was to be taken with us. Camp 1 was pitched in a meadow beside a river.

When we went to bed the sky was still perfectly clear. However, experience had taught us to expect nothing of the weather, and we were not surprised the next morning to find that it had broken. In mist and rain we began the task of carrying our loads, in three relays, up into the mountains. Our choice of a landing place had been perfect; indeed any other would have cost us weeks of extra toil. As it was we found our way over a 3,000-foot pass on to the upper basin of the Marinelli Glacier which flows fifteen miles northward into Ainsworth Bay, and is probably the longest in the whole range. In six days we had established an advanced base (Camp 3) with all the loads, at the head of this great glacier.

We avoided the worst of the forest by climbing 800 feet up a rock ramp left by the shrinkage of a small glacier which came steeply down almost to the sea-shore at Camp 1. From Camp 2, in a wide grassy combe at the upper edge of the forest, we looked down over the treetops and a tumbling icefall to the lagoon 1,500 feet below, and across to the tremendous cirque of mountains surrounding it. In fair weather or in foul it was one of the loveliest places I have ever seen.

During most of this time the weather was bad; but the morning of 25 January, when we reached the pass with the first relay, was brilliantly fine and we were greeted by a splendid view of the whole length and breadth of the Marinelli Glacier and the scores of peaks surrounding it, including a lovely mountain standing above Parry Fjord which de Agostini had named 'Luis de Savoya'.

One of our chief purposes was to examine the geological structure of the range, and to make a collection of rock samples from appropriate places. This would best be served by crossing the range to the Beagle Channel. We had also set ourselves two other objectives: to climb the highest peak in the range and Luis de Savoya. In view of the predominance of foul weather we knew we must expect, this seemed a fairly ambitious programme. We would probably have been satisfied with the accomplishment of any one of our three objectives, and we scarcely hoped to achieve all three.

Our radio proved a complete failure. In normal conditions the station on Dawson Island should have been well within its range; but, presumably because of the high mountains surrounding us, we had failed to make ourselves heard from Camp 1. So we had reluctantly decided to hump the wretched machine, which weighed twenty pounds., to Camp 2, hoping that we would have more success from a greater altitude. Again we failed, so we carried it on over the pass to Camp 3. But even there, at 3,000 feet, we could not establish contact. We had with us a small transistor set with which we could hear both Dawson Island and Punta Arenas calling us. Our silence seemed to be causing them increasing concern. Night after night while we were on the glacier, we heard them telling us to light fires, one if we were all right and two if we were in trouble. Presumably the idea was to send a plane to spot for the fires; but by then, of course, we had no means of complying with their request. Later, on two or three occasions, we were told that planes were being sent out the next day to look for us, and that we were to place ourselves in a conspicuous position; no easy thing to do among the towering mountains surrounding us. Anyway we did not see or hear anything of the planes.

On some Chilean maps of the area the name 'Cerro Darwin' is applied to a peak standing above the Beagle Channel, presumably because it is the most prominent seen from that direction. So far we had not identified the highest mountain in the range, but we knew that it was one of a group of peaks at the head of the Marinelli Glacier. As it was obviously more appropriate that this should bear the name, we had decided to call it Mount Darwin.

Camp 3 was close to the northern side of the group, and we decided first of all to concentrate upon an attempt to climb this peak. The only direct approach to the group lay up a 2,000-foot icefall, not unlike the Khombu Icefall on Everest. It looked so broken and complicated, however, that we did not fancy tackling it, heavily laden and in foul weather. The alternative was to make a long detour to the west in the hope of finding an easier line of approach. As we also hoped to find a route across the range in that direction, we decided to take three weeks' food with us.

On 26 January we started carrying our loads up another icefall. Using skis partly as a protection against falling into crevasses, we reached a broad snow ridge above the junction of two glaciers. There on the 29th we established Camp 4 (5,000 feet). The weather was continuously bad, our tracks were covered by wind and drifting snow almost as soon as we had made them, and our chief concern was to avoid losing our way among the crevasses. Nor, when they were hidden, was it very easy to determine in which direction they were running, and we had to be very careful to ensure that we were not all standing over the same crevasse at the same time. However, we only had one minor mishap, when Eduardo, who was in the lead, suddenly disappeared. Fortunately Cedomir was holding him on a tight rope and he did not drop far; for, as we found, it is much more difficult to extract a man from a crevasse when he is wearing skis.

From Camp 4, where we were held up for a day by a particularly severe tempest, we had to turn southwards to reach our objective. In a brief clearing, we saw in that direction a small saddle, 3,000 feet above us, accessible by way of a steep slope of what appeared to be wind-polished ice. Leaving a dump of twelve days' food, with the skis stuck upright in the snow to mark the spot, we set towards it. We had brought the light tent with us with the intention of using it for an attempt on Mount Darwin. But now that we were actually confronted with the prospect of facing the weather with such meagre protection, the prospect was so repulsive that we had no hesitation in leaving it behind, and accepting the burden of the pyramid, even though this meant that we still had to carry in two relays. The ice slope was less steep than it appeared from below, but even so the pyramid proved an awkward load; soaking wet and encrusted with frozen snow it must have weighed eighty pounds.

The saddle was more than 8,000 feet high, only a few hundred feet below the highest summits of the range. We reached it with the second relay at 5.30 p.m. on 1 February. A short while before the clouds had vanished, and we found ourselves looking eastward across a deep glacier combe, on the opposite side of which was the highest peak of the group, our Mount Darwin. We were delighted to see that there was a feasible route down to the floor of the combe, and from there up to the western face of the mountain.

The two other high peaks of the group flanked the head of the combe; we called them Darwin II and III. The latter stood directly above the saddle, and Cedomir suggested that we should climb it there and then. As we had already done a hard day's work and had eaten nothing since breakfast, I reacted strongly against the idea. But the clear weather was such a rare occurrence, and it would probably not last for more than a few hours, that it seemed a pity to miss the chance of climbing our first peak. So we hurriedly pitched the tent on a ledge beneath a huge, overhanging ice-cliff, and set off.

No sooner had we started climbing up the ice ridge towards the peak than my fatigue and hunger vanished in the joy of unfettered movement, of the clear, cold air about me and of the rapidly expanding scene. We reached the summit as the sun was setting in a blaze of colour. East and west our view extended over the whole extent of the range, and southward far across the snow-capped islands beyond the Beagle Channel. In the long summer twilight we had plenty of time to return to our camp. The fine spell was indeed short-lived. That night there was a very heavy storm, from which the ice-cliff gave us very little protection. In the general confusion a bag containing two days' rations was blown away.

Descending 2,200 feet to the valley below we pitched camp at the western foot of Mount Darwin. Well protected by the high mountains surrounding it, the place seemed at first so peaceful after the storms to which we had been exposed that I called it the 'Silent Combe'. Though it did not always live up to this name, it was on the whole a pleasant spot. We reduced our food ration by one third and settled down to a ten-day siege. But the weather was liable to change at any moment, and we had to be ready to take advantage of any clearing.

The morning of 4 February, though by no means fine, was at least compara-tively calm; so we started up towards the summit, now some 3,000 feet above us, intending to reconnoitre the route, and to flag crucial sections. We encoun-tered no great difficulty and succeeded in reaching the summit ridge, from which we looked down the sheer eastern face of the mountain into a boiling cauldron of cloud.

Our chance came the next morning, for the peak was clear and although it was blowing fairly hard the wind was not excessive. Helped by our step cutting and route finding of the day before, we climbed very fast and reached the top with five minutes to spare before it was once more enveloped in dense cloud. The deep contentment which came with the accomplishment of our first objective was enhanced that evening by the resumption of full rations.

20 'The Uttermost Part of the Earth'

On 6 February we climbed Darwin II. Though the day was cloudless, a tremendous wind was now sweeping across the range from the south-west. As we were climbing the northern side of the mountain, however, we were largely protected from it until we were within 300 feet of the summit. Fortunately we were then on easy ground, for when we met the full force of the gale we were unable to stand and had to crawl forward on hands and knees, digging the picks of our ice axes into the wind-packed snow. At one point, a large chunk of granite hurtled past Cedomir's head and buried itself in the snow a few feet ahead. It was hard to imagine where it came from, for we were near the top of the peak and there were no rocks in the vicinity. Cedomir added it to his collection, more for its sentimental than its scientific interest.

The actual summit was a pillar of ice, twelve feet high, and we each climbed it in turn while the others huddled on the lee side. We then descended to an ice plateau to the west from where we saw a large section of the southern side of the range, which was a great help in planning our crossing to the Beagle Channel. When we got back to the Silent Combe we were wet through from head to foot as though we had been standing under a hose for some hours.

On the 7th we recrossed the saddle in mild weather, and on the following day pitched camp on a high pass on the main divide. From there we had to return to the dump at Camp 4 for more supplies. The pass was so wide and flat that there was some danger, if the weather was bad, of our missing the tent on the way back, for our tracks were obliterated almost as soon as they had been made. So we laid out a line of ski sticks, placed fifty yards apart, on a compass bearing at right angles to our line of march.

The weather was constantly changing, and although fine spells were usually brief, they were much more frequent than they had been on the ice cap the year before. When they occurred, particularly in the early morning and evening, they brought to our surroundings that delicate colouring, that ethereal texture captured by Edward Wilson's paintings of the Antarctic.

We now had to cross a wide plateau to the west; so we had brought two pairs of skis from the dump, with which we constructed a sledge, as we preferred to drag our loads than to carry them. Most of the way we were in thick mist and had to find our way by compass, but on the 11th we descended below the cloud level and reached a high ridge running southward between two inlets from the Beagle Channel, nearly 4,000 feet below.

There was such a feeling of pleasurable excitement in the camp the next morning, that even breakfast seemed quite festive. At seven o'clock, leaving the tent standing, we set off with cries of '*A la plage*' from my companions.

A swift glissade down a wide snow gully and a scramble down a series of cliffs brought us into a wide amphitheatre of gently sloping meadows sprinkled with white and yellow flowers. The surrounding precipices disappearing into the cloud, isolated us from the frozen world above. The sun broke through and the warm air was heavy with delicious scents. Even the struggle through the dense forest did not spoil the magic of the transformation. At 10.30 we reached the shore at a point where a large glacier flowed into the bay.

We allowed ourselves four hours on the shore before starting back a different way. By following the bed of a stream we penetrated the forest belt easily, but above this we were faced by a line of crags where we became involved in three hours of difficult rock climbing. As a result it was almost dark before we reached the camp.

On the return journey to our base on the Marinelli Glacier, though we had one fine day, the weather was extremely bad, with powerful winds and exceptionally heavy snowfalls, which made the going very laborious. For two days we were unable to move, and again we reduced our ration to conserve our food supplies. When, on the 19th, we reached Camp 4, we found that the dump was buried by six feet of fresh snow. As a precaution against this eventuality we had fixed its position by compass bearings to surrounding objects, but even so we had to dig and probe for two hours before finding the tip of one of the upright skis.

We were afraid that our main depot at Camp 3 might have been similarly buried, for if so it would have been almost impossible to find, situated as it was on a flat, featureless expanse of snow at the head of the Marinelli Glacier.

Fortunately we had planted the twelve-foot aluminium wireless mast to mark the spot, and when we reached it the next day, we found that, although the mast had been snapped by the wind, it was still protruding above the surface. So perhaps the radio had been worth bringing after all!

We reckoned that we would have to start back on 28 February at the latest, so as to reach Ship Creek by 5 March. This meant that we had seven days left to achieve our final objective, the ascent of Luis de Savoya.

On the 21st, after a long haul across the huge upper basin of the Marinelli Glacier, and a climb up a small icefall, we reached, late in the evening, what seemed to be a sheltered hollow at the foot of one of the granite buttresses of the mountain. Above us was a second icefall, and we had intended to carry our camp up this the next day, so as to get close enough to the top to reach it in a short spell of fine weather. However, that very evening the weather cleared and we decided to attempt the summit the next day if it was still fine.

Hitherto, fine evenings had always been followed by bad days, but when I awoke just before three o'clock the next morning and looked outside the tent, I saw the moon shining in a clear sky. I roused the others and we made a hasty breakfast. Though it was freezing hard, the snow had a breakable crust which made the going heavy. In spite of this we climbed rapidly, and achieved 1,000 feet in the first hour. Already the view had expanded over the mountains behind us. Sixty miles away stood the lovely spire of Sarmiento, ghostly white against the dark-blue shadows of the western sky; nearer at hand, the icy ramparts of Mount Darwin were already lit by the first rays of the rising sun.

We were now faced by a series of enormous crevasses which stretched right across the steep glacier, backed by vertical or overhanging walls. Each in turn seemed to present an impassable barrier; but each time the lucky chance of a slender snow bridge and a crack in the wall beyond enabled us to overcome the obstacle. The most difficult of the walls (led by Eduardo) took an hour and a half to surmount. Though it was inevitable, I found myself becoming increasingly impatient of the delay, for I could hardly believe that the fine weather would last much longer. Moreover, it was now obvious that we would not be able to carry our camp up this difficult icefall, and this might well be our last chance to climb the peak. However, when at last we reached the top of the icefall the sky was still cloudless and there was no wind.

After climbing a long slope of soft snow, we reached the crest of a steep ridge of hard ice. From there we looked straight down 7,000 feet to the blue waters of Parry Fjord and the dark-green forest surrounding it. At the top of the ridge there was a bulging wall of ice, which seemed to extend right across the upper face of the mountain. Traversing downwards to the left, however, we found a gangway leading to a col on the summit ridge, between two bosses which looked like giant cauliflowers. We chose the right-hand one, as it seemed to be the easier to climb, but when we reached the top we found that the other was a few feet higher. From where we stood the latter appeared to be overhanging on all sides; but having returned to the col and made our way round behind, we found a way of climbing it. We reached the summit at 12.30.

It had been an exciting climb, not because it was particularly difficult, but because the issue had been in doubt until the very last moment; and once again we were just in time, for the cloud had started to form about the highest peaks of the range, though this did nothing to detract from the splendour of the view. But we did not have long to admire it, for ten minutes later we ourselves were swathed in mist.

My companions were keen to change the name of the peak to one of local application. I suggested Cerro Yagan and we decided to adopt the name.

The descent was uneventful. There was still no wind and we could afford to take our time, and savour to the full the blissful sense of relaxation following the urgency of the past few hours. We were tired when we got back to camp and were looking forward to a long lie-in the next morning. But this was not to be. Around midnight I awoke to find a storm of unusual violence raging. The wind was coming at us in intermittent gusts, funnelled through the trough we were in, which continued to increase in force. At three o'clock I crawled outside to check the guys. Soon after 4.30, when it was quite light, the tent collapsed over our heads. We thought that two of the poles had snapped, but we discovered later that one side of the tent had been driven four feet into the hard-packed snow beneath. In the pandemonium of madly flapping canvas we managed to put on our boots and windproof suits and to collect our belongings. Then I crawled outside, stood up, and was immediately blown flat, while my balaclava was whipped off my head and disappeared, flying high over the rim of the icefall.

Our activities during the next two hours must have resembled one of those slapstick comedies of the old silent films. As we struggled to dismantle the tent and pack the loads, we were constantly being hurled to the ground. Cedomir's pack, weighing nearly fifty pounds, was swept away and fell into a crevasse 200 yards off. Fortunately it lodged on a ledge twenty feet down and, by lowering Cedomir on the climbing rope, we were able to recover it. Pancho's pack started on a similar escapade but he intercepted it with a neat rugger tackle. When at last we were ready, we started off, reeling and falling like drunks. Matters improved on the icefall which was comparatively sheltered, and although crossing the Marinelli Glacier we were again exposed to the wind, it blew steadily and not in those devastating gusts. Looking back at Cerro Yagan, seeing huge clouds of snow blowing off its flanks and hearing the roar of the wind among its ridges and corries, we were devoutly thankful not to be on the mountain in such conditions.

We had decided the night before to start back at once. We still had four days in hand; but Cedomir thought that he could most profitably spend the time examining the geology along the fjord. Also I had been asked by the British Museum to make a collection of *Collembola* from forest litter, and this would give me the opportunity of doing so. Moreover, we were all more than satisfied with the accomplishment of our three main objectives, and the prospect of some days of comparative idleness along those wooded shores made a powerful appeal.

That very evening we crossed the pass and reached the head of the valley leading down to the fjord, where we camped for the last time on the glacier, completely sheltered from that infernal wind. As we were cooking supper, a tiny owl flew in through the open door, flapped once around the tent and went out again to perch on the snow four feet away. There he sat for a quarter of an hour, gazing at us with his round, unblinking eyes. He was hardly bigger than a sparrow. It is hard to imagine what brought him up on the glacier, except, perhaps, sheer curiosity.

At 10.30 the next morning we reached Camp 2 in warm, sunny weather; and there we spent the rest of the day in idleness. If we had thought it a lovely place before, it seemed exquisitely beautiful now, with the meadows around the camp full of wild flowers, the peaks and glaciers of the cirque framed by a tracery of fresh green leaves and mirrored in the placid lagoon below. Once again our starved senses were ecstatically aware of the colour and the scents and the life around us.

On 25 February we reached the shore at Camp 1, and in the halcyon days that followed we cruised slowly down the fjord, stopping at one or other of the scores of charming little bays we passed, basking in the sun, diving into the icy water to fish for edible crabs among the forests of seaweed in the clear, deep pools at low tide, eating enormous quantities of mussels and sea urchins and lying beside campfires under the starlit sky. All this time the incredible spell of fine weather lasted, and every day the ice peaks of the Darwin Range were clear, reminding us of our newly won possessions.

On the 27th we made our first and only radio contact with Dawson Island. The Naval Headquarters in Punta Arenas were immediately informed and they came back with the message that a ship would soon be sent to pick us up. This news was not altogether welcome, for it looked as though our lotus eating was to be curtailed by several days. As it turned out, however, it was perhaps fortunate that we made that one contact; for about this time it was reported in several newspapers throughout the world that we were missing. How this story originated we never discovered; the Chilean Naval Authorities were certainly not responsible.

At 5.30 on 2 March, as we were settling down in our camp at Ship Creek after another glorious day, we picked up a message from Dawson Island on the transistor radio to the effect that the patrol ship *Cabrales* had set out from Punta Arenas two days before to look for us, and asking us to light a fire beacon to guide her. We were extremely puzzled by this, and a bit disturbed; for the whereabouts of Ship Creek was known to the authorities and we could hardly have failed to notice a ship entering Broken Bay, even if she had not hooted or fired a gun to announce her arrival.

We hastily packed the camp, loaded the Zodiac and raced to the prominent headland farther along the shore. There, on a hilltop, we built a huge fire of driftwood, well soused with paraffin. We had just got it well alight, the flames leaping fifteen feet high, when Cedomir spotted a tiny object, apparently going past the entrance of the bay. Sure enough it was the ship: while we watched, we saw her alter course towards us and presently we heard the faint sound of her siren. We scrambled down the hill to the Zodiac and set off at full speed in the gathering dusk.

When we reached *Cabrales* and had been hauled aboard, we went forward to meet her commander. We were delighted to find that he was an old friend,

Commander Rebolledo, who had been second in command of *Covadonga* when she had taken us to the Baker Channel the year before. Apparently he had not realised that we had a boat with us, and was very surprised when he caught sight of us, speeding towards him through the gloom. He told us that he had in fact left Punta Arenas two days before, but that he had had another assignment to discharge before coming to Broken Bay. Either we had misunderstood the message that we had picked up a few hours earlier, or it had been wrongly transmitted from Dawson Island.

The ship had turned and was now gliding through the dark silence towards the entrance of the bay. Astern we saw our fire still blazing on the now invisible headland. Beyond, between the black-forested shores of the fjord, the mountains showed as a faint glow in the southern sky.

ADDENDA I Further Travels in Patagonia and Tierra del Fuego

First published in the *Alpine Journal*, Vol. LXVIII, November 1963, No. 307

1. MOUNT BURNEY[1]

Mount Burney has often been referred to in scientific journals as the most southerly active volcano in South America. This belief was based on a somewhat vague report that in 1910 it was seen erupting. Some specimens of andesite lava had been collected from its western foot, near the shores of Mayne Channel; but apart from this little was known about the mountain, though it is often seen from ships passing through the channels.

In March, 1962, Marangunic and I attempted to reach it from the south-west. Lack of time and the difficulty of the terrain prevented our doing so; but the country we passed through was so attractive and our one glimpse of the mountain from ten miles away so intriguing, that I decided to devote the first part of my expedition this year to a further investigation of the area. This time John Earle came with me from England, and we were joined by Jack Ewer in Punta Arenas, where we arrived on 5 January.

The easiest approaches to Mount Burney would be from the shores of Mayne Channel or Union Sound which bound the Munos Gamero Peninsula on the north-west and north respectively. But either of these would require sea transport, and although the Chilean Navy would have been willing to take us there as well as to the Beagle Channel later, there was no ship immediately available, and in any case I did not want to make too many demands on their hospitality. Besides this, I was anxious to explore the lakes we had discovered the previous year. So we decided again to approach the mountain from the south-west through the heart of the Munos Gamero peninsula. Once again I had brought a Zodiac inflatable craft and a ten horse power Evinrude outboard motor.

We set out from Estancia Skyring on 9 January, the Zodiac laden with a month's provisions and forty gallons of petrol, and sailed along the coast to the neck of a mountainous peninsula which stretches twelve miles out into

---

1 The mountain was climbed in 1973 by Shipton, Roger Perry and Pete Ratcliffe.

Skyring Sound. At this point we were met by a *peon*, whom Mr Friedli had very kindly sent from the *estancia* with four packhorses; with the help of these we carried the boat and our baggage across the isthmus the following day in two relays. By this manoeuvre we avoided making the westward passage of Punta Laura at the end of the peninsula which, in a small boat in rough weather, is a difficult and somewhat hazardous operation.

Late in the evening of the 11th, after a stormy voyage, we reached the Passo del Indio, a narrow isthmus separating the north-western corner of Skyring Sound from the system of freshwater lakes occupying a large part of the Munos Gamero peninsula. It used to be crossed by the Alacaluf Indians to get their boats from Obstruction Sound to the southern channels. So far as I know, no one but the Alacaluf had crossed the isthmus until we did so last year. Indeed I am far from sure that we found the real 'Passo'; for the terrain is exceedingly complicated, and although it has been plotted from aerial pictures, the map is inaccurate. The following morning it took us six hours to carry our baggage across the isthmus. The boat, of course, gave us the most trouble; for, even with the wooden floor boards removed, it weighed nearly 150 pounds, and was so bulky that it made an awkward load on a pack frame.

In the afternoon when the voyage was resumed, the weather was calm, and we enjoyed a delightful cruise through the network of channels forming the eastern part of the lake system; past innumerable islets, like green, floating pin cushions, and along forested shores, backed by sweeping mountain land-scapes. From the water, the country looked gentle and friendly; but, then as before, it gave me a strange sense of loneliness, due no doubt to the knowledge that it was completely devoid of human habitation, and that for all its beauty, it was in fact far from kind. It would be horribly difficult to travel there without a boat.

By seven o'clock we had entered a narrow passage leading into the main lake. We had just selected a cove in which to spend the night, when the motor stopped and refused to start again; so we had to row ashore. This was the only time we experienced trouble with the motor, and it could not have happened at a more fortunate moment; on a calm evening, close to a good landing place. Had it occurred in the normal rough weather we might have found ourselves in an awkward situation. The next morning a strong southerly wind was blow-ing straight into our cove. We made repeated efforts to launch the Zodiac, but each time it was beaten back to the shore and swamped. So we spent the day in idleness, cursing our foolish choice of a camp site. However, at 8 p.m., while we were eating our supper, the wind dropped slightly; so we hurriedly packed up, and this time we succeeded in getting the boat through the breakers and the motor started. It was dark when, after another rough passage, we reached the western side of the main lake. The next morning we had an easy run along the lee shore to its northern extremity.

Our next task was to carry the boat and our gear to the new lakes we had found last year. I knew that the distance to the nearest point was not great, but I had no idea what the going would be like. If it had been dense forest all the way, it would have been a very long and laborious job. But we were delighted to find a long rocky spur, with open ground along its crest, which offered such easy going that in a day and a half we had completed the carry. On the next bit of the voyage we were forced to go so far westward that, with the mountains closing in on either side, I began to fear that I had been mistaken in thinking that the new lakes were interconnected, and that yet another and far more difficult portage would be necessary. However, at the last moment, a channel opened to starboard and we sailed through to the biggest of the lakes. The northern shore of this marked the end of our voyage; there we made our base in surroundings which, apart from the glaciers, might well have been in the Scottish Highlands.

On the 16th we set out across a great plain which we had seen last year stretching northward to the coast. It was largely devoid of forest and, as we had rightly inferred from this, it was very swampy. Marangunic had thought that it might have been formed by huge deposits of volcanic ash filling a wide channel which had once connected the lakes with the sea; but the swamp and the deep beds of peat made it difficult to obtain much evidence to support this theory.

We started with eighteen days' food, and our normal equipment was augmented by two cine cameras and some 3,000 feet of film, as part of John's object in joining the expedition was to make a film record of it. Thus we had too much to carry at once and we had to relay. Because of the swampy nature of the ground, the going on the plain was laborious and unpleasant; but on the second day we reached the south-easterly spurs of Mount Burney which were heavily forested. That evening we camped amid the most glorious surroundings, in a wide basin formed by the East face of the mountain and a range of wooded foothills, and filled with a lovely mixture of glacier, forest, lakes and meadows, some of which were richly strewn with wild flowers.

We were now faced with the problem familiar to most of us in a bad Alpine season; whether to wait for a chance to climb our peak, or to keep moving and to risk missing such a chance. The upper part of Mount Burney was hidden in cloud; but there seemed to be a way of reaching it up the south-east ridge. If our sole object had been to climb the mountain, we would no doubt have taken a camp up this ridge and waited for a clearing. Our main purpose, however, was to explore as much of the mountain and surrounding country as possible; so we decided to concentrate on making a journey right round the mountain, hoping that any spell of fine weather that might occur would find us in a position to make the ascent. As it turned out, this was the right decision, for not once during the sixteen days that it took us to make the tour did the weather clear.

At first the way led us over a wide ice-sheet, and thereafter across a long series of ridges and combes, many of which contained glaciers. The cloud ceiling usually remained around 2,500 or 3,000 feet and, as for the most part we were travelling slightly below this level, we had a series of fine views over the channels flanking the peninsula on the north and north-west. Our camps were usually pleasantly sited near the upper edge of the forest. The weather was generally what one might expect in a bad summer in the Lake District, though colder, and occasionally we experienced severe gales.

We kept close under the faces of the mountain; those not covered with ice seemed to be composed entirely of tuff; some of them were most spectacular. We found very few outcrops of andesite lava, though the moraines were largely composed of this material. So far as we could judge, the area covered by the volcano and its subsidiary cones, is about twenty-four miles in circumference. We found no evidence of recent activity.

Eventually we reached the south-eastern combe of the mountain. This was the side of Burney that I had seen last year and, although this time we could not see the peaks of the summit ridge, I was no less impressed by the splendid ice-face, which seemed to belong to a mountain of quite a different order of magnitude. The valley below was very beautiful; it was drained by a wide river which we followed through the forest to the plain, whence we reached the place where we had left the boat. We were then blessed by a spell of milder weather, and the voyage back through the lakes to Skyring was wholly delightful.

2. MOUNT BOVÉ

From the summits of the peaks we climbed in the Darwin Range of Tierra del Fuego last year, we saw the mountains lying at the eastern end of the penin-sula. They looked very fine, and we thought that two of them, Bové and Roncagli, might be as high as Mount Darwin itself, if not higher. Like the central part of the range, this group was largely unexplored, and I had decided to spend the second half of my expedition this year in the region, approaching it from the Beagle Channel.

When we returned to Punta Arenas from Mount Burney, John and I were joined by Peter Bruchhausen, who had been with me in Patagonia three years before, and Claudio Cortez, a medical student from Santiago. Once again the Chilean Navy had generously agreed to transport us to our chosen base, and on 12 February the four of us embarked on their ship *Cabrales*.

The voyage took us through a labyrinth of channels characteristic of the whole coastline of southern Chile. The following morning we passed close to Mount Sarmiento, a landmark well known to the early navigators of the Magellan Straits, and we saw its lovely ice-spring piercing the banks of cloud which hung low over the coast. For much of the day the scenery resembled the Western Isles of Scotland as, in the eastern part of the archipelago, the forest is sparse and confined to a few sheltered valleys. Early in the morning of the 14th, we were put ashore with a month's provisions in a little bay known as Olla.

Since dawn it had been raining heavily; the precipices flanking the Beagle Channel and the massive glaciers cascading down to the water's edge had presented a sombre spectacle. As soon as we landed, however, the weather cleared and the scene was transformed. Under a warm sun and a cloudless sky, Olla Bay was idyllic. A wide, sandy beach, backed by forest, stretched in a half-mile crescent around the turquoise water of the lagoon. The peace was only disturbed by the boisterous behaviour of a party of sea-lions further along the shore. The tide was low and we collected large quantities of mussels which we ate for breakfast. Then, resisting the temptation to linger in this lovely place, we started inland, carrying supplies for seven days.

Our chief objective was to climb Bové which, seen both from Mount Darwin and from the eastern end of the Beagle Channel, appeared to be the highest peak of the group. A few years ago an attempt had been made to reach it from the east by a party of Argentine mountaineers; they had failed largely because of the weather. De Agostini's party had landed at Olla Bay when they climbed Pico Italia. [2] A map of the area reproduced in his book, *Sfingi di Ghiaccio*, had led us to suppose that we could reach the western face of Bové from the head of the Italia glacier, and so, lacking any other information about the mountain, we decided to approach it from that direction.

Our way through the forest was made easy by well-worn guanaco tracks (later, on several occasions we encountered herds of these creatures on the high glacier moraines; they are, I believe, distant relatives of the camel); and at 7.30 that evening we camped on a ridge far above the treeline. Meanwhile, Peter, who had been lagging behind, and whom I had last seen only a couple of hundred feet below the camp, had disappeared. Getting no reply from our shouts, and thinking that he must have bypassed the camp, John and I set off up the ridge. It was almost dark and raining gently when we returned after a fruitless search. But a little later, shortly before 10.30, Claudio found Peter lying on a ledge quite close to the camp, recovering from a long attack of vomiting, during which he must have lost consciousness. Evidently he was allergic to mussels.

Two days later we reached the head of the Italia glacier. The weather was bad, but we saw enough to realise that there was no way of reaching Bové from that direction; so we returned to Olla Bay, loaded the Zodiac with our

---

2 In the *Alpine Journal*, 67. 259, I stated that this party had climbed Pico Francés as well as Pico Italia; this, however, is not the case.

baggage, and moved our base eastward along the coast. We had been fortunate only to waste four days in this abortive reconnaissance; for in the mountains of Tierra del Fuego, where for weeks on end the surrounding country may be shrouded in mist, or movement prevented by gales, route finding is apt to be a long and frustrating business.

Our second sortie was more successful; we found an excellent route into the range, and on 21 February we established a camp near the head of the Frances glacier at the southern foot of Bové. As we approached it, moreover, the weather cleared and we saw that there was a way of reaching the summit from that direction. This was a great relief, for it meant that we would thus be saved many days of further reconnaissance and load carrying. Later we discovered that any alternative approach would have been either impossible or a great deal more difficult. As it was, we had now only to sit tight and await a chance to climb the mountain, using any brief clearing of the weather to familiarise ourselves with the route so as to save time when such a chance occurred.

We found that there was a remarkable absence of névé even in the highest glacier basins and that the surfaces were nearly all composed of hard ice. Though, as a rule, this made it a lot easier to move around locally, it presented us with a considerable problem in pitching the tent securely on open glacier; indeed it would have been impossible to do so in a high wind. This factor would have prevented us from travelling as freely as we did last year. I suspect that such conditions are quite exceptional even so late in the season. We experienced some severe storms, and our pyramid tent suffered a tremendous battering. I know of no other type of tent that could have withstood such weather, and there were times when I doubted even its ability to do so.

At dawn on the 25th it was calm, but rain was falling heavily. However, this stopped by 9 a.m. and we set out, not expecting to get far, as the mountain was still wrapped in cloud. The lower part of the route led up a wide gully, a thousand feet high. We had already reconnoitred this and found it to be full of the debris of avalanches falling from a line of hanging glaciers. However, by climbing very steep ice on the left flank of the gully, we were able to avoid the danger, and eventually reached the crest of the West ridge of the mountain. Though there was little visibility, it was still calm and we sensed an improvement in the weather; so we went on.

The ridge was composed of a mounting series of huge ice bosses, like gigantic cauliflowers, poised on a narrow crest, overhanging on either side. One after another they loomed above us until, shortly before 3 p.m., we reached the top of the highest. To make sure that this was the summit of the peak, we continued along the ridge; but before we had gone far the curtain of mist in front of us parted, and we looked down a sheer drop of several thousand feet to a large glacier flowing eastward. A number of such clearings occurred while we were on the summit, which revealed the view in sections. The most exciting of these was to the north where we saw Roncagli standing above a group of fine granite spires. It seemed to be somewhat lower than Bové (whose height we estimated at 8,100 feet), but from this direction it looked a difficult mountain to climb.

We were fortunate to reach the summit when we did, for during the descent we were once again in thick cloud. Moreover, soon after we reached the camp the calm spell ended, and that night the roar of the wind and the racket of frozen drift lashing the walls of the tent emphasised our luck. But we were to have another break. On 1 March we climbed Pico Frances (7,900 feet) and, arriving at the summit at five o'clock on a perfect evening, we had a superb view of the whole range as far west as Mount Darwin, and eastward for seventy miles along the Beagle Channel. Though it was late and very cold, we stayed there for an hour and a half. Beyond the sparkling clusters of ice crystals, like veined leaves, characteristic of these summit ridges, we saw, far below, the coves of Devil's Island, green and blue in the warm sunlight.

Our return to the coast was hampered by foul weather. On one occasion during a storm shortly before leaving the glacier, I fell into a crevasse, where I remained for three-quarters of an hour until I and my load could be extricated. By then the wind was very violent and, blinded by drift and often knocked over by the more powerful gusts, we had a good deal of difficulty in moving on down.

Reaching our base with several days to spare before our rendezvous with the Chilean Navy on 15 March, we spent a pleasant time cruising about the channel visiting various sea-lion rookeries along the forested shores. One morning we met two ships of the Chilean Antarctic Flotilla. They stopped to investigate our strange craft, and Claudio, anxious to get home in time for his final examinations, took this unexpected opportunity of a lift back to Punta Arenas. The rest of us awaited the arrival of a small vessel, *Beagle*, which took us to Puerto Williams, a small naval base in the eastern part of the Beagle Channel.

ADDENDA II   Crossing the North Patagonian Ice Cap

First published in the *Alpine Journal*, Vol. LXIX, November 1964, No. 309

The crossing of the Hielo Patagonico del Norte was a natural sequel to our journey over the southern ice cap in 1960/1961. I knew that it would have to be done some time, but for two summers it was shelved in favour of the Fuegan mountains. We sometimes used to discuss it on that first journey and, on the few days that we were confined to our tent in the Darwin Range, Garcia used to pass the time by drawing us maps of the general layout of the region and discussing the problems of access and egress. For he had some personal knowledge of the area, having taken part in the sixteen-man Japanese-Chilean Expedition that, in 1958, had climbed Arenales, a mountain standing near its south-eastern edge. Though he had played a major part in pioneering the way and in the work of establishing the lower camps, he had been left out of the parties that reached the summit, which had naturally caused him keen disappointment. When I met him with Marangunic in Santiago in April 1963, they suggested that we should tackle the new crossing the following season.

The project involved much the same problems as we had met before; there was no reason to expect better weather conditions and, though the distance to be covered was not so long, the way would be more complicated because of several high passes that we would have to cross in the latter part of the journey. Also, after leaving the glaciers we would still have a long way to go before reaching habitation, and this meant that we would have to carry a rubber dinghy with us for crossing rivers and lakes. On the other hand an approach to the ice cap from the north-west was known: several parties had made their way up from Laguna San Rafael on the Pacific coast in their attempts on Mount San Valentin before that mountain was finally climbed in 1952.[1] In addition, García's knowledge of a route into the range from the south-east provided us with a line of escape. Our reasons for making the journey in that direction were the same as before: we would be travelling from an uninhabited region towards habitation, and with the prevailing wind.

---

1   See *A.J.* 59. 432.

We decided to start in November in the hope that we would find an abundance of winter snow which would both provide good conditions for sledging and cover the crevassed areas. An additional advantage was that my companions would return in time to spend part of their summer vacation with their families. I wrote to the Minister of Education and the Director of the Geological Institute in Santiago, to request their release a month before the end of the summer term, and received favourable replies from both. The fourth member of the party was recruited by García and Marangunic; he was a young Spaniard, Miguel Gomez, who had come three years before with a Spanish expedition to the Peruvian Andes, and had been in South America ever since. He proved an excellent choice; a first rate mountaineer, always cheerful and always ready to do the most unpleasant jobs and to carry the heaviest loads.

This time we took skis with us but, apart from these and the boat, I equipped the party in the same way as before. We had another collapsible fibreglass sledge, and a light wooden one. Our food, too, was much the same, though I increased the daily sugar ration from eight ounces to nine ounces per man. Our equipment and food were packed in a single wooden case, and shipped to Valparaiso. I joined my companions on 15 November in Santiago, where I found that the Air Force had made arrangements for our departure on the 21st.

Although we had obtained official permission to import our baggage free of duty, it was 19 November before Marangunic and I could go down to Valparaiso to claim it from the customs. Even then we had to negotiate a mass of formalities, and the issue remained in doubt until late that evening. The next morning in Santiago we opened the case and found that it had previously been broken open and a number of things stolen, including two pairs of climbing boots, two pairs of crampons, all our windproof trousers, most of our supply of tea and eight days' rations. As a result, we spent a busy day repairing our losses.

Once again we received invaluable assistance from the Chilean government. On the 21st we were flown in an Air Force 'Otter' to Puerto Montt, and the following morning we were provided with two 'Beachcraft' planes to take us from there to Puerto Aisen. As soon as we arrived, we called on Señor Atilio Cosmelli, the Governor of Aisen Province, who received us with charming courtesy and was kind enough to take a keen interest in our project. He had already arranged for our departure that very afternoon in a small motor vessel, *Devine*.

The voyage through the channels from Puerto Aisen to Laguna San Rafael should have taken a day and a half. Unfortunately, at about noon on the 23rd, when we were still some seven hours' sailing from our destination, *Devine's* transmission shaft snapped. Luckily, the wind, which had been strong throughout most of the morning, had subsided, and the crew of three, with the aid of the dinghy and a small outboard motor, were able to tow the helpless vessel to a nearby island, where she was made fast to some overhanging trees.

Luckily, too, *Devine* carried a radio, and the captain was able to send a message to Aisen informing the Governor of our plight. He immediately despatched a privately owned vessel, *Alicia*, to our rescue, which reached us late in the evening of the 24th. We spent much of the intervening time catching fish, which was useful as we were already living on expedition rations.

The crew of *Alicia* were under the impression that they had been sent to fetch us back to Aisen. However, after a strenuous discussion, in which our cause was championed by the captain of *Devine*, and a further exchange of radio messages with Aisen, they agreed to take us on. These negotiations resulted in a late start in the morning of the 25th, and as *Alicia* could only make five knots it was nearly 5 p.m. before we reached the mouth of the Rio Tempanos, the narrow five-mile channel leading to Languna San Rafael. The crew of *Alicia* said that they had been told in no circumstances to attempt the passage of this channel, and they proposed to land us near its mouth.

Although this was only some ten miles from the San Rafael glacier, the country between was composed of swamp and dense forest, and it would have taken us at least a week to reach it with all our gear, and probably a great deal longer. This would have seriously upset our timetable and left us short of food for the journey. Fortunately, largely due to the good offices of *Devine*'s captain, the crew once again yielded to our entreaties. On the ebb tide there was a strong current running against us through the channel, carrying with it a number of large icebergs. However, we made the passage without mishap and at eight o'clock we were put ashore at the south-east corner of the lagoon.

In the 1920s an attempt had been made to dig a canal from the southern end of Laguna San Rafael to the channels leading to the Gulf of Penas with the purpose of providing shipping with a protected passage along that part of the coast. The project was abandoned because of the swampy nature of the ground. At the same time the government had built a large, three-storied hotel on the shore of the lagoon, at the point where we landed. The cost must have been enormous. Presumably the idea was to attract visitors to that remote and lonely spot; but apart from the spectacle of the San Rafael glacier, thrusting its ice-cliffs into the lagoon on a two-mile front, it would have offered few of the amenities required by the average tourist. The building was completed but never used, and there it stands, a bizarre object in that wild, uninhabited land. However, it provided us with welcome shelter from the heavy rain that persisted throughout the night.

Our satisfaction at having, after all, reached this place received a rude shock when we discovered that a kit-bag, containing the sledge harness, ski skins, priming fuel and several other important items, had been left on board. Though not disastrous, this loss darkened our horizon considerably. However, when we awoke at 5.30 the next morning, we were astonished to see *Alicia* approaching the shore. She had anchored near the upper entrance of the Rio

Tempanos, the passage of the channel being too dangerous to attempt in the dark; our kit-bag had been found and was now being returned. This action of the crew was most generous, considering that we had already put them to a great deal of extra trouble, and persuaded them to disobey the instructions of their owners. By it they had nothing to gain and a great deal to lose. They even refused any remuneration. Such kindness is typical of these people.

The glacier was still four kilometres away, across an alluvial plain. Previous parties had apparently had no difficulty in reaching it, but lately a river issuing from the near flank of the glacier had spread its delta over the plain, and we had to cross a series of meandering streams. This was not difficult with our rubber dinghy, but it took us two days to transport our baggage to the corner where the glacier emerged from the mountains. There, on the 27th we established our first camp on a raised beach, sheltered by cliffs and luxuriant forest, with provisions enough for forty-three days.

Unlike most Patagonian glaciers, the San Rafael has shrunk very little, and the ice presses close against the forest on the precipitous slopes flanking it. Though by no means steep, its whole surface is a chaotic mass of séracs and crevasses; so the only way up it was along the narrow trough between the forest and the glacier, though we were frequently forced on to the ice for long stretches, and the going was sometimes hard. For the first stage we carried the loads in four relays. Our second camp (1,200 feet) was pitched on an ice-platform among the séracs, as we could find no suitable ledge in the forest.

The second stage took us through to the upper basin of the glacier, and beyond our third camp (2,300 feet), which we established on 6 December, the going was easier. For the next five days we made our way eastward through a series of crevassed areas. We had hoped that so early in the summer these would be well covered; but the winter snowfall had evidently been exceptionally light and the crevasses were much more open than we had expected. Sometimes we used the small sledge, but mostly the going was too rough and we had to carry. Route finding was complicated, though luckily at this stage we were not much bothered by mist. Indeed during the first fortnight of the journey the weather, judged by Patagonian standards, was not at all bad; there was no severe wind and we had five fine days.

On 11 December we reached the plateau, and were then able to bring both sledges into operation. For two days, however, our progress was very slow, as we encountered several more badly crevassed areas. On the morning of the 13th, for example, after an uninterrupted run of an hour and a half, we suddenly found ourselves in the midst of a perfect maze of fissures, mostly concealed by a shallow covering of rotten snow. Though, of course, our skis were a great help in bridging the crevasses, it was difficult to determine their direction, and we had to exercise great care to avoid the risk of all of us falling into the same one. Moreover we were then in dense mist with visibility restricted to a few yards. However, this proved to be the last of these obstacles, and for the next five days we were able to steer a straight course, 10° east of south.

For two days the weather was bad and we marched mostly on a compass bearing; but though we experienced some discomfort from driving sleet and melting drift, which made us very wet, the wind was not severe, and by dawn on the 16th it was fine once more. For the next three days we travelled along a flat corridor ten miles wide, between two ranges of granite peaks, their exciting shapes, which reminded me very much of the Karakoram, constantly appearing and disappearing among banks of shifting cloud. These peaks offer a wonderful new field of mountaineering, for there are scores of them, and most will demand a very high standard of climbing. Moreover one of the ranges should not be too difficult of access from the east. With the sledges running easily over good snow, with plenty of time in between spells of pulling to sit in the warm sun, and enjoying these glorious surroundings, this part of the journey was sheer delight.

On the 18th we reached the foot of a col leading south-west across a northerly spur of the Arenales group. We had been lucky that the fine spell had enabled us to find it without difficulty, for that night the weather broke. On the 19th we were confined to our tent by a storm and, although the 20th was not much better, a temporary lull in the morning encouraged us to set out for the pass; and a few brief clearings later in the day enabled us to find a route and to carry half our loads to its crest. The rest were brought up the following day. We now entered a vast basin of glaciers which combine in a large ice-stream flowing southwards to the Baker Channel. Our objective was a depression in the range south of Arenales, which Garcia had seen from the east and which would lead us on to the route followed by his 1958 expedition; we called it the Arenales col. Crossing a second pass and keeping close under the main range, we reached the foot of it on the 24th.

It had been our intention to leave a dump at this point, and to go on with the small sledge carrying a week's provisions with the object of climbing two mountains, Pared Norte and Pared Sur, near the southern end of the range. But we were behind our schedule and, estimating the time that it would take to cross the col and reach habitation, with a reasonable allowance for delay by bad weather, we reckoned that we had only four days' food to spare and that this would hardly give us time to attempt either of the peaks. So we decided to go straight to the col, and use the time climbing from there. In fact events showed us to have been over cautious, particularly as during the next ten days we had some of the best weather of the whole trip.

Christmas morning was still and cloudless. We packed up the camp and started at 6.45 a.m., following a route that García and Gomez had reconnoitred the previous evening. There had been a sharp frost during the night (−11°C) and the snow was in perfect condition. Carrying fifty pounds each, we climbed 3,000 feet to the col (about 7,850 feet) in two hours and twenty minutes. Then, having deposited our loads on the broad snow-saddle, we set off at ten o'clock to climb Cerro Arco (9,950 feet), a mountain two miles away to the south. A powerful wind embarrassed us on the steep ice-slopes below the summit, but the weather remained clear and from the top we had a wonderful view of Arenales to the north, across the basin of the Rio Baker to Mount San Lorenzo, fifty miles away to the south-west, and over the great glaciers to the west. Pared Norte and Pared Sur, to the south, looked splendid, and we regretted that we were not to make their closer acquaintance. When we got back to the col we dug a pit in which we pitched the tent, and built a high snow wall round it for protection from the wind.

It was still clear early the next morning, but in the gaudy sunrise there were ominous signs that a storm was about to break. So, as we only had one more day's food with us, we raced down to the dump at the foot of the col, where we collected the remainder of our baggage, except for the small sledge which we decided to abandon. We were only just in time, for half an hour later the storm broke with considerable violence and everything was blotted out in mist and blinding drift. It would have been almost impossible to locate the dump in such conditions.

The snow was soft that day, which was lucky as it meant that our deep downward tracks survived the gale just long enough to guide us over the lower and most complicated section of the route. The upper section was more or less straight and we could follow a compass bearing. Even so I was very doubtful if we would manage to hit off the right part of the col and find the tent, largely hidden within its snow wall. The climb back to the col was most unpleasant, for we were soon soaked to the skin by melting drift driven against us with tremendous force, and we were often blown over by the more violent gusts. When, however, we reached the col, whether by luck or by accurate navigation we found the tent and wasted no time in scrambling through the entrance. The inside immediately became a shambles of sodden garments, slushy snow and pools of water, and we spent until ten o'clock that night drying out. The storm continued to rage until about that time, when it ceased as suddenly as it had begun.

When we awoke at five o'clock the next morning, it was very cold. Though the sun was shining, the weather again looked threatening, and we thought we were in for another storm: many of the peaks were capped by mushroom-shaped clouds and the distant views were suffused with an inky blue. We decided to move down to a wide combe, 400 feet below the col, at the southern foot of Arenales. The wet snow which had half buried the tent the day before had frozen into a solid block of ice; it was a long job digging this away, and we were not ready to start until 10.30. By then all the clouds had vanished and the day was gloriously fine.

García was keen to seize the opportunity of climbing Arenales (11,277 feet) which had been denied him on the Japanese expedition. So, though there were two other fine peaks within our reach, we decided to forgo the chance of another first ascent. We dragged the sledge down into the combe, and set off for the mountain shortly before eleven o'clock. It was a climb of 4,800 feet, but conditions were excellent and it was not difficult. A bitter south-westerly wind kept us moving fast and we reached the summit at 2.40. From there we had a superb view over the ice cap and the ranges to the north as far as San Valentin.

When we got back to the sledge, we went on down the combe so as to take advantage of the clear weather, as there seemed to be only one line through the crevasses, which would have been very difficult to find in bad visibility. The following day we made our way along a terrace between two formidable icefalls. García had warned us that the Japanese expedition had encountered great difficulty here, negotiating a series of immense crevasses. But that had been in March and we hoped that at the end of December we would have less trouble. Even so, the two-mile passage took us all day. The crevasses were among the largest I had ever seen; once again I was thankful we were equipped with skis, for some of the chasms were spanned only by the slenderest of bridges and the snow was soft. Beyond the terrace we had a short section of icefall to negotiate, followed by the descent of a 2,000 foot rock wall; but with García to guide us these obstacles presented no great difficulty, even in bad weather. After that we had some ten miles to go to the snout of the Colonia glacier, which we reached on 2 January.

Our final obstacle was Lago Colonia, some six miles long and flanked on both sides by steep precipices. The rubber dinghy, which had survived the journey without a single puncture, was too small to take us all with our luggage; in fact we would have had to make three relays. Except on rare occasions it would have been impossible to row the boat back against the prevailing westerly wind; moreover even in calm weather a strong wind was liable to spring up without warning. We therefore constructed a raft with our air mattresses and skis. This carried one man and the baggage, and was towed behind the dinghy which accommodated the rest of us. For oars we used snow-shovels fixed to the end of poles and, until it became too rough, an anorak was hoisted over each craft to serve as a sail.

At first it was relatively calm, but the wind and the waves increased as we went. We kept close to the precipitous southern shore, though there were few places where we could have landed. About half way, however, there was a small beach where we put in for some refreshment. The second part of the voyage was most exciting, for it was very rough. However we managed to maintain our direction and eventually we reached the far end of the lake, where we were hurled unceremoniously ashore by the breakers. There we lit a mighty fire, to dry ourselves and to celebrate the end of our journey.

Two or three miles beyond the end of the lake we found some untenanted houses, and we had to go another ten miles down the Rio Colonia before we reached a small farm where we could hire some pack ponies. For the next few days we marched in comfort and deep contentment along broad valleys flanked by snow peaks, through mile upon mile of green meadows and woods where wild strawberries abounded. The sun shone and the air was clear and still. Always we met with the same generous hospitality and kindness, which is everywhere to be found in Patagonia; always we were fed, housed, provided with transport and accompanied on the next stage; payment for these services, if it was accepted at all, was a secondary consideration and not even the poorest people seemed to expect it.

We crossed the Rio Baker, a noble river as wide as the Danube at Budapest, below its junction with the Rio Colonia. From there we marched to the Rio Cochrane, another tributary of the Baker, where there was a *gendarmerie* post with a radio station. A message was transmitted to the Air Force post at Balmacera, and a few hours later a Beachcraft arrived to collect us.

The journey had gone remarkably smoothly. This was very largely due to the skill and efficiency of my companions, for much of the detailed planning, particularly in the field, was theirs. Normally, I believe, this part of Patagonia is not more favoured by fine weather than the parts further south. If this is the case, we were extremely lucky; in the six weeks occupied by the crossing we had fifteen fine days; the good spells occurred when we most needed them and the bad spells were comparatively short and rarely severe. Altogether it had been a glorious trip, full of variety, through some of the loveliest mountain country I have seen in Patagonia or anywhere else. The region still offers wide scope for those who enjoy untravelled ground; for mountaineers it is an almost untouched field.[2]

---

2 The general location of the area described is latitude 47° S., longitude 73° E.

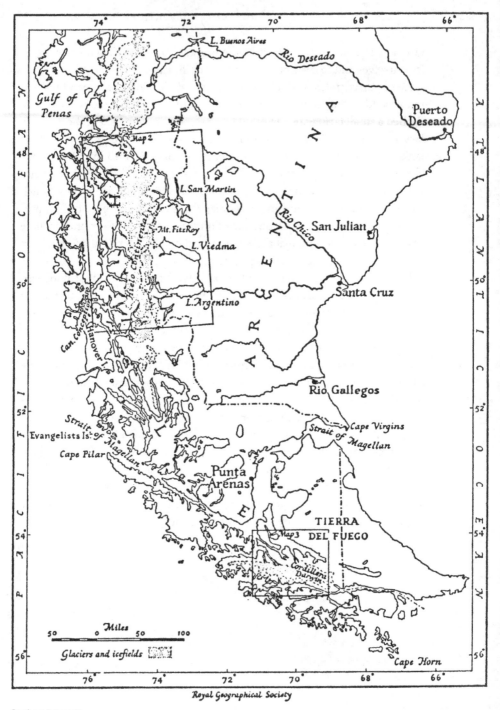

Southern Patagonia

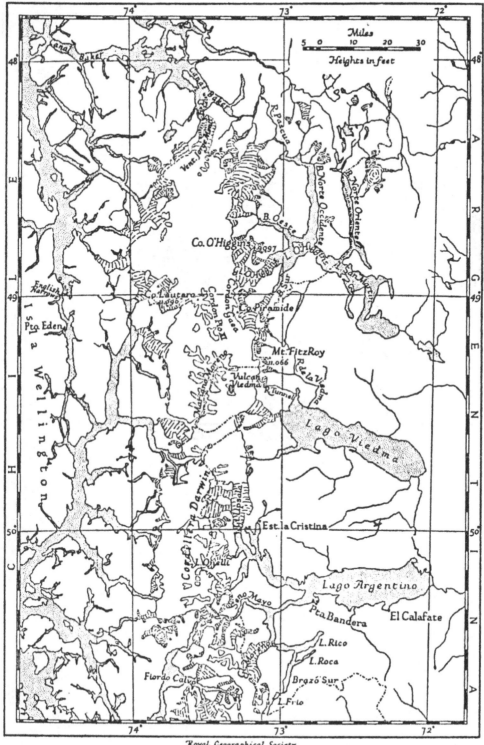

Great Lakes of Patagonia

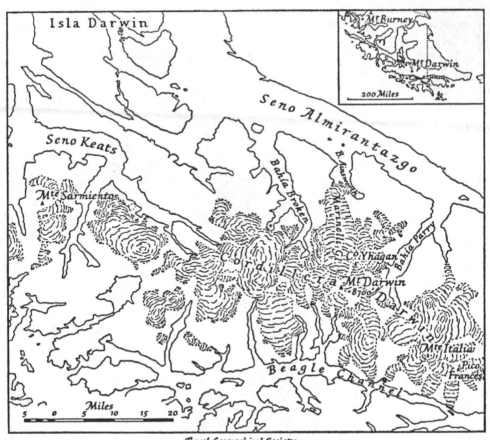

Tierra del Fuego

Explorations in Patagonia. The Onelli Glacier with ice calving off the cliffs two miles away. Several minutes later the tidal well from this swept the beach.

A Patagonia glacier wildly contorted to reveal seasonal snow grain.

The *Covadonga* in sheltered waters near Puerto Eden.

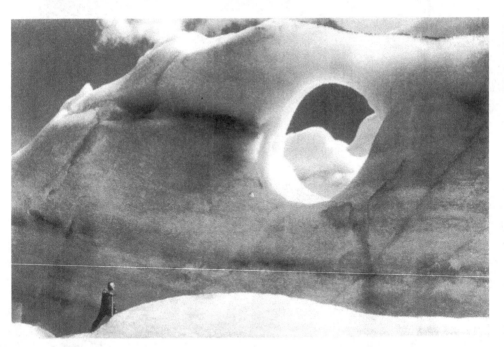

A section of a Moulin (water hole) sliced and turned to a vertical position by the action of the Seno Mayo Glacier.

An Alacaluf Indian hut, 'like a primitive version of an Asian yort'

The South Patagonian ice cap journey, 1962. Shipton carrying sledge sections on the Jorge Montt Glacier. The Canal Baker is in the background.

The mists clear to reveal the first mountains.

Marangunic and García with the sledge near the head of the Viedma Glacier.

Clearer conditions in 1973 revealed the splendor of the scenery on the northern end of the ice cap. Here climbers, having ascended Cerro Lautero, approach Cerro Mimosa, another volcanic peak in the vicinity. *Photo: Leo Dickinson.*

A view north from the summit of Cerro Don Bosco. The South Patagonian ice cap is flanked by the Moreno range (left) and the Fitzroy group (right).

Tierra del Fuego, 1962. Aspects of the camp on the Marinelli Glacier.

Cerro Yagen.

Eduardo García, Commander Robolledo, Cedomir Marangunic and Francisco Vivanco on the *Cabrales*.

The North Patagonian ice cap journey, 1964. An unnamed peak towering 4,500 feet about the ice cap.

Approaching Cerro Arenales.

Miguel Gomez on the airbed raft used to cross Lago Colonia at the end of the trip.

Approaching Mount Bové. *Photo: John Earle*